WILLS
AND WHERE TO FIND THEM

WILLS

AND WHERE TO FIND THEM

Compiled by

J. S. W. GIBSON

PHILLIMORE

Published for the

BRITISH RECORD SOCIETY

1974
Published by
PHILLIMORE AND CO. LTD.
Head Office : Shopwyke Hall, Chichester,
Sussex, England

© J. S. W. Gibson, 1974

ISBN 0 900592 59 1

This book has been issued as an
Extra Volume
to members of the British Record Society

The Publishers and the Author of this book wish to
make it clear that they acknowledge that 'Wills and
Their Whereabouts' by Anthony J. Camp, a 4th
edition of which has recently been published and is
available from Mr. Camp at 162 Westbourne Grove,
London, W.11. is the definitive book in the field of
testamentary records. The author wishes also to
record his indebtedness to Mr. Camp's painstaking
researches of which he has made considerable use in
the present volume which is intended for less ex-
perienced genealogists than is Mr. Camp's book.

Printed by the Compton Press Ltd.,
Compton Chamberlayne, Salisbury
Wiltshire

CONTENTS

CONTENTS

PREFACE

Nearly all who use wills and their associated records are local or family historians. The local historian will want to know where wills relating to a particular place, or small group of places, are to be found. The genealogist will want much the same, although over a wider area, as people moved around and may have owned scattered property.

This guide is designed primarily for such searchers and endeavours to indicate the different 'courts' that might have had pre-1858 jurisdiction over any specific parish or area. All places were subject to at least a two-tier system : in England and Wales the over-riding Prerogative Court of Canterbury (P.C.C.), and the local court. Frequently it was three-tier : a consistory (diocesan) court, with superior or concurrent jurisdiction (often only in special circumstances or at certain times), and the normal lowest court, the archdeaconry. Then some places fell into exempt or 'peculiar' jurisdictions, invariably inferior to P.C.C., and sometimes to another court such as that of a dean and chapter.

The reasons why a will was proved in a particular court are really immaterial, and are usually unknown (at least beforehand) to the searcher. A local historian will want *all* wills relating to a place, whatever property the testator owned elsewhere. A genealogist often won't know more than the names of people for whom he is searching – the will may tell him more precisely where they lived or what they owned. It is essential, therefore, that *all* possible courts are searched : not just for one place, but all around in widening circles. A place may well be near the boundary between one jurisdiction and another – be it county, diocese, archdeaconry or peculiar – and a neighbouring or superior court may have been used for no obvious reason. Contrary to normal expectation, the wills of people of small means may appear in P.C.C.; less frequently those of the wealthy may be found in a local court. People may have died away from home. The search can never be too wide.

The arrangement of this book is, therefore : first, a short section on the various classes of records which relate to the whole of England and Wales, the all-important P.C.C. and its associated courts (the equivalent Prerogative Court of York, with jurisdiction over northern counties, is described on page 150), the Estate Duty Office abstracts and indexes, and the Principal (Probate) Registry;

second, the historic English counties; and subsequent sections on Wales, Ireland and Scotland, also arranged by counties, and on the Channel Islands and the Isle of Man.

Counties are described throughout as they were before the many changes since the mid-19th century. In the case of earlier boundary changes (some of which took place before 1858) the records of all possible jurisdictions should be consulted. The most far-reaching reorganisation of all comes into force early in 1974, but at the time of writing there appear to be no plans to change the present *location* of any testamentary records although the titles of record offices are changing in some cases.

The post-1857 history of the ecclesiastical areas (province, diocese or archdeaconry) does not concern the searcher for wills. Although most counties are still in the same province, the dioceses and arch-deaconries have frequently changed, but to describe these changes would be to provide irrelevant detail. Even before 1858, a number of alterations were made to ecclesiastical jurisdictions. However, the Act of Parliament which governed these (6 and 7 William IV, c.77) laid down that no change was to be made in testamentary jurisdiction for at least a year, and in most cases this effectively meant that they continued as before until 1858.

Nearly all counties are accompanied by an outline map showing the approximate boundaries of different jurisdictions and peculiars. These are meant as a general indication, as the scale is too small for precision; moreover, as already emphasised, *all* courts within reasonable distance should be considered. Generally places outside the main jurisdictions in a county are listed together alphabetically, with a letter key to the court in which they lay and a number key to their position on the map. For detailed research the parish maps published by the Institute of Heraldic and Genealogical Studies (Northgate, Canterbury) should be consulted. In each county section, the different courts are normally described in their relationship only to that county, and the fact that a consistory court, for instance, might have jurisdiction over neighbouring counties will not necessarily be mentioned. The full extent of a court's authority can be established from the index.

An index or calendar of some kind is generally essential in order to locate a will. The records in this book are therefore described in the context of indexes to them. No attempt is made to differentiate between registered copies of wills and original wills, unless they are housed or indexed separately. The same is the case for administrations (admons.) and their related documents, such as act books, bonds and so on. Inventories may be filed with original wills and admons., or separately. Thus indexes to inventories alone sometimes exist, but often they do not; and sometimes, but by no means always, they are referred to in the indexes to wills and admons. Except in Scotland, they are generally scarce after the mid-18th century, and not very informative after the late 17th century.

In describing the indexes, prominence has been given to those that have been printed and published, as they are so much more accessible. There are also microfilms at the Society of Genealogists of many of the original calendars. Normally, apart from these, non-printed indexes are only available at the offices where the records themselves are held. Earlier calendars have been ignored when they have been superseded by printed, card or TS indexes, or by one of the excellent series of late-19th century MS indexes made when some of the local courts were centralised at the Principal Probate Registry. Defects in modern indexes, when they occur, are mentioned. Most of the early MS indexes are chronological within the initial letter, and these have been described as 'calendars'.

An attempt has been made to indicate, where easily ascertainable, the quantities of records in different courts. These indications are usually very approximate, and inadequate at present as a basis for statistical conclusions. Often, the way records are indexed makes it difficult to calculate their numbers at all; and sometimes calculations may have been based on misleading information. The main purpose of their present inclusion is to emphasise the great quantitative difference in importance between the normal archdeaconry court, with its tens of thousands of wills and admons., and the peculiars, often with less than five hundred; and, sometimes, the relative importance of consistory and archdeaconry courts. It is hoped that this attempt will lead to more detailed and accurate information becoming available so that in a future edition more useful conclusions can be drawn from the figures.

Where it has seemed that no confusion can arise the titles of courts have been abbreviated, usually by the omission of the word 'court' itself. It is the existence of the group of records, rather than its full official title, that seems of importance.

The Court of Probate Act, 1857, became operative on 11 January 1858, bringing to an end the jurisdiction of the old ecclesiastical courts, and substituting a centralised system. For the purpose of this book the latest terminal date of all courts in England, Wales and Ireland, is taken to be 1857. In fact, in the larger courts at least, there are likely to be a few wills and admons. between 1 and 10 January 1858 – but to quote 1858 as the terminal date might mislead by suggesting it covered the whole year, which it certainly does not. The wills proved in the post-1857 district registries (of which there are of course copies at the Principal Registry) are now often held in local record offices. There has been no attempt to make a comprehensive survey of these, but they have been mentioned when drawn to my attention.

The compilation of this guide to the location of wills would have been infinitely more arduous but for the work of predecessors – the earliest being the Command Papers of 1828-1830. Apart from a condensed version of these by George Marshall, in 1895, the first (and very successful) modern guide was *Wills and their Whereabouts*, compiled by S. G. Bouwens and published by the Society of Genealogists in 1939 (with an updated edition by Helen Thacker in 1951). Before the war most testamentary records were still scattered in diocesan registries, often the cramped offices of solicitors, and an understanding of the working of the courts was essential to make any headway. By 1963, when Phillimore published a complete revision and extension of that book, by A. J. Camp, nearly all the records were in properly appointed (usually county) record offices, in the care of professional archivists. Consequently the freshly-gathered information was arranged according to the office and county in which the records then were – often different from the county to which some of them related. Archival detail (omitted in this guide) was provided on the different *classes* of testamentary records and the frequency and length of periods of inhibition.

Fortunately, the ever-continuing cataloguing and creation of modern consolidated indexes to wills and other records, preserving the archive groups but freeing the searcher from the need to consult a variety of calendars, makes the understanding of testamentary procedure far less necessary for the average user. The Introduction discusses the background to the system, and the Glossary explains the technical terms most likely to be encountered. For an exhaustive but simply-presented description, *Genealogical Research in England and Wales,* by David E. Gardner and Frank Smith, vol. 2 (Bookcraft, Utah, 1959), is recommended.

In the compilation of this book I have had the great advantage of being able to visit virtually all the major probate record-holding offices, and one of its pleasures has been the personal contact with and invariable helpfulness of archivists, both then and in subsequent correspondence. A side-advantage has been the opportunity of giving a 'stranger's' description of the location of the different offices, which it is hoped will be useful to future visitors. Existing leaflets or guides should be obtained before a visit, and a prior appointment to see specified records made by letter or telephone (which will establish current opening hours). At the office, the catalogues will always be more detailed, informative and up-to-date than this book (the information for which was assembled between

October 1973 and January 1974), the purpose of which is to guide the searcher to the right record office. Most offices, moreover, maintain indexes to wills in deposited private records, quite apart from official probate archives; and this may also apply to those county and other record offices not holding probate records, and so excluded from this guide.

It is particularly appropriate that this book should be published for the British Record Society, as it bears testimony time and again to the really great contribution of the Society, through its Index Library, to the publication of indexes to wills and admons. Apart from the northern counties, where there have been active local societies, virtually every English county has one or more volumes to its advantage. This work is due to the devotion of a very few people, over several generations. The first volume was published in 1888. Amongst these the names of W. P. W. Phillimore, T. M. Blagg, E. A. Fry and C. Harold Ridge stand out, and must be taken for the whole – editors, transcribers and indexers.

To their worthy successor, Dr. Marc Fitch, the present flourishing programme of the Society is almost entirely due : both the recently published volumes and others, well advanced, particularly for P.C.C. and for the London courts, which are mainly the outcome of his own prodigious industry; and the work in progress on indexing many other courts, much of which is financed by his personal munificence or that of the Fund which bears his name. Few historians cannot have made use of the Society's indexes at some time or other, and far too few give any thought or credit to the time and work that has gone into the provision of the keys which can unlock the doors to this treasure-house of raw material.

No one can have detailed knowledge of a whole country, and in compiling this guide I am greatly aware that much of it was previously strange territory to me. Archivists have helped a great deal, and have frequently corrected or verified detail; but on occasion even they have been unable to answer some questions. That there are major errors in descriptions of courts, their jurisdictions, location of their records, and their indexes, seems unlikely; but that there are incorrect points of detail, or at least differences of interpretation, on the jurisdictions and counties in which individual places lay at different times, on the precise dates covered by different courts, on the style of indexes, seems inevitable. I offer my apologies in advance, with the hope that no one is seriously misled, and with the request that all such errors be brought to my attention for correction in a future edition.

11 Westgate, Chichester.   J. S. W. Gibson

ACKNOWLEDGMENTS

A guide of this nature is only the sum of the information provided by many. It is therefore a particular pleasure to be able to make some small acknowledgment of all those who have been so helpful throughout. Where possible I am acknowledging them personally, but there must be others whose names are unknown to me, and to them I am equally grateful.

I have received help from archivists and librarians at the following record offices, libraries and university departments: The Public Record Office: Miss D. Gifford and Mrs J. Hoare; Lambeth Palace Library: Mr E. G. W. Bill and Miss M. Barber; Somerset House (Principal Registry, Family Division): The Record Keeper; Bedfordshire: Miss P. Bell and Mr A. F. Cirket; Buckinghamshire: Mr E. J. Davis; Cambridge University: The Keeper of the University Archives, Miss H. E. Peek, and Dr E. S. Leedham-Green, and the Archivist to the Bishop and the Dean and Chapter of Ely, Mrs D. M. Owen; Cheshire: Mr B. C. Redwood; Cornwall: Mr P.L. Hull and Mrs C. North; Cumberland and Westmorland: Mr B. C. Jones and Mrs A. Rossiter; Devon: Mr P. A. Kennedy and his staff; Exeter Cathedral Library: Mrs A. Erskine; Exeter City Record Office: Mrs M. Rowe and her staff; Dorset: Miss M. E. Holmes and Miss J. Hofmann; Durham University, Department of Palaeography and Diplomatic: Mr J. E. Fagg; Northumberland: Mr R. M. Gard; Essex: Mr K. C. Newton; Gloucester (City Library, Archives Department): Miss K. Collins; Bristol: Miss M. E. Williams and Mrs Phillips; Hampshire: Miss M. E. Cash and Mr C. R. Davey; Hertfordshire: Mr P. Walne and Miss E. Lynch; Huntingdonshire: Dr D. E. Cottrell; Kent: Dr F. Hull; Lancashire: Mr R. Sharpe France and Mr Campbell; Leicestershire: Dr L. A. Parker and Mr T. J. Falla; Lincolnshire: Mr C. M. Lloyd and his staff; Greater London Council, County Hall: Miss J. Coburn and Mrs J. Kenealy; Middlesex Records: Mr W. J. Smith and Mr R. Samways; The Guildhall Library: Dr A. E. J. Hollaender and other staff; St. Paul's Cathedral Library: Mr A. R. B. Fuller; Norfolk and Norwich: Miss J. M. Kennedy and Mr P. Rutledge; Northamptonshire: Mr P. I. King; Nottinghamshire: Mr A. J. M. Henstock and Mr R. Brocklesby; Oxford University, Bodleian Library, Department of Western Manuscripts: Dr D. M. Barratt; Somerset: Mr I. P. Collis, Mr D. M. M. Shorrocks and their staff; Lichfield (Joint Record Office, Public Library): Miss J. Isaac; Ipswich and East Suffolk: Mr W. R. Serjeant; Bury St. Edmunds and West Suffolk: Mr K. Hall; East Sussex: Mr S. C. Newton and Mr M. J. Burchall; West Sussex: Mrs P. Gill and Mr T. McCann; Stratford-upon-Avon, Shakespeare's Birthplace Trust: Dr L. Fox; Wiltshire: Mr M. G. Rathbone and Miss P. Rundle; Worcestershire: Mr E. H. Sargeant and Miss M. Henderson; York, The Borthwick Institute of Historical Research: the late Mrs N. K. M. Gurney and Dr D. M. Smith; Leeds (City Libraries, Archives Department): Mr J. M.

Collinson; The National Library of Wales, Department of Manuscripts
and Records: Miss N. C. Jones; The Scottish Record Office: Mr P.
Gouldesbrough; The Public Record Office of Northern Ireland: Mr B.
Trainor; Jersey (Judicial Greffe, Royal Court): The Judicial Greffier, and
Mr P. D. Harris, Assistant Judicial Greffier; Guernsey (Ecclesiastical
Court): Mr E. Bourgaize.

For general advice and help I am also grateful to the following, in
addition to some of those already mentioned: Mr D. Harrington, Dr P.
Spufford (on whose work my Introduction is based), Mr D. J. Steel, Mr
F. W. Steer, Mr B. S. Trinder and Mr C. Tucker; and the librarians of
the Society of Antiquaries, Mr J. H. Hopkins, and the Society of
Genealogists, Mr L. W. Lawson Edwards.

During my journeyings around the country various old friends and
relations have given me hospitality and in return had their homes turned
into species of testamentary offices: John and Georgina Blight, Nicholas
Cooper, Charles and Susan Gibson, Hester and Helen Gibson, Bill and
Margaret Gibson, Michael and Wendy Sanger-Davies, Peter and Margaret
Spufford, Patrick and Julia Stevens, and Keith and Judy Wallace-Dunlop.
I thank them all for their welcome and tolerance.

My printers, the Compton Press, in particular Julian Berry and
Humphrey Stone, have co-operated to produce this book in an amazingly
short time, in spite of three-day-week working and constant alterations in
proof to what in any case would be a complicated piece of book production. My publishers, Phillimore and Company, occupy a unique position:
no other publishers in the country possess a genealogical library which
includes most of the printed works referred to in this guide, some of
them very rare, and even the occasional MS or TS. It was at the
suggestion of the Chairman, Philip Harris, that I first undertook its
compilation, and throughout I have received the greatest support and
encouragement from him and his colleague, Noel Osborne, and the rest
of their staff at Chichester.

J.S.W.G.

INTRODUCTION
THE BACKGROUND TO WILLS

It is the avowed intention of this guide to make the understanding of testamentary procedure largely unnecessary for the normal user of wills and their associated records. Accordingly a detailed discussion is deemed out-of-place, and the purpose of this introduction is only to give the most general of background information.

The centralised state systems governing wills and letters of administration (admons.) (of the estates of intestates) since 1858 in England and Wales, and in Ireland, are described on pages 6 and 195-6; and for Scotland, since 1876, on page 199. The Estate Duty Office abstracts, which for England and Wales from 1812 effectively provide a consolidated index, are described on page 4.

Before 1858, in England, Wales and Ireland the probate of wills and granting of letters of admon. were matters for the church courts, a complex system that had grown up in medieval times, although it was not until the mid-16th century that it became at all common for wills to be made. Broadly speaking, in England it was normal for a will to be proved in the court of the archdeaconry in which the testator died. If, however, his possessions fell into two archdeaconries, it was necessary for the will to be taken to the (consistory) court of the bishop for probate, or if in two bishoprics (dioceses), to the prerogative court of the relevant archbishop, and, if in both archbishoprics (provinces), to the prerogative court of the senior archbishop, Canterbury (P.C.C.). Letters of admon. and disputes were dealt with by the same hierarchy. The procedure was the same for Wales, except that there were no archdeaconry courts.

In practice, at times it seems that the exception was almost as common as the rule. The function of the archdeaconry court was frequently assumed by the consistory court, either directly or else through a commissary, or this court might exercise jurisdiction over particular clergy or parishes to the exclusion of the archdeacon. The superior courts (P.C.C. for England and Wales, York for the northern province, Armagh for Ireland and to a lesser extent the commissary of Edinburgh for Scotland) were always much used by the executors of testators of wealth, property or standing, whether or not this was essential. Their records were probably better maintained, and the possibility of disputes being taken to a higher court minimised. By the 19th century this became so markedly the case that business in the inferior courts was much reduced and some even fell into disuse.

Throughout England there were 'peculiar' jurisdictions, again dating from medieval times, of parishes or groups of parishes, exempt from the archdeacon's and frequently the bishop's authority. At times of episcopal visitation, the archdeacon's court would be 'inhibited', that is, closed down, for several months, and all business would have to be taken to the consistory court. The same might happen with some ecclesiastical peculiars, on visitation by a dean or by a dean and chapter. In theory this also happened with the consistory court at times of archiepiscopal visitation, or at times of vacancy between the death or translation of one bishop and the appointment of another, though in fact the same courts and officials often seem to have carried on without break in the records. This guide indicates the hierarchy of courts connected with any place or district, and the superior courts during inhibition.

Although the centralised system that operates in England and Wales today has only been in existence since 1858, there was a forerunner for a brief period in the 17th century. This was during the Commonwealth (1653-1660), when all ecclesiastical courts were abolished, and a Court of Civil Commission, in place of P.C.C., had sole testamentary jurisdiction. This had effectively been the case for some years before, as many church courts were practically closed down from the outbreak of the Civil War. Within a year or two of the Restoration the old system was re-established.

The most numerous and useful class of testamentary records is that of the wills themselves. A will was normally made by the testator when he was on his deathbed, though occasionally during an illness from which he recovered, or before a seemingly risky undertaking, such as setting out on a long journey, possibly overseas. Apart from the men with family commitments struck down in the prime of life, the other two most common types of testator were the wealthy whose affairs were abnormally complex, and elderly single women, whether widows or spinsters, who had no obvious heirs and wished to distribute a large number of small legacies amongst grand-children, nephews and nieces, cousins and friends. None of these groups is typical of the population.

It must be emphasised how relatively uncommon was the making of wills among the population in general. For example, in Essex there were some 80,000 wills proved in the 300 years between the 1520s and 1820s in various local courts having jurisdiction over most of the county. Around 1700 it was estimated there were 35-40,000 houses in the county. There was thus an average of hardly more than two wills per household in three centuries, though this admittedly does not take into account wills proved in P.C.C. Part of the reason for this infrequency was that people often settled inheritance long before death – it is not unusual when a will has been made to find some children (known to be surviving) omitted, or left a token amount such as a shilling. This is more likely to indicate that they have already been 'set up' in their livelihood long beforehand, or, in the case of daughters, provided with dowries, than to be a sign of disapproval.

The process of proving a will, or of obtaining letters of administration for an intestate, generated quite a number of documents. These are mentioned in the glossary, but the most important and interesting was the inventory, which from the mid-16th to the early 18th century (and much later in Scotland) would be likely to list all of a man's household goods, room by room, and the tools of his trade, crops, debts or loans, and so on – though land and buildings would be excluded.

Unlike wills and inventories, letters of administration and their associated bonds and entries in court act books offer only minimal information, such as the name of the next-of-kin, to whom they were usually granted – but in the absence of a will, they may still provide some vital scrap of evidence.

The systems in Ireland and Scotland were to a great extent similar to England and Wales, stemming in the same way from medieval ecclesiastical jurisdiction. In Ireland the relevant courts were those of the Protestant bishops – there were no archdeaconry courts involved, and virtually no peculiars – under the superior jurisdiction of the prerogative court of Armagh. In Scotland, although episcopal jurisdiction was abolished in the 16th century, the commissariot districts remained based on the former dioceses until 1823, again without other inferior courts or peculiars, and with superior jurisdiction in the commissary court of Edinburgh. The post-1823 organisation is fully described on page 197.

The Channel Islands were in the diocese of Winchester, and the Isle of Man, in the diocese of Sodor and Man, was in the province of York, but both have retained separate administrative systems to this day – indeed, uniquely, in Guernsey testamentary business is still conducted in an ecclesiastical court.

Wills and inventories are amongst the most personal documents that the local and family historian can deal with. As few others can, they reveal the way a person thought, the way he lived. As much as any they can bring back to us the human beings of flesh and blood and individuality, who otherwise are all too apt to remain as mere names in fading ink and on weathered stones.

GLOSSARY

Account The 'true and just account' which executors or administrators sometimes had to render.

Act The endorsement on a will indicating probate has been granted; the record of a grant in an act book.

Act Book A day-by-day account of the official grants of probate of wills, letters of administration (admon.), and other testamentary business.

Administration, Letters of (usually abbreviated to *Admon.*) A grant to the next-of-kin (or some other person or persons) who applied to administer the property of an intestate.

Administration (Letters of) with Will annexed A grant, usually to the next-of-kin, when the will did not specify any executors or they were unable to act, or renounced, or had died. The will is then attached to the admon. bond. Sometimes filed under admons. instead of wills.

Administrator A man vested with the right to administer an estate, normally, in the case of an intestate, the next-of-kin; but one might be appointed when the executor, or next-of-kin, was a minor. An administratrix is a woman.

Admon. See *Administration, Letters of.*

Archdeaconry Normally the lowest of the ecclesiastical courts with testamentary jurisdiction. In larger dioceses there might be several, often co-terminous with counties (*cf.* Berkshire in the diocese of Salisbury), whilst just one might cover the whole of a smaller diocese (*cf.* Oxford). It was not unusual for the bishop's consistory court to appropriate this jurisdiction (*cf.* Lichfield), or for a commissary to be appointed for an archdeaconry (*cf.* Buckingham in the diocese of Lincoln).

'Bona Notabilia' A Latin term meaning considerable goods, technically worth £5 and more. When the deceased had 'bona notabilia' in more than one jurisdiction, a will should have been proved in a superior court.

Bond A signed and witnessed obligation, the conditions of which might include the proving of a will, administration of an intestate's estate, rendering an account or inventory, or guardianship of a minor.

xvii

Calendar In this guide, this generally implies an index, chronological within initial letter, normally contemporary with the records. A modern fully alphabetical index is to be preferred.

Caveat A warning notice that a will is to be disputed.

Citation A summons to appear before a court.

Commissariot In Scotland the district within the jurisdiction of a commissary court. In 1823 the old districts were abolished, and most commissariots thereafter coincided with the old sheriffdoms (counties) and the sheriff court districts, with which they were merged in 1876. See also *Sheriffdom* and *Sheriff Court*.

Commissary A person who held authority or a commission to exercise jurisdiction on behalf of an archbishop, bishop or other dignitary; the title continued to be used in Scotland in spite of the abolition of episcopal authority.

Commissary Court A court acting with delegated power from the bishop, normally as a consistory court but in one archdeaconry only – in contrast to an archdeaconry court which was subject to the archdeacon. In Scotland, one of the courts which took over the jurisdiction of the pre-reformation church courts.

Confirmation In Scotland, the completion of the probate of a testament by the executors.

Consistory Court The bishop's ecclesiastical court, with superior jurisdiction to an archdeaconry court. Theoretically wills of testators with 'bona notabilia' in two archdeaconries within the same diocese would be proved in the consistory court, and often the wills of clergy were reserved to it. In many dioceses it displaced the archdeaconry court entirely (*cf.* Lichfield), or had jurisdiction over certain parishes exempt from the archdeacon's jurisdiction (*cf.* Canterbury). In large dioceses powers were often delegated from the consistory court of the diocese to commissary courts acting in different archdeaconries (*cf.* Buckingham in the diocese of Lincoln). The consistory court would normally have jurisdiction during periodic visitations of the bishop to different archdeaconries, when the archdeaconry court would be *inhibited*.

Curation Guardianship over orphaned minors, under 21 but over 14 (boys) or 12 (girls). See also *Tuition*.

Dean (and Chapter) Clergy who were members of a cathedral chapter, often with peculiar jurisdiction over parishes in the patronage of that cathedral.

Diocese   The district over which a bishop has authority.

Executor (often abbreviated to *Exor.*)   A man appointed by the testator to see that the provisions of a will are carried out. An executrix is a woman.

Grant   Approval of the submission of the executor or administrator, denoting probate or letters of administration.

Guardianship   See *Curation* and *Tuition*.

Hono(u)r   See *Manor*.

Inhibition   The period during the visitation of a bishop to an arch-deaconry, when the archdeacon's court would be closed and probate business conducted in the consistory court. In theory the visitation of an archbishop to a diocese would have the same effect on a consistory court, but in post-medieval times this was likely to be *pro forma* only. Some peculiars were entirely exempt from visitation and inhibition, others were subject to visitation by a dean or a dean and chapter. Visitations would normally last several months at intervals of several years.

Intestate   A person who died without making a will.

Inventory   A list of personal and household goods left by the deceased, with their appraised value. Occupation was usually given, or can be inferred from tools of trade. They were common in the later 16th and 17th centuries, but became much less detailed and frequent in the 18th century; except in Scotland where they continued to a much later date.

Jurisdiction   The area over which a court claimed the right to grant probate or letters of administration. Peculiars within this area would be exempt from the jurisdiction of the court concerned.

Letters of Administration   See *Administration*.

Liberty   See *Manor*.

Manor   Occasional manorial courts had peculiar or exempt jurisdiction over a parish or part of a parish. An *Honour* (*cf.* Knaresborough, Yorks.) or *Liberty* (*cf.* Frampton, Dorset) might be a group of manors with such exempt jurisdiction.

Nuncupative Will   A will made orally, normally by a testator on his deathbed, written down and sworn to by witnesses, but not signed by the deceased.

Peculiar (*Testamentary*)   A parish or group of parishes, not necessarily adjacent or even in the same district or county, which were usually exempt from the testamentary jurisdiction of the archdeaconry and often the consistory court. Ecclesiastical peculiars were often subject to a dean or dean and chapter, though they might be administered by a locally appointed official; a bishop's peculiars might be administered by the consistory court; a number were royal or archbishop's peculiars, usually locally administered; and there were some lay, manorial or collegiate, peculiars. See also *Inhibition*.

Personalty   Personal property (goods, chattels, credits, etc.) as opposed to *real property*. In Scotland, until 1868, and in the Channel Isles only personalty (moveable property) could be bequeathed, and a document so excluding *realty* is technically known as a *testament*.

Prebend   So far as testamentary matters are concerned, this was a type of ecclesiastical peculiar, in the jurisdiction of a prebendary, who was appointed by the dean and chapter of a cathedral; accordingly it was usually subject to their visitation and inhibition.

Prerogative Court   See *Province*.

Probate   Evidence that a will has been accepted and that the executor has been granted permission to carry out its provisions.

Proved   A will has been proved when probate has been granted.

Province   The dioceses over which an archbishop has authority, i.e., before 1858, in England and Wales, the provinces of Canterbury and York, and in Ireland, the province of Armagh. The *prerogative courts* of the archbishops had superior jurisdiction to all others, and Canterbury was superior to York.

Realty, Real Property, Real Estate   Property or interests in land, as opposed to *personalty*. In Scotland, until 1868, and in the Channel Isles realty (heritable property) could not be bequeathed, and in England there were certain limitations on its bequest, so that it does not always appear in wills.

Registers and Registered Wills   Volumes of copy wills, made at the time of probate. It is these the searcher will normally see, though sometimes only original wills are available. At times only the registered copies survive. These are not to be confused with archbishops' and bishops' registers, which record their provincial and diocesan activities, but also include occasional wills, particularly in medieval times.

Renunciation   When an executor declines to apply for probate.

'Sede Vacante'   See *Vacancy*.

See   Often used as a synonym for *diocese,* though technically the seat of the bishop or the diocesan centre.

Sentences The final judgment on a disputed will, often entered in an act book.

Sheriff Court In Scotland, since 1876 the court with testamentary jurisdiction over anyone dying within its district, usually a county or part of a county. There are several such districts in each modern sheriffdom. Its official, the sheriff clerk, has custody of current testamentary records and also often of the 1823-1876 records of the commissary court of the former sheriffdom, which the modern sheriff court district has replaced.

Sheriffdom In Scotland, an administrative area, generally in the mid-19th century coinciding with a county, which between 1823 and 1876 acted as a commissariot district. In more recent years their number has been reduced and each now incorporates several counties and sheriff court districts. See also *Commissariot*.

Surrogate A deputy appointed by the ecclesiastical court to deal with testamentary and other matters.

Testaments Normally a synonym for a *will*, but technically a document which excludes *realty* (heritable property), as in Scotland and the Channel Isles.

Testator A man who has made his will. A testatrix is a woman.

Tuition Guardianship over orphaned minors, under 15 (boys) or 13 (girls). See also *Curation*.

Vacancy A break in the official business of the court on the death or translation of the bishop or other chief official. The court might be closed and business carried on in another court, but often this was *pro forma* only, i.e., the same actual officials carried on, powers from the alternative court being delegated to them.

Warrants (of testaments) In Scotland, normally the drafts from which the entries in the register were made up, but occasionally including original wills.

Will A written statement by which a person regulates the disposition of property and rights after his death, normally signed and witnessed. See also *Testament*.

ABBREVIATIONS

The following abbreviations are used throughout the book. The names of local record publishing societies may be abbreviated after the first reference to them in a county section.

Admon.	Administration (Letters of)
Index Lib.	Index Library, the series of indexes to wills and other records published by the British Record Society
Inv.	Inventory
M/f	Microfilm
MS	Manuscript
P.C.C.	Prerogative Court of Canterbury
P.R.O.	Public Record Office
SG	Society of Genealogists
S.R.O.	Scottish Record Office
S.R.S.	Scottish Record Society
TS	Typescript

ENGLAND AND WALES

THE PREROGATIVE COURT OF CANTERBURY
and other Courts having
General Jurisdiction before 1858

The Prerogative Court of (the Archbishop of) Canterbury (usually abbreviated to P.C.C.) had over-riding jurisdiction in England and Wales; and sole jurisdiction when a testator held possessions ('bona notabilia') in more than one diocese or peculiar in the province of Canterbury – that is, England south of Cheshire and Yorkshire (except for Nottinghamshire), and virtually all of Wales; also over those with estate in England or Wales who died overseas or at sea.

During the Commonwealth (1653-1660) this court, nominally in the form of a Court of Civil Commission, had sole testamentary jurisdiction over all England and Wales, and this was effectively the case from the outbreak of the Civil War in 1642, and for a time after the Restoration, as many provincial courts were practically shut down.

Moreover the wills and admons. of men and women of substance are usually (and often of those of lesser means) to be found in this court even when a lower court could have been used. Registration of Irish wills, and during the 18th century of bi-national Hollanders', is not uncommon. It will therefore be seen that any search should always include P.C.C.

The records of the court are now at the Public Record Office (P.R.O.). There are printed indexes to wills to 1700 and to admons. to 1660. After these dates it is necessary to consult the calendars (MS to 1852, and printed thereafter), which are arranged in one or more volumes per year (over 200 in all). Names are listed chronologically within their initial letter, and admons. are in a separate section at the end of each year. A fully alphabetical index to the 18th century wills and admons. is being prepared by the Society of Genealogists. The index is now complete for the period 1750-1800, though not available for public use. The Society will undertake searches for a fee. There are also printed abstracts to all wills for the year 1750. There are, at the P.R.O., several separate classes of 'supplementary wills' which are now or shortly will become available, of which the most numerous are unproved and nuncupative wills, 1660-1857 (3,000).

Prerogative Court of Canterbury (Public Record Office, Chancery Lane, London, WC2A 1LR. Tel. 01-405 0741)

Note: printed indexes are Index Library unless otherwise stated.

Printed indexes:

wills,   1383-1558 (36,000) (vols. 10 and 11).

1558-1583 (14,000) (vol. 18).

1584-1604 (21,000) (vol. 25).

1605-1619 (20,000) (vol. 43).

1620-1624 (8,500) (*Probates and Sentences* 1620-24, by J. and G. F. Matthews, 1911).

1620-1629 (16,000) (vol. 44).

1630-1639 (*Sentences and Complete Index Nominum,* by J. and G. F. Matthews, 1907).

1630-1655 (70,000) (*Year Books of Probates,* by J. and G. F. Matthews, vols. 1-8, 1903-27).

1653-1656 (27,000) (vol. 54).

Jan. 1657/8-June 1658 (4,000 abstracts) (*Register Wootton,* by W. Brigg, 6 parts, chronological with indexes).

1657-1660 (30,000) (vol. 61).

1661-1670 (19,492) (*Wills, Sentences and Probate Acts,* by J. H. Morrison, 1935).

1671-1675 (9,500) (vol. 67).

1676-1685 (20,000) (vol. 71).

1686-1693 (37,000) (vol. 77).

1694-1700 (18,500) (vol. 80).

1750   (4,382) (*Register Greenly,* by G. Sherwood, a list of all persons named (40,000), arranged in 8 groups, topographically – not indexed).

admons., 1559-1580 (5,400) (*Administrations in the Prerogative Court of Canterbury,* by R. M. Glencross, 2 vols.).

1581-1595 (6,000) (vol. 76).

1596-1608 (7,000) (vol. 81).

1609-1619 (7,250) (vol. 83).

1620-1630 (8,179) (*Letters of Admon.,* by J. H. Morrison).

1631-1648 (8,000) (vol. 88, in press).

1649-1654 (20,000) (vol. 68).

1655-1660 (23,000) (vols. 72, 74 and 75).

invs., 1702 (125), 1718-1782 (5,500) (List and Index Soc., vols. 85 and 86 – calendar with index).

Other indexes:

wills, 1701-1858 (10 Jan.); admons., 1661-1858 (10 Jan.) (calendars, printed from 1853; ref. for wills, PROB. 11, admons., PROB. 6).

supplementary wills (unproved, nuncupative, etc.), 1626-1838 (3,000) (PROB. 20); (miscellaneous), 1623-1857 (200) (PROB. 21, 22, 23).

invs., 1417-1660 (500) (PROB. 2); 1661-1725, paper (2,000) (PROB. 5, card index in progress); post-1660, parchment (3,000) (PROB. 4, card index in progress); 1722-1857 (among Exhibits, PROB. 31 – indexed in PROB. 33); miscellaneous, among Filed Exhibits, mainly London, PROB. 32.

Inventories in P.C.C. have been filed separately from the wills and admons., and very few proportionately have survived. Only with their transfer to the P.R.O. have more than a very few for the eighteenth century begun to be available. Many are in a very bad condition, and their use by the public is dependent on the progress of measures being taken for their repair. There is a printed index to inventories for 1718-1782, and a TS index to the few surviving before 1660. Work is in progress on indexing the much more numerous post-1660 inventories (an estimated 35,000) which are in two main classes of 'paper' and 'parchment' documents. TS lists have been prepared of those at present available, and additions will be made to these lists from time to time. The continuing card indexes, which include future additions to the classes, may be consulted on request.

The Public Record Office is in Chancery Lane; prior application should be made for a reader's ticket; nearest tube station : Chancery Lane. The P.C.C. indexes are in a special 'probate' room on the first floor, through the 'Long Room' and up a staircase. A leaflet on *Probate Records* is available.

The Prerogative Court of York fulfilled the same function (Commonwealth apart) for the northern province – from 1541 the counties of Cheshire, Cumberland, Durham, Lancashire, Northumberland, Nottinghamshire, Westmorland and Yorkshire (before 1541 Cheshire and the southern part of Lancashire were in the province of Canterbury) – see page 150.

Associated courts

The Court of Delegates was the court of appeal for the two prerogative courts of Canterbury and York. Its records are at the Public Record Office and there is a printed index to 1857.

The Court of Arches (not to be confused with the Deanery of the Arches) was another court of appeal for the province of Canterbury mainly from 1660, and the archiepiscopal registers also contain wills and admons. for those with possessions in more than one diocese in the province, mainly before 1500. There are printed indexes to both.

Before 1559 the court of the prior and chapter of Christ Church, Canterbury, exercised jurisdiction during vacancies, but in practice most wills proved at such times (mainly in 1500-1 and 1503) are to be found also in P.C.C., or at least included in the printed indexes. However there is a separate printed index.

The Court of Delegates (Public Record Office)
  Printed index: wills and admons., 1651-1857 (550) (*The Genealogist*, vol. 11, pp. 165-71, 224-27, vol. 12, pp. 97-101).

The Court of Arches (Lambeth Palace Library, London SE1 7JU)
A court of appeal for the province of Canterbury, apart from royal peculiars.
Printed index: wills, admons. and invs. (in disputed cases), 1660-1857 (3,250) (Index Lib., vol. 85 – index of testators, pp. 543-569).
Calendar: muniment books, 1554-1588, 1624-1631, 1635-1642, sentences, 1560-1561, 1622-1623, 1639-1640 (wills, admons. and invs. produced as exhibits were copied into the muniment books) (TS).

Archiepiscopal Registers (Lambeth Palace Library)
A miscellaneous collection, including wills from throughout the province which might normally, or also, appear in P.C.C., and from the archbishop's peculiars, such as Bocking, Essex.
Printed index: wills, c.1350-c.1600 (*Index to Wills recorded in the Archiepiscopal Registers at Lambeth Palace*, by J. Challoner Smith, 1919, reprinted from *The Genealogist*, N.S., vol. 34, pp. 53-64, 149-66, 219-34, and vol. 35, pp. 45-51, 102-126; admons., c.1350-c.1600 (*The Genealogist*, vol. 7, pp. 204-12, 271-84, N.S. vol. 1, pp. 80-82).
Printed abstracts: wills, etc., are to be found in the registers of archbishops Pecham, Winchelsey, Langham and Bourgchier (Canterbury and York Soc.) and of archbishop Chichele (1414-1443).

Court of the Prior (later Dean) and Chapter of Christ Church, Canterbury (Cathedral Archives and Library, Canterbury)
Jurisdiction during archiepiscopal vacancy in place of P.C.C., mainly in 1500-01 and 1503, but most wills are also to be found in the P.C.C. indexes.
Printed index: wills, c.1278-1559, admons., 1500-1501, 1503 (928) (Kent Arch. Soc., Records Branch, vol. 3).

The Estate (or Stamp) Duty Office
From 1796 abstracts of most, and from 1812 copies of nearly all, wills and admons. in England and Wales had to be deposited at the Legacy Duty Department of the Stamp Office. Regrettably the full copies have now been destroyed (except for those relating to Cornwall, Devon and Somerset, for which see under those counties, and to Ireland, for which see page 194). The abstracts are now in the P.R.O. and continue after 1811 to 1857 (and later), though for a number of courts they do not start until after 1800. At present these abstracts are only available for public search to about 1822, but more will be released annually (under a 150-year rule).

The indexes for the whole period are particularly valuable. Prior to 1812 they are arranged in three groups: P.C.C. wills, P.C.C. admons.; and 'Country Courts', wills and admons., arranged court by court. From 1812 the grouping alters and becomes vastly more useful, as *all* wills are indexed in one consolidated series, whatever the court. P.C.C. admons. remain in a separate series; and all

4

admons. from the 'Country Courts' are indexed in a third (consolidated) series. Unlike the calendars to P.C.C. wills and admons. described on pages 1-3, these indexes are not on the open shelves, and individual volumes of the index have to be ordered first (ref. I.R. 27). The catalogue of these index volumes is available in the probate room, and there is a copy at the Society of Genealogists.

The copy wills, abstracts and their indexes are described in two articles in the *Genealogists' Magazine* (vol. 15, no. 11, pp. 393-97, by A. J. Camp, and vol. 16, no. 6, pp. 269-72, by D. T. Hawkings). There is also a good description of the indexes, whose use is not absolutely straightforward, and their scope, in Gerald Hamilton-Edwards' *In Search of Ancestry* (3rd edition, Phillimore, 1974), pp. 58-60.

Wills in the Public Record Office

As well as possessing numerous small collections of original or copy wills, the Public Record Office also contains some very large ones, quite apart from the P.C.C. and Stamp Office records mentioned above. Most of these very probably appear in P.C.C. or some other court. The publication *List of Wills, Admons., etc., in the Public Record Office* (Baltimore Book Co., 1968) is based on an unrevised TS in the Round Room dated 1932, and as a survey is both out of date and incomplete.

The Universities of Oxford and Cambridge

The Chancellors of the Universities of Oxford (1436-1814) and Cambridge (1501-1765) had probate jurisdiction over persons who had matriculated in the Universities and were in residence as members of the University, or of a College, at the time of their deaths – see pages 105 and 19.

Society of Genealogists (37 Harrington Gardens, London SW7 4JX. Tel. 01-373 7054)

The Society in its unique library and MSS collection includes virtually all printed indexes to wills and admons., much TS and MS material (including indexes), and thousands of abstracts. Of particular importance is its collection of microfilms of calendars of wills and admons. – these were microfilmed by the Church of Jesus Christ of Latter-Day Saints some years ago, so usually are of 19th century and earlier indexes, which may well have been superseded since, but are useful for those able to get to London more easily than the local record offices concerned. Details are given under the relevant counties.

5

WILLS SINCE 1858

Since 11 January 1858 a centralised system has been in operation in England and Wales, with a principal probate registry in London and a chain of district probate registries in important centres. A similar system came into operation in Ireland at the same date (see page 195), and to an extent in Scotland in 1876 (see page 199). Testamentary matters for the Channel Islands and the Isle of Man are still in the jurisdiction of local courts.

In England and Wales a consolidated index of grants of probate and letters of administration within the year has been printed annually. These indexes may be consulted without charge at the principal registry in London or in any of the district registries. Wills and admons. within the past hundred years are 'current' legal documents, and may be consulted on payment of a small fee, and for a further fee photocopies and certified official copies are obtainable.

There are copies of all these wills and admons. since 1858 at the Principal Registry (Family Division, Somerset House, Strand, London WC2R 1LP, tel. 01-405 7641, ext. 3959), formerly known as the Principal Probate Registry. Somerset House is a well-known London landmark, and the Registry is on the opposite side of the courtyard to the main entrance on the Strand. Wills and admons. over a hundred years old can be consulted without charge by holders of a search permit, obtainable on prior application to the Record Keeper at Somerset House, though this of course only applies at present to those between 1858 and 1873.

The original wills and admons., or copies, were retained by the district registries, but these have generally now been transferred (for all but comparatively recent years) to local record offices. Some of these have been mentioned under the counties concerned, but no attempt has been made in this guide to include reference to all such deposits, nor to indicate the districts which they actually covered.

BEDFORDSHIRE

Bedfordshire was in the province of Canterbury, and in the diocese of Lincoln until 1837 when ecclesiastically it was transferred to Ely. The county of Bedford formed an archdeaconry, and probate matters were effectively delegated to the archdeaconry court, very few wills at Lincoln referring to Bedfordshire. The records of the archdeaconry and of the peculiars of Biggleswade and Leighton Buzzard (together covering the whole county except for the parish of Everton, in the archdeaconry of Huntingdon) are now all at the county record office, where there is an excellent modern card index to all testamentary records.

The record office is adjacent to the public library in the county council buildings, close to the centre of Bedford. There is very limited public parking. The office issues leaflets *How to Trace the History of a Family* and *Introduction to the Record Office* which mention the courts for which wills and admons. are held.

Prerogative Court of Canterbury and other courts having general jurisdiction – see page 1.
  Invs., 1650-1660 (TS at SG).

Archdeaconry of Bedford (County Record Office, County Hall, Bedford MK42 9AP. Tel. Bedford (0234) 63222, ext. 277)
  Jurisdiction: the whole county except peculiars and the parish of Everton.
  Index: wills, 1480-1857, and admons., 1670-1857 (occasional entries, 1558-1652) (30,000) (card index); m/f of calendar to 1857 at SG.
  Printed abstracts: wills, 1480-1526 (396) (Beds. Hist. Record Soc., vol. 37, pp. 1-80, and vol. 45); invs., 1562-1591 (15) (vol. 32, pp. 92-108), 1617-1619 (166) (vol. 20, pp. 1-143).

Peculiar of Biggleswade (Bedford County Record Office)
  A prebend of the dean and chapter of Lincoln, but there is no Biggleswade material in the records at Lincoln.
  Index: wills, 1540-1559, 1639, wills and admons., 1713-1857 (card index, consolidated with archdeaconry of Bedford).
  Printed index: wills and admons., 1639, 1730-1740 (13) (formerly at Lincoln District Probate Registry) (Index Lib., vol. 57, p. 367).

Peculiar of Leighton Buzzard (also some Leighton Buzzard wills proved in the peculiar court of Aylesbury, Bucks.) (Bedford County Record Office)

> A Prebend of the dean and chapter of Lincoln, but only one will (1634) and one admon. (1638) are in the Lincoln records (see page 81).
>
> Jurisdiction: Leighton Buzzard and its former hamlets of Billington, Eggington, Heath and Reach and Stanbridge. (For the jurisdiction of the peculiar of Aylesbury see page 15. There are also at the Bedford County Record Office photocopies of Leighton Buzzard wills proved between 1700 and 1720 in two registers of this court.)
>
> Index: wills, 1537-1554, 1701-1846, admons., 1712-1842 (card index, consolidated with archdeaconry of Bedford).
>
> Note: some of these records were formerly at the Bodleian Library, Oxford, and still appear in an index there too.

Diocese of Lincoln, Episcopal Registers (Lincolnshire Archives Office, page 81).

> The diocese included Bedfordshire, and a very few wills for the county are to be found,
>
> Printed index: wills, 1320-1547 (Index Lib., vol. 28, pp. 1-17).
>
> Printed abstracts: the above (*Early Lincoln Records,* by A. Gibbons, 1888).

Consistory Court of Lincoln (Lincolnshire Archives Office)

> Records in this court refer mainly to Lincolnshire, as court records of the bishop's commissary generally were kept with the archdeaconry records, but some Bedfordshire testators occur.
>
> Printed indexes: wills, 1506-1652 (Index Lib., vols. 28 and 41), admons., 1540-1659 (vol. 52); also, miscellaneous wills, 1549-1730 (vol. 57, pp. 430-56).

Consistory Court of Ely (Cambridge University Library, page 18)

> Replaced the consistory court of Lincoln in 1837, but Bedfordshire testators are unlikely to be found.

Archdeaconry of Huntingdon (Huntingdon Record Office, page 65)

> Jurisdiction: the Bedfordshire parish of Everton (but there are no references to it in the index of places in the printed volume, to 1652).

A few wills proved at Lambeth Palace, 1379-1453, 1556, 1607 (13), and admons., 1463-1586 (3), and wills in the archdeaconry of Huntingdon, 1525-1627 (7), are abstracted in Beds. Hist. Record Soc., vol. 2, pp. 1-59. There are numerous abstracts of Bedfordshire wills, arranged by parish, in *Genealogica Bedfordiensis,* 1538-1700, by F. A. Blades.

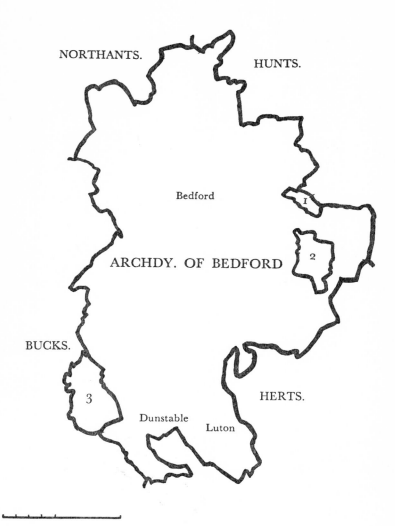

NORTHANTS.

HUNTS.

Bedford

1

2

ARCHDY. OF BEDFORD

BUCKS.

3

HERTS.

Dunstable

Luton

BEDS.

Peculiar of Biggleswade, 2

Archdeaconry of Huntingdon
  Everton, 1

Peculiar of Leighton Buzzard, 3
Leighton Buzzard and
its former hamlets of
Billington
Eggington
Heath and Reach
Stanbridge

BERKSHIRE

Berkshire was in the province of Canterbury and diocese of Salisbury (Sarum) until 1836 when it was transferred to the diocese of Oxford.

The main probate records are those for the archdeaconry of Berkshire, which covered virtually the whole county except for peculiars. These are now at the Bodleian Library, Oxford, and there is a printed index to 1710, with a good 19th century MS index to 1857. Records of the peculiars of Faringdon and Langford, and some of those of the dean and canons of Windsor in Wantage, are also at the Bodleian; as are those for the consistory court of Oxford, in which a few post-1836 Berkshire wills are to be found.

The consistory court of Salisbury had jurisdiction over the archdeaconry, mainly during inhibitions, until 1836, and some Berkshire wills are therefore amongst its probate records at the Wiltshire Record Office at Trowbridge, to which there is a good 19th century MS index. Nine Berkshire parishes were peculiars of the dean of Salisbury; the records of these and, after 1669, of the dean and canons of Windsor in Wantage, are also at Trowbridge.

The Bodleian Library is in the centre of Oxford, and the headquarters of the Department of Western Manuscripts is Duke Humfrey's Reading Room. There are no public carparks nearby, and car parking in Oxford generally is very difficult. Prior application for a reader's ticket should be made. Long delays are likely unless documents are ordered in advance. The department issues a leaflet on *Genealogical Sources within the diocese of Oxford*.

Prerogative Court of Canterbury and other courts having general jurisdiction – see page 1.

Archdeaconry of Berkshire (Department of Western MSS., Bodleian Library, Oxford OX1 3BG. Tel. Oxford (0865) 44675)
   Jurisdiction: the county except for peculiars. See also the consistory court.
   Printed indexes: wills and admons. (19,000), 1508-1652 (Index Library, vol. 8, and Oxford Hist. Soc., vol. 23); wills, admons. and invs. (9,600), 1653-1710 (Index Library, vol. 87, in press).
   Other indexes: wills, admons. and invs., 1711-1857 (MS. 19th cent.); m/f of calendar to 1857 at SG.

Consistory Court of Salisbury (Wiltshire Record Office, County Hall, Trowbridge, BA14 8JG. Tel. Trowbridge (02214) 4036)
  Jurisdiction: until 1836, over the archdeaconry of Berkshire, mainly during inhibition; all rectors in the diocese.
  Indexes: wills, 1526-1836, admons. and invs., 1584-1836 (MS, 19th cent., with modern additions).

Consistory Court of Oxford (Bodleian Library, Oxford)
  Jurisdiction: from 1836, over the archdeaconry of Berkshire; however there are very few wills for the county.
  Index: wills, admons. and invs., 1836-1857 (MS, 19th cent.).

Peculiar of the Dean of Salisbury (Wiltshire Record Office)
  Jurisdiction: included Arborfield, Blewbury with Upton and Ashton Upthorpe, Hurst, Ruscombe, Sandhurst, Sonning and Wokingham; and the peculiars of Faringdon and Wantage during inhibition.
  Indexes: wills, admons. and invs., 1538-1857 (MS, 19th cent. calendars, with modern additions) (see also Miscellaneous Wills, below).

Peculiar of Faringdon (Bodleian Library, Oxford)
  This was a Salisbury prebend, a peculiar in the jurisdiction of the dean of Salisbury during inhibition, above.
  Jurisdiction: (Great) Faringdon with Little Coxwell.
  Index: wills, admons. and invs., 1547-1853 (MS, 19th cent., consolidated with other 'Oxford' peculiars).

Peculiar of Langford (Bodleian Library, Oxford)
  This jurisdiction was held by a prebend of Lincoln; one will only (Mary Cross of Standlake, 1706: Index Lib., vol. 57, 'misc. wills', p. 435) is found there.
  Jurisdiction: Langford (partly Oxon.) and Little Faringdon.
  Index: wills, admons. and invs., 1560-1833 (MS, 19th cent., consolidated with other 'Oxford' peculiars).

Peculiar of the Dean and Canons of Windsor in Wantage (Bodleian Library, Oxford, and Wiltshire Record Office)
  See also peculiar of the dean of Salisbury, above.
  Jurisdiction: Hungerford, West Ilsley, Shalbourne (partly Wilts.) and Wantage in Berkshire; Ogbourne St. Andrew and Ogbourne St. George in Wiltshire. These may have been separate peculiars, but at least after 1660 appear to have been jointly administered.
  Index: wills, admons. and invs., 1582-1668, relating to Wantage and its hamlets only (MS, 19th cent., with other Oxford peculiars) (Bodleian Library).
  Chronological list: wills, admons. and invs., 1669-1840 (MS, 19th cent.) (Wiltshire Record Office).

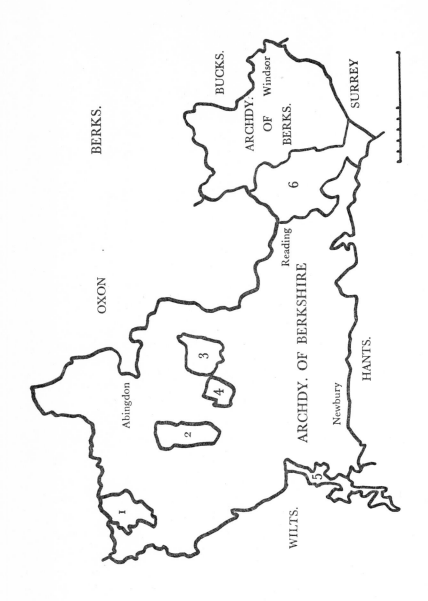

Court of the Dean of Windsor (The Aerary, St. George's Chapel, Dean's Cloister, Windsor Castle, Berks. Tel. Windsor (07535) 68286)

Jurisdiction: in the freehold of the College within the Lower Ward of Windsor Castle.

Printed abstracts: wills 1396-1638 (18 only) (*The Manuscripts of St. George's Chapel,* by Canon J. Dalton, 1957, pp. 24-26; includes John Byles of Staines, Middx., 1436; Wm. Bagenhale of Leighton Buzzard, Beds., 1438; Wm. Wyse of All SS. London Wall, 1449; Wm. More, BVM Oxford, 1492; John Cretynge, of Caxton, Camb., 1500; John Palmer, of Barsby, Leics., 1638).

Wills, 1662-1735.

Miscellaneous Wills (*many relating to the court of the dean of Salisbury*) (Wiltshire Record Office)

Index: wills, 1555-1730 (and a few to 1805) (TS, superseding printed index below, and including recent additions).

Printed index: the above (relating to Berkshire, Dorset and Devon) (*The Genealogists' Magazine,* vol. 5, pp. 140-41 *et seq.,* compiled by C. R. Everett; but has been found to be incomplete).

Berkshire parishes outside the jurisdiction of the archdeacon of Berkshire.

F=Peculiar of Faringdon
S=Peculiars of the Dean of Salisbury
W=Peculiars of the Dean and Canons of Windsor

Arborfield, S 6
Aston Upthorpe, S 3
Blewbury, S 3
Little Coxwell, F 1
Great Faringdon, F 1
Hungerford, W 5
Hurst, S 6
West Ilsley, W 4

Ruscombe, S 6
Sandhurst, S 6
Shalbourne
　(partly Wilts.), W 5
Sonning, S 6
Upton, S 3
Wantage, W 2
Wokingham, S 6

BUCKINGHAMSHIRE

Buckinghamshire was in the province of Canterbury, and in the diocese of Lincoln until 1845 when it was transferred to the diocese of Oxford. The county of Buckingham formed an archdeaconry (except for peculiars and four parishes in the diocese of London, archdeaconry of St. Albans), and probate matters were effectively delegated to the archdeaconry court, very few wills at Lincoln (or, after 1845, at Oxford) referring to Buckinghamshire. The records of the archdeaconry are now in the county record office at Aylesbury where there is in preparation a good modern card index to wills, which already covers 1483-1624 and 1720-1857; those for the peculiars are in the Bodleian Library, Oxford (where there is a good 19th century index), except for that of the Provost of Eton, which remain at Eton College.

The county record office in Aylesbury is in the county council building, adjacent to the public library, and there is a multi-storey car park nearby. The office issues a leaflet *Notes for the Guidance of Genealogists*, which describes the wills and admons. held.

Prerogative Court of Canterbury and other courts having general jurisdiction – see page 1.

Archdeaconry of Buckingham with the Commissary of the Bishop of Lincoln (Buckinghamshire Record Office, County Offices, Aylesbury HP20 1UA. Tel. Aylesbury (0296) 5000, ext. 586/8)
  Jurisdiction: the whole county except for the peculiars (below; some late 17th and early 18th century wills and admons. for these are to be found in the archdeaconry records) and the parishes of Aston Abbots, Granborough, Little Horwood and Winslow.
  Indexes: wills, 1483-1624 (card index), 1625-1632 (calendar), 1632-1708 (MS, 19th century), 1709-1720 (calendar) (card index, 1625-1720, in preparation), 1720-1857 (35,000) (card index); admons., 1598, 1632-1857 (10,000) (calendar); m/f of calendar, to 1857, at SG.

Archdeaconry of St. Albans (Hertford County Record Office, page 61)
  Jurisdiction: Aston Abbots, Granborough, Little Horwood and Winslow in Buckinghamshire. See also *Consistory Court of London* (page 64) during inhibition.

Diocese of Lincoln, Episcopal Registers (Lincolnshire Archives Office, page 81).
The diocese included Buckinghamshire, and a very few wills for the county are to be found.
Printed index: wills, 1320-1547 (Index Lib., vol. 28, pp. 1-17).
Printed abstracts: all the above (*Early Lincoln Wills*, A. Gibbons, 1888).

Consistory Court of Lincoln (Lincolnshire Archives Office)
Records of this court refer mainly to Lincolnshire, as court records of the bishop's commissary generally were kept with the archdeaconry records, but some Bucks. testators occur.
Printed indexes: wills, 1506-1652 (Index Lib., vols. 28 and 41); admons., 1540-1659 (vol. 52); wills ('miscellaneous'), 1549-1730 (vol. 57, pp. 430-56).
For other indexes and records see page 80.

Peculiars of Aylesbury, Bierton, Buckingham, Monks Risborough and Thame (Oxon.) (Department of Western MSS., Bodleian Library, Oxford, page 105)
Jurisdiction: the places named; and Buckland, Stoke Mandeville, and Quarrendon (Bierton); Halton (Monks Risborough); Towersey (Thame).
Index: wills, admons. and invs., 1547-1857 (MS, 19th cent., consolidated for all peculiars, with Oxon. and Berks. peculiars. Some late 17th and early 18th century wills, etc., are among the Buckingham archdeaconry records, above, but are listed in this index. Records of the individual peculiars commence: Aylesbury, 1624; Bierton, 1547 (but very incomplete before 1660); Buckingham, 1559, 1607-1623, 1674, 1701 onwards; Monks Risborough, 1605; Thame, 1547 (very incomplete before 1660)).
Aylesbury and Buckingham were Lincoln prebends; Bierton and Thame were parts of the peculiar of the dean and chapter of Lincoln; but separately administered from 1547; see below. Monks Risborough was a peculiar of the archbishop of Canterbury and was never inhibited.

Peculiar of the Dean and Chapter of Lincoln (Lincolnshire Archives Office)
Jurisdiction: included the peculiars of Aylesbury and Buckingham and some records for Bierton before 1547.
Printed index: wills, admons. and invs., 1534-1834 (Index Lib., vol. 57, pp. 265-366: Bierton (5), 1540-1544; Buckingham (1), 1673); also under 'miscellaneous' wills, 1542-1730 (vol. 57, pp. 430-56, Aylesbury (1), 1580; Buckingham (5), 1580, 1671-1673).

Peculiar of the Provost of Eton (Eton College Records, Penzance, Eton College, Windsor, Berks. SL4 6DB. Tel. Windsor (07535) 62937)
 Jurisdiction: the parish of Eton.
 Wills and admons., 1457-1643 (225), 1665-1666 (2).

Consistory and Archdeaconry Courts of Oxford (Bodleian Library, Oxford, page 104)
 Jurisdiction: included Caversfield, Ipstone (or Ibstone), Lillingstone Lovell and Stokenchurch. After 1845 the consistory court replaced that of Lincoln for the archdeaconry of Buckingham, but few wills are likely to be found any more than at Lincoln.

Buckinghamshire parishes outside the jurisdiction of the archdeacon of Buckingham.

Aston Abbots
 (archd. of St. Albans), 4
Aylesbury (pec.), 6
Bierton (pec.), 7
Buckingham (pec.), 2
Buckland (pec. of Bierton), 9
Caversfield (detd.)
 (archd. of Oxford)
Eton (pec.), 14
Granborough
 (archd. of St. Albans), 3
Halton
 (pec. of Monks Risborough), 10
Little Horwood
 (arch. of St. Albans), 3

Ibstone or Ipstone
 (archd. of Oxford), 13
Lillingstone Lovell
 (archd. of Oxford), 1
Monks Risborough (pec.), 12
Quarrendon (pec. of Bierton), 5
Stoke Mandeville
 (pec. of Bierton), 8
Stokenchurch
 (archd. of Oxford), 13
Towersey (pec. of Thame), 11
Winslow (archd. of St. Albans), 3

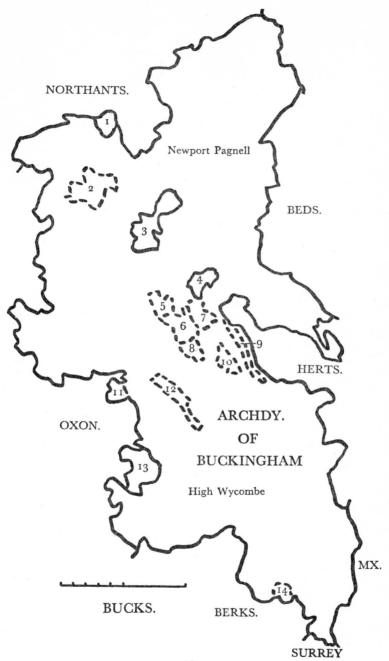

NORTHANTS.

Newport Pagnell

BEDS.

HERTS.

ARCHDY.
OF
BUCKINGHAM

High Wycombe

OXON.

MX.

BUCKS.

BERKS.

SURREY

17

CAMBRIDGESHIRE
AND THE ISLE OF ELY

Cambridgeshire was in the province of Canterbury, mainly in the diocese of Ely, except for a few parishes in the eastern part of the county in the diocese of Norwich. For probate purposes the archdeaconry court of Ely only had jurisdiction over the south-western deaneries of Bourne, Shingay and Cambridge itself, and the parishes of Haddenham and Wilburton in the Isle of Ely; the remainder, peculiars and the university apart, being subject to the consistory court direct.

The records of the consistory, archdeaconry and university courts are now all housed in Cambridge University Library, and administered by the Keeper of the University Archives. Very good modern card indexes to the records of the court of the Chancellor (later the Vice-Chancellor) of the University and to the archdeaconry court have now been compiled. Work is at present in progress on the very much bulkier consistory court records.

The Ely Diocesan and Capitular records, in the care of the archivist to the bishop and dean and chapter of Ely, also in Cambridge University Library, to which there is a recent printed catalogue, contain some testamentary records, in particular admons. for the consistory court from 1563 to 1694. A summary list of chapter records is available in the Manuscript Reading Room.

The University Library is situated on the west of Cambridge, out of the centre of the city, and there is ample parking. Application should be made in advance to the Keeper of the Archives.

Prerogative Court of Canterbury and other courts having general jurisdiction – see page 1.
   Inventories, 1650-1660 (TS at SG).

Consistory Court of Ely (often called *Ely and Cambridge*) (Keeper of the University Archives, Cambridge University Library, West Road, Cambridge CB3 9DR. Tel. Cambridge (0223) 61441, ext. 345 or 344).
   Jurisdiction: see introductory note; and the archdeaconry when inhibited.

   Indexes: wills, 1449-1857 (calendar); also 1621-1658 (MS, modern); admons. (see also below) and invs., 1662-1857 (MS, modern). A consolidated index to all these records is now in preparation; m/f of calendar to 1857 at SG.
   Printed index: miscellaneous wills, 1800-1841 (55 only) (*Ely Episcopal Records*, 1891, pp. 16-18).

Consistory Court of Ely (Archivist to the Bishop and Dean and Chapter of Ely, Cambridge University Library)
Printed list: admons., 1562-1582 (1,000) (*Ely Episcopal Records*, pp. 154-84).
Unindexed: admons., 1582-1611.
Index: admons., 1611-1620, 1660-1667, 1687-1694 (calendars).
These records are catalogued in *Ely (Diocesan) Records*, by Mrs D. M. Owen, 1971, pp. 35-36; see also p. 29.

Audience Court of the Bishop of Ely (Diocesan Archivist, Cambridge University Library, as above)
Jurisdiction: a few clergy and wealthy or noble subjects of the diocese.
Printed abstracts: wills, 1382-1527 (33) (*Ely Episcopal Records*, pp. 193-223).

Archdeaconry of Ely (Keeper of the University Archives, Cambridge University Library, as above)
Jurisdiction: the south-western deaneries of Bourne and Shingay, and Cambridge deanery (53 parishes) and the parishes of Haddenham and Wilburton in the Isle of Ely; see also the consistory, above.
Index: wills, admons. and invs., 1513-1857 (22,500) (card index; and to be published shortly in Index Library).

Court of the Chancellor of the University of Cambridge (Keeper of the University Archives, Cambridge University Library, as above)
Jurisdiction: over members of the university and certain so-called 'privileged' persons. The court later became known as the *Court of the Vice-Chancellor.*
Index: wills, 1501-1765, admons., 1541-1746, invs., 1498-1744 (modern card index).
Printed index: wills and admons., 1501-1765 (1,300) (*Wills Proved in the Vice-Chancellor's Court at Cambridge* – 'unreliable', and now superseded by the card index above).

Archdeaconry of Sudbury (with the Commissary Court of Bury St. Edmunds) (Suffolk Record Office, Bury St. Edmunds, page 124)
Jurisdiction: Cambridgeshire parishes in the eastern deanery of Fordham. See also consistory court of Norwich, below.
Indexes: wills and admons., 1354-1700 (card index); 1700-1800 (modern MS); 1800-1857 (card index).
Printed index: wills, 1354-1538 (Proc. Suff. Inst. Arch., vol. 12).

Consistory Court of Norwich (Norfolk Record Office)
Superior jurisdiction to the archdeaconries of Sudbury, above, and Norfolk.
Printed indexes: wills, 1370-1603 (Index Lib., vols. 69 and 73, and Norf. Rec. Soc., vols. 16 and 21), 1604-1818 (Norf. Rec. Soc., vols. 28, 34 and 38).
For other records and indexes, see page 92.

Peculiar of Thorney (Keeper of the University Archives, Cambridge University Library, as above)
  Jurisdiction: parish and lordship of Thorney in the Isle of Ely.
  Indexes: wills, admons. and invs., 1774-1857 (calendar).
  See also *Archdeaconry of Huntingdon*, page 65.
Peculiar of King's College, Cambridge (King's College, Cambridge)
  Jurisdiction: in the precincts of the college only.
  Unindexed: wills and admons., 1449-1794.
Peculiar of Isleham (Cambs.) *and Freckenham* (Suffolk) (Suffolk Record Office, Bury St. Edmunds)
  Isleham in the diocese of Ely and Freckenham in the diocese of Norwich were a peculiar of the bishop of Rochester. There are a few wills for both in the consistory court of Norwich (see above), this court claiming jurisdiction during visitations by the bishop of Norwich. There are also some wills in the *Consistory and Archdeaconry Courts of Rochester* (see page 72) and post-1649 wills and admons. in the records of the *Archdeaconry of Huntingdon* (page 65).
  Index (Isleham): wills, 1556-1581, 1647-1857, admons., 1662-1851 (card index, by Rev. J. A. Humphries).
Court of the Dean and Chapter of Ely (Diocesan Archivist, Cambridge University Library, as above)
  Jurisdiction: inhabitants of the College (i.e. the Cathedral Close). See also consistory court of Ely.
  Wills, admons. and invs., 1664-1776 (79).
Archdeaconry of Norfolk (Norfolk Record Office)
  Jurisdiction: the parishes of Outwell and Upwell (partly in Norfolk).
  See also consistory court of Norwich, above.
  For records and indexes, see page 92.

Archdeaconry of Sudbury
  (in diocese of Norwich), 4
Ashley cum Silverley
Burwell
Cheveley
Chippenham
Wood Ditton
Fordham
Kennett
Kirtling
Landwade
Newmarket
Snailwell
Soham
Wicken

Archdeaconry of Norfolk
  (in diocese of Norwich), 2
Outwell
Upwell
Welney
Peculiar of Isleham, 3
Peculiar of Thorney, 1

Archdeaconry of Ely
  (deaneries of Cambridge, Bourne and Shingay, and parishes of Haddenham and Wilburton)
Cambridge (all parishes), 6
Abington by Shingay, 7
Barnwell, 7
Bassingbourne, 7
Bourne, 7
Boxworth, 7
Caldecot, 7
Caxton, 7
(Cherry) Hinton, 6
Conington, 7
Croxton, 7
Croyden cum Clapton, 7
Elsworth, 7
Eltisley, 7

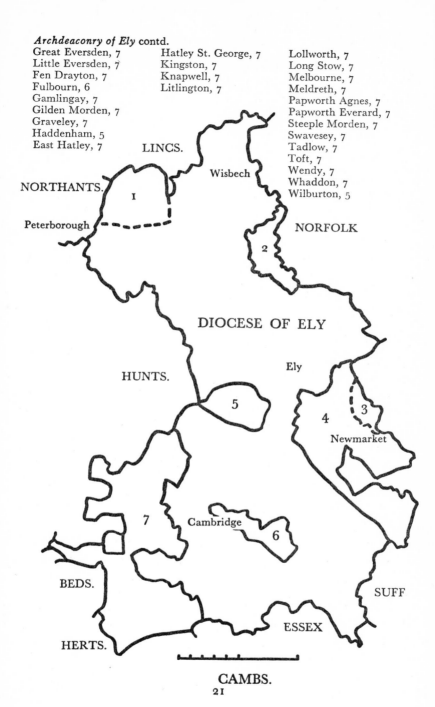

LINCS.

NORTHANTS.

Wisbech

Peterborough

NORFOLK

DIOCESE OF ELY

HUNTS.

Ely

Newmarket

Cambridge

BEDS.

SUFF

HERTS.

ESSEX

CAMBS.

21

CHESHIRE

Cheshire was in the province of York and almost wholly in the diocese of Chester from its creation in 1541; before that it formed part of the diocese of Lichfield (and Coventry), in the province of Canterbury. The township of Wirswall only remained in that diocese.

The probate records relating to the county of Cheshire in the consistory court of Chester are now mainly at the Cheshire Record Office (having been separated from those for Lancashire and Wales). The court was divided into two, estates below £40 being an 'infra jurisdiction', clergy and esquires excepted. There are printed indexes to all wills and admons. to 1830 – the 'infra' wills are separately indexed before 1665, are included as appendices with the main series 1665-1800, and are jointly indexed thereafter. There is a TS index 1831-1857, and also one to wills transcribed in the Bishop's Registers, 1492-1829 (printed to 1650). There are no surviving records relating to the county in the consistory court of Lichfield.

The record office is situated in Chester Castle (sign-posted 'Crown Court'), on the road to North Wales immediately on the town side of Grosvenor Bridge crossing the river; car parking for visitors to the record office in the castle square. The office issues leaflets on the facilities and general sources available, probate records and *Compiling a Family Tree*.

For a map of the county, showing its situation in relation to neighbouring counties and jurisdictions, see the 'Province of York', page 152.

Prerogative Court of Canterbury and other courts having general jurisdiction – see page 1.
    Printed index: wills, 1650-1660 (Lancs. and Ches. Record Soc., vol. 4, pp. 250-80) and admons., 1650-1660 (vol. 4, pp. 281-300).

Prerogative Court of York and other courts having jurisdiction in the province – see page 150.

Consistory Court of Chester (Cheshire Record Office, The Castle, Chester CH1 2DN. Tel. Chester (0244) 602574)

Jurisdiction: the county from 1541.

Printed indexes: wills and admons., 1545-1650 (main series) (Lancs. and Ches. Record Soc., vols. 2 and 4), 1590-1665 ('infra' series) (vol. 52), 1660-1800 (main series, with 'infra' series as appendices) (vols. 15, 18, 20, 22, 25, 37, 38, 44 and 45), additional wills and admons., 1670 (vol. 63, pp. 183-87) and additional 'infra' wills and admons., 1693 (vol. 63, pp. 193-199), wills and admons., 1801-1820 (consolidated) (vols. 62, 63 and 78), 1821-1830 (Cheshire separate) (vols. 107, pp. 159-205, and 113, pp. 143-186). Wills 'formerly in the diocesan registry', 1487-1800 (vols. 33, 43, and 52).

Other index: wills and admons., 1831-1857 (14,000) (TS); m/f of calendar to 1849 at SG.

Printed abstracts: selected wills and invs., 1525-1544 (54) (Chetham Soc., vol. 33), 1483-1589 (106) (vol. 51), 1596-1639 (67) (vol. 54), 1477-1746 (200, incl. admons.) (N.S., vol. 3; incl. in Part 2, p. 198, 220 wills now lost), 1572-1696 (180) (vol. 28, with an appendix of Ches. wills proved at York or Richmond, 1542-1649), 1563-1807 (63) (vol. 37); 1301-1752 (123) ('not now found in any probate registry', Lancs. and Ches. Record Soc., vol. 30).

Consistory Court of Lichfield (Lichfield Joint Record Office, page 119)

Jurisdiction: before 1541 throughout the county, but no records appear to have survived. After 1541, the township of Wirswall only.

Diocese of Chester, Episcopal Registers (Chester Record Office)

Printed index: wills, 1492-1650 (Lancs. and Ches. Record Soc., vol. 2, pp. xi-xix).

Other index: wills, 1492-1829 (TS).

B=Peculiars of the Bishop of Exeter
D=Peculiars of the Dean and Chapter of Exeter
S=Royal Peculiar of St. Buryan

St. Agnes, D 5
St. Anthony in Roseland, B 7
Boconnock with Bradoc, D 3
St. Breoke, B 2
Budock, B 6
(St.) Buryan, S 9
Egloshayle, B 2
St. Erney, B 4
St. Ervan, B 2
St. Eval, B 2
Falmouth, B 6
(St.) Germans, B 4
(St.) Gerrans, B 7
St. Gluvias, B 6
St. Issey, B 2

Landrake, B 4
Lawhitton, B 1
St. Levan, S 9
Lezant, B 1
Mabe, B 6
St. Merryn, B 2
Mylor, B 6
Padstow, B 2
Perranzabulo, D 5
Little Petherick
 (or St. Petroc Minor), B 2
South Petherwyn, B 1
Sennen, S 9
Trewen, B 1
St. Winnow, D 3

CORNWALL

Cornwall was in the province of Canterbury and diocese of Exeter. It formed an archdeaconry which covered the county, except for peculiars, and included three parishes in Devon.

The records of the consistory court of the archdeaconry of Cornwall and those of the royal peculiar deanery of St. Buryan are now at the Cornwall County Record Office. There is a printed index to both to 1799 and a modern card index to both, 1800-1857.

All probate records for the diocese of Exeter deposited in the probate registry there were destroyed by enemy action in 1942. These included the consistory and episcopal principal registry records, which related generally to Cornwall; 22 Cornish parishes which were bishop's peculiars, with specific jurisdiction in the consistory (there are printed indexes to 1799 to these lost documents); and five Cornish parishes which were peculiars of the dean and chapter of Exeter. From 1812 copies of all wills, whatever the court, had to be deposited with the Estate (or Stamp) Duty Office in London. So far as the courts whose records were destroyed at Exeter are concerned, these copy wills have now been distributed to the relevant county record offices. The Cornwall Record Office has a card index to those now there. Abstracts of wills and admons. for these (and other) courts from 1796 are still at the Public Record Office in London.

The Cornwall County Record Office is a building on the Old County Hall site, on the western outskirts of Truro near the railway station; there is ample car parking in the main car-park nearby.

Prerogative Court of Canterbury and other courts having general jurisdiction – see page 1.
Invs., 1650-1660 (TS at SG).

Consistory Court of the Archdeaconry of Cornwall and Royal Peculiar of St. Buryan (Cornwall County Record Office, County Hall, Truro TR1 3AY. Tel. Truro 3698)
    Jurisdiction: the county except for peculiars; generally excluding beneficed clergy not possessed of 'bona notabilia' in any other diocese and persons possessed of personalty in more than one jurisdiction in the diocese.
    Printed index: wills and admons., 1600-1799 (and a very few pre-1600) (61,500) (Index Lib., vols. 56 and 59); for St. Buryan, 1700-1799 (100), see vol. 59, pp. 242-43.

Archdeaconry of Cornwall and Peculiar of St. Buryan, contd.
> Other indexes: wills, admons. and invs., 1800-1857 (15,900) (card index; for eventual publication in Index Lib.); m/f of calendar to 1857 at SG; 1600-1799 (new card index, to supersede printed index above, A-B and in progress).
> Unindexed: invs., 1600-1799.

Episcopal Consistory Court of Exeter (Devon Record Office, Concord House, South Street, Exeter EX1 1DX. Tel. Exeter (0392) 79146/7).
> Virtually all the records of this court were destroyed in 1942; see also page 33.
> Jurisdiction: over the whole of the diocese when there were not 'bona notabilia' within two or more subordinate courts, and 22 Cornish parishes which were peculiars of the bishop.
> Printed index (to the destroyed records): wills and admons., 1532-1800 (Index Lib., vol. 46 and Devonshire Assoc., vol. 2 – calendar).

Episcopal Principal Registry of Exeter (Devon Record Office)
> Virtually all the records of this court were destroyed in 1942; see also page 33.
> Jurisdiction: over all beneficed clergy in the diocese, and all persons in the diocese during inhibition of the archdeaconries or having 'bona notabilia' in more than one jurisdiction within the diocese.
> Printed index (to the destroyed records): wills and admons., 1559-1799 (Index Lib., vol. 35 and Devonshire Assoc., vol. 1, pp. 1-215, calendar).

Peculiars of the Dean and Chapter of Exeter (Devon Record Office)
> Virtually all the records of this court were destroyed in 1942; see also page 34.
> Jurisdiction: over four Cornish parishes. No surviving index.

Estate (or Stamp) Duty Office (Public Record Office, Chancery Lane, London WC2. Tel. 01-405 0741; and Cornwall County Record Office)
> See introductory note. The abstracts, from 1796, should include wills and admons. for, amongst others, the courts whose records were destroyed in 1942. For details see page 32.
> Indexes: abstracts of wills and admons., from 1796 (Public Record Office).
> Wills (relating to Cornwall), 1812-1857 (card index) (Cornwall County Record Office).

See under Devon (pages 33-35) for other surviving original documents and abstracts from the destroyed records of the above courts.

CUMBERLAND AND WESTMORLAND

Cumberland and Westmorland were in the province of York and in the dioceses of Carlisle and Chester, apart from one parish in the diocese of Durham. The major part of Cumberland and the northern half of Westmorland were in the diocese of Carlisle. The records of the consistory court, to which there is a 19th century index, are at the Record Office in Carlisle, together with those of three manorial courts. The south-western part of Cumberland (the deanery of Copeland), and the southern part of Westmorland (the deaneries of Kendal and Lonsdale, both partly in Lancashire), were in the diocese of Chester, in the western division of the archdeaconry of Richmond (Yorks.). The records of this part of the archdeaconry are now at the Lancashire Record Office at Preston; there is a 19th century index, chronological within letter, to 1720. Wills relating to the western deaneries but found in the records of the eastern deaneries (at Leeds) have mostly been transferred to Preston. Before 1541 the archdeaconry of Richmond formed part of the diocese of York; and in 1856 the deanery of Copeland was transferred to the diocese of Carlisle. The parish of Alston in Cumberland with the chapelry of Garrigill was in the diocese of Durham throughout, and so was Upper (Over) Denton until about 1777.

The Record Office is in the ancient castle in Carlisle, just north of the centre of the city and of the cathedral (it is not to be confused with the crenellated buildings known as the Courts in the centre of the city, near the railway station); there is ample car parking. The office issues a leaflet *Notes for Genealogical Searchers* which gives details of probate records and of all parishes in the counties.

Prerogative Court of Canterbury and other courts having general jurisdiction – see page 1.

Prerogative Court of York and other courts having jurisdiction in the province – see page 150.

Consistory Court of Carlisle (Archives Department, Cumbria County Council, The Record Office, The Castle, Carlisle. Tel. Carlisle (0228) 24248)

Jurisdiction: see introductory note.

Indexes: wills and admons., 1558-1644, 1661-1857 (MS, 19th cent., calendar, includes some wills no longer existing); 1661-1750, A-E (and in progress) (card index); m/f of calendar to 1857 at SG.

CUMBERLAND & WESTMORLAND

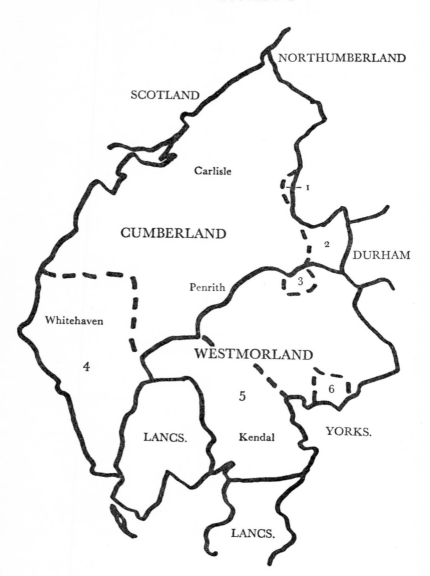

Parishes outside the jurisdiction of the consistory court of Carlisle.

Archdeaconry of Richmond, Diocese of Chester:

Cumberland (Deanery of Copeland), 4

Arlecdon
Beckermet St. Bridget
Beckermet St. John
Bootle
Brigham
Buttermere
Cleator
Clifton
Cockermouth
Corney
Dean
Distington
Drigg
Egremont
Embleton
Ennerdale
Eskdale
Gosforth
Harrington
Hensingham
Irton
Lamplugh
Lorton
Loweswater
Millom
Moresby
Mosser
Muncaster
Ponsonby
St. Bees
Setmurthy
Thwaites
Ulpha
Waberthwaite
Wasdalehead
Nether Wasdale
Whicham
Whitbeck
Whitehaven
Workington
Wythop

Westmorland (Deaneries of Kendal and Lonsdale), 5

Ambleside
Barbon
Beetham
Burnside
Burton in Kendal
Casterton
Crook
Crosthwaite
Firbank
Grasmere
Greyrigg
Holme
New and Old Hutton
Hutton Roof
Hugill (Ings)
Kendal
Kentmere
Killington
Kirkby Lonsdale
Langdale
Mansergh
Middleton
Preston Patrick
Rydal
Selside
Long Sleddale
Over Staveley
Troutbeck
Underbarrow
Windermere
Winster
Witherslack

Diocese of Durham

Alston with
 Garrigill, Cumb., 2
Upper Denton, Cumb., 1

Peculiar of Ravenstonedale, 6

Peculiar of Temple Sowerby, 3

Consistory Court of Carlisle, contd.
  Printed list: selected 'foreign' wills, 18th and 19th cent. (77) (*Genealogists' Magazine,* vol. 15, pp. 420-21).
  Printed abstracts: wills, 1353-1386 (157), in the Registers of the Bishops of Carlisle (Cumb. and Westm. Antiq. and Arch. Soc., Extra Series, vol. 9, 1893).

Consistory Court of the Commissary of the Archdeaconry of Richmond, Western Deaneries (Lancashire Record Office, Preston, page 74)
  Jurisdiction: the deanery of Copeland in Cumberland, and those parts of the deaneries of Kendal and Lonsdale in Westmorland.
  Indexes: wills and admons., 1457-1720 (MS, 19th cent., calendar), 1720-1857 (36,000) (calendar). The indexes to the western deaneries printed by the Lancs. and Cheshire Record Society do not include non-Lancashire wills.
  Printed abstracts: selected wills and invs., 1442-1579 (Surtees Soc. vol. 26).

Consistory Court of Durham (Department of Palaeography and Diplomatic, University of Durham, page 44)
  Jurisdiction: over the parish of Alston with the chapelry of Garrigill, and, until c. 1777, Upper (or Over) Denton, all in Cumberland.

Manor of Docker (Cumbria Record Office, Carlisle)
  Wills and admons., 1686-1770 (a few only).

Manor of Ravenstonedale (Cumbria Record Office, Carlisle)
  Index: wills and admons., 1670-1857 (MS, 19th cent.).

Manor of Temple Sowerby (Cumbria Record Office, Carlisle)
  Index: wills and admons., 1580-1816 (MS, 19th cent.).

DEVON

Devon was in the province of Canterbury and diocese of Exeter.

All probate records for the diocese of Exeter deposited in the probate registry there were destroyed by enemy action in 1942. These included the episcopal consistory, principal registry and archdeaconry of Exeter records (to which there are printed indexes to 1799 to the lost documents), the consistory court of the dean and chapter of Exeter, the peculiar courts of the dean of Exeter and of the custos of the cathedral and the college of vicars choral, and the consistory courts of the archdeacons of Barnstaple and Totnes.

From 1812 copies of all wills, whatever the court, had to be deposited with the Estate (or Stamp) Duty Office in London. Copies of all Devon wills from this collection have now been deposited in the Devon Record Office, so there should still be a virtually complete record for the period, 1812-1857, enhanced by the inclusion of P.C.C. wills for the county. These are arranged alphabetically, and there is a separate TS index. From 1796 abstracts of wills and admons. had similarly to be sent to this Office. These abstracts remain in the Public Record Office, London, and continue after 1811 (at present, under a 150-year rule, they are available to 1823). Unlike the complete copies, which were indexed in one series, the abstracts are still arranged by courts.

The parishes of North Petherwin, St. Giles in the Heath and Werrington were in the archdeaconry of Cornwall, whose records survive at Truro; there is a list at the Devon Record Office. Similarly the parish of Uffculme was a Salisbury prebend, and the records of this court and during inhibition those in the court of the dean of Salisbury are at the Wiltshire Record Office at Trowbridge; there is a list at the Devon Record Office.

Stockland and Dalwood were detached parishes in the county and archdeaconry of Dorset (diocese of Bristol) until 1836, when they were transferred to Devon and the archdeaconry of Exeter; at the same time Thorncombe, a detached Devon parish, was transferred to Dorset, though some wills continued to be proved at Exeter.

Some probate records, relevant material in act books, lists of wills proved and admons. granted, survive for the peculiars of the dean and chapter, the peculiar of Woodbury, and the archdeaconry of Exeter, in the Exeter Cathedral Library, to which there are TS lists. Act books for the archdeaconry of Barnstaple are deposited at the Devon Record Office, and there is a 5 volume TS index to the destroyed wills for this court, copies in the Devon County, Exeter City, Exeter University and New York Public Libraries.

The Devon Record Office also has a large collection, made by Miss Moger, of abstracts of wills, 1532-1846 (47 TS volumes, with an index to testators A-C only), and testamentary causes, 1537-1857, mainly in the episcopal consistory court, with a 3 volume index. There are other smaller collections of 'stray' wills, and the Devon Record Office keeps a card index of wills formerly in private custody and now deposited amongst family, estate and solicitors' records.

The Exeter City Record Office was established earlier than the County Record Office, and so in its collections has material relating to the county generally as well as the city. There is a consolidated card index to all testamentary records there.

The Devon Record Office is in the centre of Exeter, near the cathedral; it has a small car-park reserved for users of the office. A leaflet on *Family History* is issued. The Cathedral Library is in part of the Bishop's Palace, adjacent to the cathedral. The City Record Office is in the main city library building.

Prerogative Court of Canterbury and other courts having general juris-diction – see page 1.
> Post-1811 wills should also be in the Estate Duty Office collection at the Devon Record Office, below.
> Abstracts: Devon wills (MS, the Tuckett collection, at Devon County Library; and 8 vols., TS, skeleton pedigrees compiled from these wills, arranged alphabetically, at the Exeter Record Office).

Estate (or Stamp) Duty Office Wills (Devon Record Office, Concord House, South Street, Exeter EX1 1DX. Tel. Exeter (0392) 79146/7)
> See introductory note; should include wills from all Devon courts, apart from men who died on active service and who were exempt from duty.
> Index: copy wills, 1812-1857 (TS; and the wills arranged alpha-betically).

Estate (or Stamp) Duty Office Abstracts (Public Record Office, Chancery Lane, London WC2A 1LR. Tel. 01-405 0741)
> See introductory note; should include abstracts of all wills and admons. from all courts, arranged by court.
> Indexes: wills and admons., 1796-1811 (refs. IR 26/333-344, IR 27/84-85), 1812-1857 (from 1824 the indexes only are available, under a 150-year rule, but more abstracts will become available annually).
> These copies and abstracts of wills and admons. are described in two articles in the *Genealogists' Magazine* (vol. 15, no. 11, Sept. 1967, pp. 393-97, by A. J. Camp, and vol. 16, no. 6, June 1970, pp. 269-73, by D. T. Hawkings – the latter relates specifically to Devon).

Episcopal Consistory Court of Exeter (Devon Record Office)
Virtually all the records of this court were destroyed in 1942.
Jurisdiction: over the whole of the diocese when there were not 'bona notabilia' within 2 or more subordinate courts, and 14 Devon parishes which were peculiars of the bishop.
Printed index (to the destroyed records): wills and admons., 1532-1800 (22,000) (Index Lib. vol. 46 and Devonshire Assoc., vol. 2 – calendar with index).
Other indexes: surviving testamentary material, c. 1530-1699, 1700-1857 (card indexes). See also Miss Moger's abstracts, below.
Printed abstracts: invs., 1531-1699 (266) (Devon and Corn. Record Soc., N.S., vol. 11, 1966).

Episcopal Principal Registry of Exeter (Devon Record Office)
Virtually all the records of this court were destroyed in 1942.
Jurisdiction: over all beneficed clergy in the diocese, and all persons in the diocese during inhibition of the archdeaconries or having 'bona notabilia' in more than one jurisdiction within the diocese.
Printed index (to the destroyed records): wills and admons., 1599-1799 (17,500) (Index Lib., vol. 35, and Devonshire Assoc., vol. 1, pp. 1-215 – calendar with index).
Other indexes: as above (card index). See also Miss Moger's abstracts, below.
Printed abstracts: invs., as above.

Episcopal Registers and Exhibit Books (Devon Record Office)
A few pre-Reformation wills, mostly of canons and benefactors of the cathedral; and some later material in exhibit books.
Printed calendars: 1257-1441 (*Episcopal Registers of the Diocese of Exeter,* by F. C. Hingeston-Randolph, 10 vols., 1886-1915), 1420-1455 (*Register of Edmund Lacy,* Devon and Corn. Record Soc., vols. 7, 10, 13, 16 and 18 (index), 1963-72).
Indexes: exhibit books, c.1590-1710, containing further testamentary material (calendars).

Consistory Court of the Archdeaconry of Barnstaple (Devon Record Office)
Virtually all the records of this court were destroyed in 1942.
Jurisdiction: the archdeaconry except for peculiars; see also episcopal principal registry.
Index (to destroyed records): wills, 1721-1745.
Act books, containing testamentary matters, 1682-1855.
Also, at Devon County Library, Exeter City Library, Exeter University Library, and New York Public Library, but not Devon Record Office:
Index (to the destroyed records): wills and admons., 1563-1857 (TS, 5 vols., showing name and parish).

Consistory Court of the Archdeaconry of Exeter (Exeter Cathedral Library, Capitular Archives, Bishop's Palace, Exeter EX1 1HX. Tel. Exeter (0392) 72894)
> Virtually all the records of this court were destroyed in 1942.
> Printed index (to the destroyed records): wills and admons., 1547-1799 (46,000) (Index Lib., vol. 35, and Devonshire Assoc., vol. 1, pp. 216-673).
> Acts books, intance papers from 1679, testamentary causes, 1727-1852, accounts of wills, 1843-1856.

Consistory Court of the Archdeaconry of Totnes
> The records of this court were completely destroyed in 1942 and no indexes survive.

Consistory Court of the Archdeaconry of Cornwall (Cornwall Record Office, Truro, page 25)
> Jurisdiction: included the Devon parishes of North Petherwin, St. Giles in the Heath and Werrington.

Consistory Court of Bristol (Dorset Division) and Archdeaconry of Dorset (Dorset Record Office, page 38)
> Jurisdiction: included the detached Dorset parishes of Stockland and Dalwood, transferred to Devon and the archdeaconry of Exeter in 1836. Some records of Thorncombe (a detached Devon parish until 1836) may be found in this court after that date.

Peculiars in the Consistory Court of the Dean and Chapter of Exeter (Exeter Cathedral Library)
> Virtually all the records of this court were destroyed in 1942.
> Act books from 1593; admons., 1747-1756; testamentary causes, 1749-1843 (of which latter see Miss Moger's Abstracts, below) (TS lists).
> A few general records relating to the dean and chapter, chiefly pre-Reformation, also survive in this Library.

Peculiar of the Dean of Exeter
> Records of this peculiar were destroyed in 1942.
> Jurisdiction: the Cathedral Close at Exeter, and the parish of Braunton.
> Abstracts and indexes: 1632-1857 (Phillimore and Co., Ltd., Shopwyke Hall, Chichester, Sussex).

Peculiar of the Custos of the Cathedral and College of the Vicars Choral of Exeter Cathedral (Exeter Cathedral Library)
> Most of the records of this peculiar were destroyed in 1942.
> Jurisdiction: the parish of Woodbury.
> Act book, 1786-1850; list of wills and admons., 1635-1790; invs. (endorsed 'not exhibited for want of stamp'), 1679-1707 (TS lists).
> Abstracts and indexes: 1633-1850 (Phillimore and Co. Ltd., as above).

Prebend of Uffculme (Wiltshire Record Office, County Hall, Trowbridge, page 140)

A Salisbury prebend; see also the peculiar court of the dean of Salisbury, and Miscellaneous Wills, pages 141 and 143.

Index: wills, admons. and invs., 1552-1857 (19th cent. MS with modern additions).

Miss Moger's Abstracts (Devon Record Office, Exeter Record Office and Devon County Library)

Abstracts made by Miss Olive Moger as a professional genealogist.

Devon wills; arranged alphabetically (47 TS vols., with a card index to testators, A-C only).

Testamentary causes (mainly in the episcopal consistory court, but also some from the archdeaconry of Exeter (A-L) and the peculiars of the dean and chapter), series I, 1557-1700 (with a supplement up to 1749), series II, 1700-1857 (with a supplement from 1575 onwards), plus 3 index vols.; also a card index, incomplete at the end of the alphabet, to Series I only (in Devon Record Office only).

Court of the Mayor and the *Orphans' Court of Exeter* (City Record Office, Castle Street, Exeter EX4 3PQ. Tel. Exeter (0392) 73047)

Index: wills (on Mayor's Court Rolls), 1263-1701; (in miscellaneous deeds), 1327-1510; (Orphans' Court), 1555-1765; invs. (Orphans' Court), 1560-1774 (209); and all other wills, admons. and invs. in deposited records (consolidated card index).

Printed list: wills (miscellaneous deeds), 1327-1510 (Hist. MSS. Comm. Report, 1916, pp. 281-82, and (Orphans' Court), 1555-1765 (pp. 414-16).

Manor of Cockington (Exeter Record Office)

Wills, admons. and invs., 1540-c.1700.

Oswyn Murray Collection of Abstracts (Devon County Library)

Devon wills, arranged alphabetically (39 vols.).

Wills at Plymouth (Archives Department, Central Library, Drake Circus, Plymouth)

There are several large deposits of estate documents and family papers, calendared separately, which include probate and other copies of wills.

Other collections

Printed abstracts: *Devonshire Wills: a collection of annotated testamentary abstracts,* by Charles Worthy (1896); *Extracts from* (302) *Wills proved in P.C.C., relating to the parishes of Shute and Colyton,* by S. A. Smith (with a MS index at SG).

Other abstracts: some Devon wills (Vivian Collection, British Museum Add. MSS. 34546-52 and 34810, incl. some lost wills).

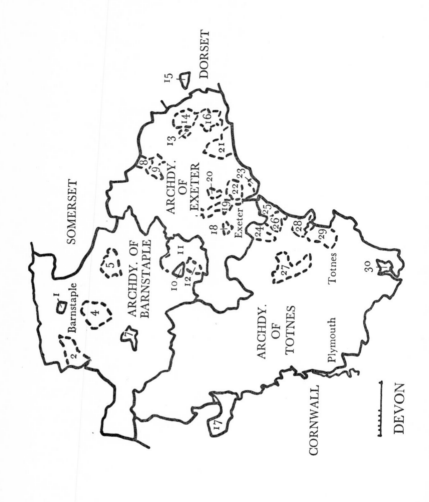

Parishes in Devon outside the jurisdiction of the archdeaconries of Barnstaple, Exeter and Totnes.

AC=Archdeaconry of Cornwall; AD=Archdeaconry of Dorset (dioc. of Bristol); AE=Archdeaconry of Exeter (outlying parishes); BE=Peculiars of the Bishop of Exeter; C=Manor of Cockington; DC=Peculiars of the Dean and Chapter of Exeter; DE=Peculiar of the Dean of Exeter; U=Prebend of Uffculme; VC=Peculiar of the Vicars Choral.

Arlington, AE 1
Ashburton, *DC* 27
Bickington, *DC* 27
Bishop's Nympton, BE 5
Bishop's Tawton, BE 4
Bishop's Teignton, BE 26
Branscombe, *DC* 21
Braunton, DE 2
Buckland, *DC* 27
Chudleigh, BE 24
Clyst Honiton, DC 20
Cockington, C 29
Coffinswell, *DC* 28
Colebrook, *DC* 12
Colyton, *DC* 16
Crediton, BE 11
Culmstock, *DC* 8
Dalwood, AD & AE 14
Dawlish, *DC* 25
Down St. Mary, AE 10
Exmouth, *DC* 23
Heavitree, DC 19
Ide, *DC* 18
Kennerleigh, BE 11
Kingskerswell, *DC* 28
Landkey, BE 4
Littleham (nr. Exmouth), *DC* 23

Marldon, BE 29
Monkton, *DC* 13
Morchard Bishop, BE 11
Northcott, AC 17
Paignton, BE 29
North Petherwin, AC 17
South Pool, AE 30
St. Giles in the Heath, AC 17
St. Giles in the Wood, AE 7
St. Marychurch, *DC* 28
Salcombe, *DC* 21
Sandford, BE 11
Shute, *DC* 16
Sidbury, *DC* 21
Southpool, AE 30
Staverton, *DC* 27
Stockland, AD & AE 14
Stoke Canon, *DC* 19
Stoke Gabriel, BE 29
Swimbridge, BE 4
East Teignmouth, *DC* 25
West Teignmouth, BE 26
Thorncombe, AE & AD 15
Topsham, *DC* 19
Uffculme, U 9
Werrington, AC 17
Woodbury, VC 22

DORSET

Dorset was in the province of Canterbury and diocese of Bristol. The archdeaconry of Dorset covered the whole county except for the many peculiars.

The records of the Dorset division of the consistory court, of the archdeaconry court, of the peculiars of Corfe Castle, Great Canford and Poole, Milton Abbas, Sturminster Marshall, and Wimborne Minster, of the prebend of Stratton, and of the manors of Burton Bradstock and Frampton are all at the Dorset Record Office. There are printed indexes to 1792 (later for the peculiars) and a consolidated card index to 1857 for nearly all these courts. The bulk of the wills are in the archdeaconry court, as the consistory court only acted during inhibition. Before 1542 and the creation of the diocese of Bristol, the county had been in the diocese of Salisbury, but records for that consistory court do not exist that early; and after 1836, when for ecclesiastical purposes the county returned to the diocese of Salisbury, the probate courts continued without change.

A number of Dorset parishes were within the jurisdiction of peculiar courts attached to the diocese of Salisbury. These were the peculiars of the dean of Salisbury, the dean and chapter of Salisbury, the royal peculiar of Gillingham, and the prebend peculiars of Chardstock, Fordington, Lyme Regis and Halstock, Netherbury in Ecclesia, Preston, and Yetminster and Grimston. The records of these are at the Wiltshire Record Office. There are printed indexes to 1800 to all places in Dorset. This volume also includes Dorset wills found in other Salisbury courts, and other 'strays'.

Also at the Wiltshire Record Office is a TS index to 'miscellaneous wills', which includes many from Dorset parishes in the peculiar of the dean of Salisbury. A printed index to these that appeared in the *Genealogists' Magazine* has now been superseded as many more have since come to light, which are incorporated in the TS index.

The Dorset Record Office is part of the County Hall complex in Dorchester, on the western edge of the town. There is a small carpark reserved for visitors to the office.

Prerogative Court of Canterbury and other courts having general jurisdiction – see page 1.
see page 1.
Invs., 1650-1660 (TS at SG).

Archdeaconry of Dorset (Dorset Record Office, County Hall, Dorchester DT1 1XJ. Tel. Dorchester (0305) 3131)
Jurisdiction: the whole county except peculiars, inhibited by the consistory.

Printed indexes: wills and admons., 1660-1792 (also a few fragments, 1568-1659) (14,000) (Index Lib., vol. 22, pp. 25-179); unproved wills, 1680-1837 (90) (vol. 53, pp. 169-70); invs., 1686-1790 (1,800) (vol. 53, pp. 133-63).
Other index: wills, admons and invs., 1660-1857 (card index); m/f of calendar to 1857 at SG.

Consistory Court of Bristol (*Dorset Division*) (Dorset Record Office)
Jurisdiction: the archdeaconry during inhibition.
Printed index: wills, admons. and invs., 1681-1792 (2,000) (Index Lib., vol. 22, pp. 1-24); admons., 1727-1729 (45) (vol. 55, p. 131).
Other index: wills, admons. and invs., 1680-1857 (card index); m/f of calendar to 1854 at SG.
Printed abstracts: wills, 1559-1572 (Som. and Dorset Notes and Queries, vol. 24, pp. 69 et seq.).

Peculiar of the Dean of Salisbury (Wiltshire Record Office, County Hall, Trowbridge, page 141)
Jurisdiction: included 28 Dorset parishes or chapelries, and prebendal peculiars during inhibition.
Printed index: wills and admons., 1500-1801 (5,000) (Index Lib., vol. 53, pp. 45-127).
Other index: wills, admons. and invs., 1557-1857 (19th cent. MS calendar, with modern additions).
See also Miscellaneous Wills, below.

Peculiar of the Dean and Chapter of Salisbury (Wiltshire Record Office)
Jurisdiction: included Stourpaine and Durweston in Dorset.
Printed index: wills and admons., 1604-1799 (100) (vol. 53, pp. 43-44)
Chronological list: wills, admons. and invs., 1600-1857 (MS, 19th cent.).

Manor of Burton Bradstock (Dorset Record Office)
Index: wills and admons., 1757-1809 (card index).

Peculiar of Great Canford and Poole (Dorset Record Office)
Printed indexes: wills, 1639-1799 (643) (vol. 22, pp. 209-27); admons., 1681-1799 (427) (vol. 22, pp. 228-37) (both calendars); (invs., 1587-1719 (18) described in vol. 53, p. 129, as relating to this peculiar do in fact refer to Wimborne Minster).
Other indexes: wills, admons. and invs., 1639-1857 (card index); m/f of calendar to 1857 at SG.

Prebend of Chardstock (Wiltshire Record Office)
See also peculiar of the Dean of Salisbury.
Printed index: wills, admons. and invs., 1639-1799 (200) (vol. 53, pp. 1-5).
Other index: wills, admons and invs., 1800-1857 (MS, modern).

Royal Peculiar of Corfe Castle (Dorset Record Office)
Printed list: wills, admons. and invs., 1577-1587 (30) (documents missing), 1602-1771 (556) (vol. 22, pp. 255-64).
Printed indexes: wills, 1732-1797 (19), admons., 1770-1799 (11) (vol. 22, p. 246).
Other index: wills, admons. and invs., 1577-1849 (card index); m/f of calendar to 1849 at SG.

Manor and Liberty of Frampton (Dorset Record Office)
Printed index: wills, admons. and invs. (in court books), 1678-1755 (69) (Som. and Dorset Notes and Queries, vol. 27, pp. 229-33).
Other index: the above (card index).

Prebend of Fordington and Writhlington (Wiltshire Record Office)
Note. There are in fact no wills for Writhlington (Som.). See also peculiar of the Dean of Salisbury.
Printed index: wills, admons. and invs., 1660-1799 (180) (vol. 53, pp. 6-9).
Other index: wills, admons. and invs., 1800-1855 (MS).

Royal Peculiar of Gillingham (Wiltshire Record Office)
Printed list: wills, admons. and invs., 1658-1799 (550) (vol. 53, pp. 10-19).
Chronological list: wills, admons. and invs., 1800-1857 (MS).

Prebend of Lyme Regis and Halstock (Wiltshire Record Office)
See also peculiar of the Dean of Salisbury.
Printed list: wills, admons. and invs., 1664-1799 (350) (vol. 53, pp. 20-23).
Chronological list: wills, admons. and invs., 1800-1857 (MS).

Peculiar of Milton Abbas (Dorset Record Office)
See also archdeaconry and consistory courts.
Printed index: wills, admons. and invs., 1675-1811 (92) (vol. 22, pp. 247-53).
Other index: as above (card index).

Prebend of Netherbury in ecclesia (Wiltshire Record Office)
See also peculiar of the Dean of Salisbury.
Printed index: wills, admons. and invs., 1608-1799 (600) (vol. 53, pp. 24-34).
Other index: wills, admons. and invs., 1800-1857 (MS).

Prebend of Preston and Sutton Pointz (Wiltshire Record Office)
See also peculiar of the Dean of Salisbury.
Printed index: wills, admons. and invs., 1761-1799 (16) (vol. 53, p. 35).
Index: wills, admons. and invs., 1800-1834 (8) (MS).

Peculiar of Sturminster Marshall (Dorset Record Office)
Printed list: wills and invs., 1641-1799 (313) (vol. 22, pp. 238-41),
admons., 1719-1799 (114) (vol. 22, pp. 242-45).

Prebend of Stratton (Dorset Record Office)
See also archdeaconry and consistory courts.
Index: wills and admons., 1584-1671 (card index).

Peculiar of Wimborne Minster (Dorset Record Office)
Printed indexes: wills, 1590-1823 (940) (vol. 22, pp. 181-99); admons.,
1666-1814 (377) (vol. 22, pp. 200-08); invs., 1587-1719 (vol. 53,
p. 129, described by mistake as belonging to Great Canford and Poole).
Other indexes: wills, 1590-1857, admons., 1591-1668. invs. (card index);
m/f of calendar to 1857 at SG; wills, 1557-1638, admons., 1591-1668,
invs., 1563-1686 (from Wimborne parish records, separately indexed
to the above, MS).

Prebend of Yetminster and Grimston (Wiltshire Record Office)
See also peculiar of the Dean of Salisbury.
Printed index: wills, admons. and invs., 1654-1799 (200) (vol. 53, pp.
36-39).
Other index: wills, admons. and invs., 1800-1856 (MS).

*Miscellaneous Wills (many relating to the peculiar of the Dean of
Salisbury)* (Wiltshire Record Office)
Index: wills, 1555-1730 (and a few to 1805) (TS, superseding printed
index below).
Printed index: the above (relating to Dorset, Berkshire and Uffculme,
Devon) (*Genealogists' Magazine*, vol. 5, pp. 140-41 *et seq.*, compiled
by C. R. Everett; but is now incomplete).

Dorset Probate Registry (Dorset Record Office)
Copy wills, 1858-1941.

Other Dorset Wills
Index Library, vol. 53, also includes the following indexes to Dorset wills
found in other courts:
p. 40. Archdeaconry of Salisbury, 1625-1725 (10).
p. 41. Consistory Court of Salisbury, 1560-1729 (5).
p. 42. Archdeaconry of Wiltshire, 1557 (1).
pp. 171-84. Miscellaneous wills and admons. from various courts,
borough records, and other collections.

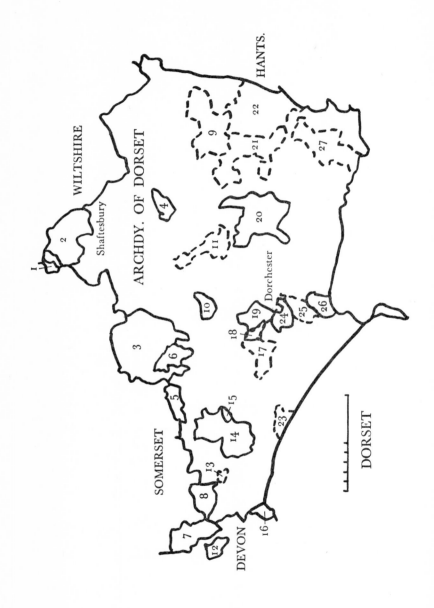

WILTSHIRE

Shaftesbury

ARCHDY. OF DORSET

HANTS.

SOMERSET

Dorchester

DEVON

DORSET

42

Parishes in Dorset in jurisdictions other than the archdeaconry of Dorset.

Note: records of the prebends of Chardstock, Lyme Regis and Halstock, Netherbury in Ecclesia, Preston and Sutton Poyntz, and Yetminster and 'Grimston are to be found also in the peculiar court of the dean of Salisbury (in addition to the parishes in the direct jurisdiction of that court). Places in the liberty of Frampton also appear in the archdeaconry and consistory records.

BB=Burton Bradstock; C=Chardstock; CC=Corfe Castle; CP=Great Canford and Poole; DC=Dean and Chapter of Salisbury; DS=Dean of Salisbury; E=Diocese of Exeter; F=Frampton; FW=Fordington and Writhlington; G=Gillingham; LR=Lyme Regis and Halstock; MA=Milton Abbas; N=Netherbury; P=Preston and Sutton Poyntz; SM=Sturminster Marshall; ST=Stratton; WM=Wimborne Minster; Y=Yetminster and Grimston.

Alton Pancras, DS 10
Anderson, DS 20
Beaminster, N & DS 14
Bere Hacket, DS 3
Bere Regis, DS 20
Bettiscombe, F 13
Bincombe, F 25
Bloxworth, DS 20
Bourton, G 1
Burton
  Bradstock, BB 23
Great Canford, CP 22
Castleton, DS 3
Caundle Marsh, DS 3
Chardstock, C & DS 7
Charminster, DS 19
Chetnole, Y & DS 6
Clifton Maybank, DS 3
Nether Compton, DS 3
Over Compton, DS 3
Compton Valence, F 17
Corfe Castle, CC 27
Corfe Mullen, SM 21
Dalwood (archd. of
  Dorset, detd.), 12
Folke, DS 3
Fordington, FW 24
Frampton, F 17

Gillingham, G 2
Grimston, Y 18
Halstock, LR & DS 5
Hamworthy, SM 21
Haydon, DS 3
Hermitage, DS 3
Holnest, DS 3
Kingston, CC 27
Leigh, Y & DS 6
Lillington, DS 3
Longburton, DS 3
Lyme Regis,
  LR & DS 16
Lytchett Minster,
  SM 21
Mapperton, DS 15
Milborne Stileham,
  DS 20
Milton Abbas, MA 11
Motcombe, G 2
Netherbury, N & DS 14
Oborne, DS 3
Poole, CP 22
Preston, P 26
Ryme Intrinsica, DS 3
Sherborne, DS 3
Stockland (archd. of
  Dors., detd.), 12

Stockwood, DS 3
Stourpaine, DC 4
Stratton,
  ST & DS 18
Sturminster Marshall,
  SM 21
Sutton Pointz,
  P & DS 26
Thorncombe, E 8
Thornford, DS 3
Tomson, DS 20
Turners Puddle, DS 20
Wambrook, C & DS 7
Wimborne Minster,
  WM 9
Winterborne Came,
  F 25
Winterborne
  Herringstone, F 25
Winterborne Kingston,
  DS 20
Winterborne Tomson,
  DS 20
Woolland, MA 11
North Wootton, DS 3
Yetminster, Y & DS 6

DURHAM AND NORTHUMBERLAND

The counties of Durham and Northumberland were in the province of York, and, apart from peculiars, in the diocese of Durham.

The records of the consistory court of Durham are now at the Department of Palaeography and Diplomatic in the University of Durham. There is a printed index to wills and admons., 1540-1599. The pre-1837 records of the peculiar of Hexham and Hexhamshire are at the Borthwick Institute at York, but there is a register of wills, 1694-1706 (the property of the Society of Antiquaries of Newcastle-upon-Tyne), at the Northumberland Record Office. The records of the prebend of Tockerington (Throckrington) are also at the Borthwick Institute.

The Department of Palaeography and Diplomatic is at present situated on the southern outskirts of Durham, at the junction of South Road and Stockton Road (traffic lights), opposite the New Inn.

For a map of the counties, showing the position of peculiars, see the 'Province of York', page 152.

Prerogative Court of Canterbury and other courts having general jurisdiction – see page 1.

Prerogative Court of York and other courts having jurisdiction in the province – see page 150.

Consistory Court of Durham (The Department of Palaeography and Diplomatic, University of Durham, South Road, Durham DH1 3LE. Tel. Durham 61478)

Jurisdiction: the two counties (except for peculiars) and the borough of Berwick-upon-Tweed.

Indexes: wills, admons. and invs., 1540-1857 (calendar) and also, wills and invs., 1540-c.1610 (card index). These are better than the printed index, below, and a TS index by J. W. Robinson, at Newcastle-upon-Tyne Reference Library and SG, of wills 1540-1812, admons., 1565-1812 (over 10,000), which is probably incomplete.

Printed index: wills and admons., 1540-1599 (2,500) (Newcastle-upon-Tyne Records Committee Publications, vol. 8, 1928 – this includes cross-references to the printed abstracts below).

Printed abstracts: selected wills and invs., 11th cent. 1649 (c.900) (Surtees Soc., vols. 2, 38, 112 and 142); also wills and admons., 1501-1502 (15), and for Durham clergy, wills and invs., 1509-1603 (19) (vol. 22, appx. 1, pp. 1-11, and appx. 10, pp. 103-145).

Peculiar of the Archbishop of York in Hexham and Hexhamshire (Borthwick Institute, St. Anthony's Hall, York (page 151); and Northumberland Record Office, Melton Park, North Gosforth, Newcastle-upon-Tyne NE3 5QX. Tel. Wideopen (089-426) 2680)

> Jurisdiction: Allendale, West Allen, St. Mary Bingfield, Hexham, Nine Banks, St. John Lee, St. Oswald, and Whitley, all in Northumberland. After 1660 the records of the court are merged with the prerogative court (page 151).

> Jurisdiction: see map. After 1660 the records of the court are merged with that of the prerogative court.

> Printed index: probate act book, 1593-1602 (260) (Yorks, Arch. Soc. Record Series, vol. 60, pp. 184-189) (Borthwick Institute).

> Wills, 1694-1706 (Northumberland Record Office, on loan from the Society of Antiquaries of Newcastle-upon-Tyne; photocopy at Borthwick Institute).

Prebend of Tockerington (Borthwick Institute, York)

> Jurisdiction: Throckrington in Northumberland.

> Wills, admons. and invs., 1741-1744 (few).

Collections at Newcastle-upon-Tyne Reference Library

> These collections are fully described in the *Genealogists' Magazine*, vol. 14, no. 7 (Sept., 1963), p. 196.

> Index: Durham wills, 1540-1812 (TS, listed above).

> Abstracts: Northumberland and Durham wills (14 vols. in 2, from Canon Raine's MSS. belonging to Society of Antiquaries of Newcastle, with index); wills and admons., 1576-1735 (6 vols. MS by J. J. Howe, with index); Northumberland wills, late 18th and early 19th cent. (122) (by J. C. Hodgson, with index).

ESSEX

Essex was in the province of Canterbury and diocese of London. It comprised the archdeaconries of Essex and Colchester, and part of that of Middlesex (Essex and Hertfordshire division). A large number of parishes scattered through these three archdeaconries were in the jurisdiction of the Essex and Hertfordshire division of the commissary court of London. The records of these four courts and those of four peculiars are all now at the Essex Record Office, and the wills are all in one consolidated printed index for the complete period to 1857. The parishes in these jurisdictions have not therefore been separately listed.

A few parishes on the outskirts of London were in the jurisdiction of the London division of the commissary court of London (Guildhall Library; printed index to 1570, and in progress); six Essex parishes were in the peculiar of the dean and chapter of St. Paul's; and Havering, Hornchurch and Romford were in the peculiar of New College, Oxford.

The Essex Record Office in County Hall is near the centre of Chelmsford, close to the railway and bus stations, and there is a multi-storey carpark nearby. Leaflets *Notes for Students* and *Indexes to Personal Names* are available.

Prerogative Court of Canterbury and other courts having general jurisdiction – see page 1, and also the Dean and Chapter of Canterbury, below.

Court of the Dean and Chapter of Canterbury (Chapter Library, Canterbury)
> Jurisdiction: during the *sede vacante* periods of the diocese of London.
> Printed abstracts: Essex wills and admons., 1293-1559 (39), (Trans. Essex Arch. Soc., vol. 21, pp. 234-269).

Commissary Court of London (Essex and Hertfordshire Division), Archdeaconries of Colchester and Essex, and Archdeaconry of Middlesex (Essex and Hertfordshire Division) (Essex Record Office, County Hall, Chelmsford, Essex CM1 1LX. Tel. Chelmsford (0245) 67222, ext. 2104)
> Jurisdiction: the whole county except for the peculiars and 14 parishes in the London division of the commissary court of London. See also consistory court of London, below.
> Printed indexes: wills, 1400-1857 (81,000) (Index Lib., vols. 78, 79 and 84).
> Other indexes: admons., commissary court of London, 1619-1857; archdeaconry of Colchester, 1663-1857; archdeaconry of Essex, 1559-1857; archdeaconry of Middlesex, 1660-1857 (calendars).

Commissary Court of London (*London Division*) (Guildhall Library, Basinghall Street, London EC2P 2EJ. Tel. 01-606 3030)
Jurisdiction: 14 parishes on the outskirts of London; see also consistory court of London.
Printed indexes: wills and admons., 1374-1570 (Index Lib., vols. 82 and 86; 1571-1625 in press, 1626-1700, waiting publication).
Other indexes: wills and admons., 1571-1629 (modern MS); 1629-1857 (calendar).

Consistory Court of London (Greater London Record Office, Room B21, County Hall, Westminster Bridge, London SE1 7BP. Tel. 01-635 6851)
Jurisdiction: concurrent with the commissary and archidiaconal courts over the whole diocese (except peculiars).
Printed indexes: wills, 1492-1719 (Index Lib., in preparation).
Other indexes: wills, 1492, 1508, 1514-1669 (calendar).
Chronological lists: wills, 1669-1857, admons., 1540-1857 (MS).
Printed abstracts: wills, 1492, 1508, 1514-1547 (London Record Soc., vol. 3, 1967).
See also Episcopal Registers, below.

Peculiar of the Dean and Chapter of St. Paul's (The Library, St. Paul's Cathedral, London EC4)
Indexes: wills, 1535-1672 (MS, 19th cent.), 1672-1840, admons., 1646-1837 (calendars).
Printed list: selected wills, 1226-1642 (79) (Hist. MSS. Comm. 9th Report, Appx., pp. 45-48).

Peculiar of the Archbishop of Canterbury in the Deanery of Bocking (Essex Record Office)
Printed indexes: wills, 1627-1857 (Index Lib., vols. 79 and 84).
Abstracts: wills, 1627-1857, wills from P.C.C., 1649-1660; admons., 1665-1683, 1722-1738, 1756-1853 (TS, by S. W. Prentis, at Essex Record Office and SG).
See also *Archiepiscopal Registers,* page 4.

Peculiar of Good Easter (Essex Record Office)
See also peculiar of the dean and chapter of Westminster, below.
Printed indexes: wills, 1613-1847 (Index Lib., vols. 78, 79 and 84).
Abstracts: wills, 1613-1847; wills from P.C.C., 1649-1660; admons., 1613-1847 (TS, by S. W. Prentis, at Essex Record Office and SG).

Peculiar of the Liberty of the Sokens (Essex Record Office)
Printed indexes: wills, 1644-1855 (Index Lib., vol. 79, pp. vii-viii, and vol. 84).
Abstracts: wills, 1644-1855; admons., 1632-1749 (TS, by Dr. E. A. Wood, at Essex Record Office and SG).

B=peculiar of Bocking; GE=peculiar of Good Easter; H=peculiar of Hornchurch; L=commissary court of London (London division); P=peculiar of the dean and chapter of St. Paul's; S=peculiar of the Sokens; W=peculiar of Writtle with Roxwell; Z=royal peculiar of the dean and chapter of Westminster (not marked on map).

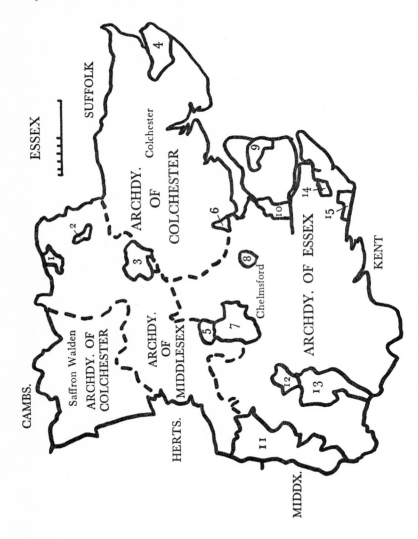

Peculiar of Writtle with Roxwell (Essex Record Office)
Printed indexes: wills, 1607, 1637-1851 (Index Lib., vols. 78, 79 and 84).
Printed abstracts: invs., 1635-1749 (250) (*Farm and Cottage Inventories of Mid-Essex*, ed. F. W. Steer, 1950, 2nd edn., Phillimore, 1969).
Other abstracts: wills, as above; wills from P.C.C., 1649-1660; admons., 1637-1857 (TS, by S. W. Prentis, at Essex Record Office and SG).

Royal Peculiar of the Dean and Chapter of Westminster (City of Westminster Archives Dept., Public Library, Buckingham Palace Road, London SW1. Tel. 01-730 0446)
Jurisdiction: from 1504, the parish of St. Mary Maldon; and, to the Dissolution only, the prebends of Newport, Creshall and Good Easter. See also consistory and archdeaconry courts and peculiar of Good Easter.
For records and indexes see page 87.

Peculiar of Hornchurch (New College, Oxford)
See also archdeaconry of Essex, above.
Index: wills, 1767-1839 (10), admons. (3), 1766, 1832, 1836 (calendar by F. W. Steer at Essex Record Office and SG).

Diocese of London, Episcopal Registers (Guildhall Library)
Wills and admons., 1313-1548 (TS).

Walthamstow Wills
Printed abstracts: 1335-1559 (Walthamstow Antiq. Soc., no. 9, 1921).

Parishes in Essex outside the main jurisdiction of the commissary court of London (Essex and Herts. division) and the archdeaconries of Colchester, Essex and Middlesex.

Barling, P 14
Belchamp St. Pauls, P 1
Bocking, B 3
Chingford, L 11
Creshall, Z
Good Easter, GE 5 & Z
Epping, L 11
Havering, H 13
Heybridge, P 6
Hornchurch, H 13
Kirkby-le-Soken, S 4
Latchingdon, B 10
Leyton, L 11
Loughton, L 11
Maldon St. Mary, Z
Milton in Prittlewell, B 15

Navestock, P 12
Nazeing, L 11
Newport, Z
Romford, H 13
Roxwell, W 7
Runsell in Danbury, B 8
Southchurch, B 15
Stisted, B 3
Thorpe-le-Soken, S 4
Tillingham, P 9
Waltham Holy Cross, L 11
Walthamstow, L 11
Walton-le-Soken, S 4
Wickham St. Pauls, P 2
Woodford, L 11
Writtle, W 7

GLOUCESTERSHIRE AND BRISTOL

Gloucestershire and the city of Bristol were in the province of Canterbury. Most of the county was in the diocese of Gloucester, but the city of Bristol and 16 neighbouring parishes were in the diocese of Bristol; this diocese also included the archdeaconry of Dorset, but probate matters for this were administered separately throughout. The diocese of Gloucester was formed out of the dioceses of Worcester and Hereford in 1541, and the following year the diocese of Bristol was formed out of this, with four parishes from Bath and Wells (the Dorset archdeaconry came from the diocese of Salisbury).

The records of the consistory court of Gloucester are now at the archives department of Gloucester City Library (although administered by the Gloucestershire Record Office), together with those of the peculiars; there are printed indexes to wills, 1541-1800, and admons., 1684-1800; and the archives department has published a booklet, *Wills Proved in Gloucestershire Peculiar Courts*, which supplements earlier printed indexes to these. There is also a TS index to admons. in the consistory, 1570-1603, with 1604-1683 in progress, which it is hoped will eventually be published. The city library is situated centrally, but there are public car parks nearby.

Parishes at the north-eastern tip of Gloucestershire, some of them detached, have changed both county and diocese at different times, and it is wise to consult the records of adjacent jurisdictions if there is any doubt.

The records of the consistory court of the bishop of Bristol in the deanery of Bristol are in the Bristol Archives Office; there are printed indexes to wills to 1792 and to admons., 1770-1793; and an index to inventories is in preparation. The archives office is in the Council House in the centre of Bristol (adjacent to the cathedral); there are metered and multi-storey car-parks nearby.

Prerogative Court of Canterbury and other courts having general jurisdiction – see page 1.
Invs., 1650-1660 (TS at SG).

Consistory Court of Gloucester (Gloucestershire Records Office, Archives Dept., City Library, Brunswick Road, Gloucester GL1 1HT. Tel. Gloucester (0452) 20020)

   Jurisdiction: see introductory note; from 1541, the county except for the city of Bristol and other parishes in the diocese of Bristol, and for peculiars.

   Printed indexes: wills, 1541-1650 (24,000) (Index Lib., vol. 12), wills, 1660-1800, admons., 1684-1800 (38,000) (vol. 34) (these are calendars with separate indexes).

   Other indexes: wills and admons., 1801-1857 (15,000) (calendar); admons., 1570-1603 (TS), 1604-1683 (TS, in progress) (11,000).

Consistory Court of the Bishop of Bristol in the Deanery of Bristol (Bristol Archives Office, The Council House, Bristol BS1 5TR. Tel. Bristol (0272) 26931, ext. 440)

   Jurisdiction: from 1542, all parishes in the city of Bristol, 16 neighbouring parishes in Gloucestershire, and Abbots Leigh in Somerset.

   Printed indexes: Wills, 1559 (10), 1570 (1) (Index Lib., vol. 22, pp. 269-70), 1546 (1), 1568-1792 (12,000) (vol. 17, pp. 1-100); admons., 1770-1793 (2,000) (vol. 17, pp. 100-16).

   Other indexes: wills, 1793-1857 (5,000), admons., 1793-1857 (2,388) (calendars); m/f of calendar to 1857 at SG; invs., 1609-1767 (index in preparation calendar 1611-1643, with copy at SG).

   Unindexed: admons., 1661-1769 (6,528).

   Printed abstracts: wills, 1559 (10), 1570 (1) (Trans. Bristol and Glos. Arch. Soc., vol. 64, 1943, pp. 118-38).

Bristol Great Orphan Books (Bristol Archives Office)

   Jurisdiction: the estates of orphans in the city.

   Printed index: wills, 1379-1674 (850) (Index Lib., vol. 17, pp. 117-136).

   Printed abstracts: wills, 1379-1605 (*Notes or Abstracts of the Wills contained in . . . the Great Orphan Books and Book of Wills . . .* by Rev. T. P. Wadley, 1886).

   Other abstracts: wills, in register of recognizances, 1331-1601.

Peculiar of Bibury (Gloucester City Library, as above)

   Jurisdiction: Bibury and Barnsley with the chapelries of Aldsworth and Winson. Disputed inhibition.

   Printed index: wills and invs., 1619-1833 (350) (*Wills Proved in Glos. Pec. Cts.,* Glos. City Lib. – this supersedes Index Lib., vol. 12, p. 206, which lists only 23 wills).

Peculiar of Bishops Cleeve (Gloucester City Library, as above)

   Jurisdiction: Bishops Cleeve and Stoke Orchard. See also consistory.

   Printed indexes: wills, 1635-1796 (50) (Index Lib., vol. 12, p. 207); wills and invs., 1622-1765 (100) (additional to those above, *Wills Proved in Glos. Pec. Cts.,* Glos. City Lib.).

WARWICKS.

WORCS.

Tewkesbury

1

HEREF.

Gloucester

2

ARCHDY.
OF
HEREFORD

OXON.

DIOCESE
OF
GLOUCESTER

Cirencester

3

MON.

WILTS.

DIOCESE
OF
BRISTOL

Bristol

SOM.

GLOS.

Peculiar of Withington (Gloucester City Library, as above)
Jurisdiction: Withington and Dowdeswell. See also consistory.
Printed indexes: wills, 1624-1752, admons., 1662-1748, 1753-1776 (Trans. Bristol and Glos. Arch. Soc., vol. 40, 1917, pp. 89-113); wills and admons., 1624-1752 (100) (*Wills Proved in Glos. Pec. Cts.*, Glos. City Lib.).

Consistory Court of Worcester (Worcestershire Record Office, page 146)
Jurisdiction: before 1541 most of the county, and the city of Bristol, though very few wills are to be found.
Printed index: wills and admons., 1451-1541 (Index Lib., vol. 31, pp. 1-8, 81-102; calendars with separate indexes).

Consistory Court of Bath and Wells (Somerset Record Office, page 113)
All probate records were destroyed in 1942. No printed index.
Jurisdiction: before 1542, the Bristol parishes of St. Thomas, St. Mary Radcliffe, Temple or Holy Cross; but see wills in the Great Orphan Books, above.

Consistory Court of Hereford (National Library of Wales, page 59)
Jurisdiction: before 1541, 32 Glos. parishes west of the Severn.
Wills, admons. and invs., c.1500-1541 (7 only, 1500-1539) (in course of indexing).

Gloucester Probate Registry (Gloucester City Library, as above)
Wills: 1858-1941.

Consistory Court of the Bishop of Bristol in the Deanery of Bristol All parishes in the city of Bristol; the Gloucestershire parishes of : Almondsbury Alveston Clifton Compton Greenfield Elberton Filton Henbury Horfield St. George Bristol Littleton-on-Severn Mangotsfield Olveston Stapleton Stoke Gifford Westbury-on-Trym Winterbourne St. Michael and Abbots Leigh (Som.), Bedminster (Som.) (from 1845 only)	*Peculiar of Bibury,* 3 Aldsworth Barnsley Bibury Winson *Peculiar of Bishops Cleeve,* 1 Bishops Cleeve Stoke Orchard *Peculiar of Withington,* 2 Dowdeswell Withington *Archdeaconry of Hereford* Parishes west of the Severn, before 1541 in the diocese of Hereford. *Diocese of Bath and Wells* Bristol parishes of St. Mary Redcliffe, St. Thomas, Temple or Holy Cross, and Abbots Leigh – before 1541. *Note.* The detached parish of Shenington, formerly in Glos., was in that diocese until 1837 when it was transferred to the diocese of Worcester.

HAMPSHIRE
(also known as the county of Southampton)

Hampshire (including the Isle of Wight) was in the province of Canterbury and virtually entirely in the diocese and archdeaconry of Winchester.

The records of the consistory, the archdeaconry and the many peculiar courts are all now in the county record office. Modern card indexes already cover most of the wills in the consistory and archdeaconry courts, and all the wills in the peculiars are in a third, consolidated, card index. Admons. could only be granted by the consistory court; some work has been done on an index to these, and more is planned.

The record office is a purpose-planned conversion of a church in the centre of Winchester. There is limited car-parking at the office, and a multi-storey car-park about half a mile distant.

Prerogative Court of Canterbury and other courts having general jurisdiction – see page 1.
  Copy wills, 1603, 1644-1674 (235) at Hampshire Record Office.
  Invs., 1650-1660 (TS at SG).

Consistory Court of Winchester (Hampshire Record Office, 20 Southgate Street, (St. Thomas's Church), Winchester SO23 9EF. Tel. Winchester (0962) 63153/4)
  Jurisdiction: virtually the whole county.
  Index: wills, 1502-1560 (and a few pre-1500) (card index); 1561-1652 (card index in preparation; meanwhile, calendars); 1660-1857 (card index) (50,000 in all). Also, wills, 1502-1857 (TS of calendars, at SG). Admons., 1561-1616 (TS, by year), 1617-1857 (calendars). A small collection of wills from Winchester Diocesan Registry, 1592-1635, 1665-1694 (TS calendar, by A. J. Willis, also at SG).
  Printed index: wills, 1553-1825 (unclassified, few), 1502, 1541, 1557, 1617-1640 (with gaps) (consistory), 1617-1626 (archdeaconry) (*Wills, Administrations and Inventories with the Winchester Diocesan Records,* by A. J. Willis, 1968 – these form part of a small collection formerly at the Winchester Diocesan Registry, transferred to the record office in 1968; for the main collection of wills and admons. see the card index above, which also includes those indexed by Willis).

54

HAMPSHIRE

Archdeaconry Court of Winchester (Hampshire Record Office)
  Jurisdiction probably included places in peculiars at times; see also the
    consistory court.
  Index: wills, 1572-1652 (card index in preparation; meanwhile, calen-
    dars); 1660-1857 (card index) (56,000 in all). Also, wills, 1572-1792
    (TS of calendars, at SG).
  Printed index: see under consistory court.

Hampshire Peculiars (Hampshire Record Office)
  Wills, the earliest are 1561 and the latest in most courts are 1770s, but
    a few 19th cent. (13,000) (consolidated card index).

Archdeaconry of Berkshire (Bodleian Library, Oxford, page 10)
  Jurisdiction included the Hampshire parish of Stratfield Mortimer.

*Archdeaconry Court of Surrey and Commissary Court of the Bishop of
Winchester* (Greater London Record Office, page 129)
  Jurisdiction included the Hampshire parish of Frensham.

Peculiar Court of the Dean and Chapter of Salisbury (Wiltshire Record
Office, Trowbridge, page 141)
  Jurisdiction included the Hampshire parish of Bramshaw.

Note. Hurstbourne in Hampshire was technically within the jurisdiction
of the *Prebendal Court of Hurstbourne and Burbage* (Wiltshire Record
Office), but the peculiar apparently covered Burbage (in Wiltshire) only,
and there are no Hurstbourne wills.

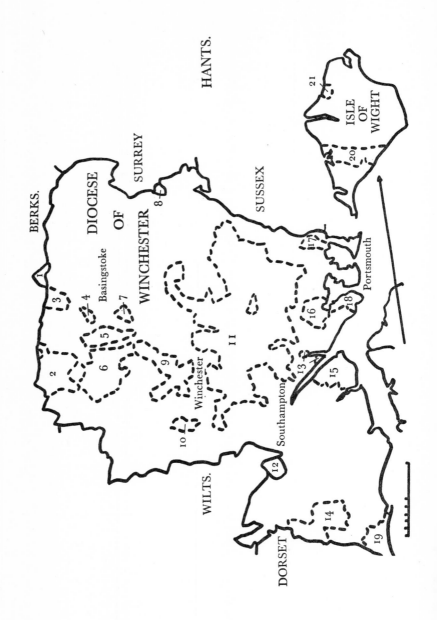

BERKS.

DIOCESE

OF

WINCHESTER

SURREY

HANTS.

SUSSEX

WILTS.

DORSET

Basingstoke

Winchester

Southampton

Portsmouth

ISLE
OF
WIGHT

1
2
3
4
5
6
7
8
9
10
11
12
13
14
15
16
17
18
19
20
21

Hampshire parishes and places in peculiars. All were also subject to the consistory court and most are also likely to appear in the archdeaconry court.

Allington, 11
New Alresford, 11
Old Alresford, 11
Alverstoke, 18
Ashmansworth, 2
North Baddesley, 11
Baughurst, 3
Binstead (IoW), 21
Bishopstoke, 11
Bishop's Waltham, 11
Braishfield, 11
Brambridge, 11
Bramshaw (dioc. of
  Salisbury), 12
Brickmerston, 15
Brighstone (IoW), 20
Brockhampton, 17
Burghclere, 2
Bursash, 15
Bursledon, 13
Cadlands, 15
Calbourne (IoW), 20
Catisfield, 16
Charlecott, 6
Cheriton, 11
Chilbolton, 9
Chilcombe, 11
Combe
  (nr. Petersfield), 11
Compton, 11
Cranborne, 9
Crawley, 9
Dean (nr. Fareham), 16
Denmead, 11
Droxford, 11
Durley, 11
Easton, 11
Exbury, 15

Exton, 11
Fareham, 16
Fawley, 15
Freefolk, 6
Frensham (archd. of
  Surrey), 8
Froxfield, 11
Gosport, 18
Hamble, 13
Hambledon, 11
Hannington, 4
Harbridge, 14
Hardley, 15
Havant, 17
Highclere, 2
Hill, 11
Hoe, 11
Holbury, 15
Holdenhurst, 19
Houghton, 10
Hunton, 9
Hursley, 11
Hurstbourne Priors, 6
Hythe, 15
Kilmeston, 11
Langley, 15
Leigh, 17
Lepe, 15
Littleton, 9
Medstead, 11
Meonstoke, 11
East Meon, 11
West Meon, 11
Merdon, 11
Michelmersh, 11
Midlington, 11
Morestead, 11
Newtown (IoW), 20

Otterbourne, 11
Overton, 5
Ovington, 11
Ower, 15
Owslebury, 11
Oxenbourne, 11
Polhampton, 5
Privett, 11
Ramsdean, 11
Ringwood, 14
St. Mary Bourne, 6
Shamblehurst, 11
Shedfield, 11
Silkstead, 11
Soberton, 11
Stanswood, 15
Steep, 11
Stone, 15
South Stoneham, 11
Stratfield Mortimer
  (archd. of Berks., dioc.
  of Salisbury), 1
Sutton Scotney, 9
Swanmore, 11
Tadley, 3
Tichborne, 11
Twyford, 11
Upham, 11
Bishop's Waltham, 11
North Waltham, 7
Warnford, 11
Whitchurch, 6
Winchester, St. Cross or
  St. Faith, 11
Winnall, 11
Wonston, 9
East Woodhay, 2

RADNORS.

SHROPSHIRE

HEREF.

WORCS.

DIOCESE OF HEREFORD

BRECON

ARCHDY. OF BRECON

MONMOUTHS.

GLOS.

Hereford

Archdeaconry of Brecon
  (*diocese of St. Davids*)
  (B)
Clodock
Dulas
Michaelchurch Escley
Ewyas Harold
Llancillo
St. Margaret
Rowlstone
Walterstone
Fwddog (in Cwmyoy,
  Mon.), B 9

*Peculiar of Little
  Hereford*, 1

*Peculiar of Moreton on
  Lugg*, 5

Peculiar of Bullingham, 6

Consistory of the Dean of Hereford (D)

Allensmore, D
Blakemore, D
Breinton, D
Brockhampton, D 7
Canon Pyon, D 2
Clehonger, D
Dewsall, D 8
Dinedor, D
Eaton Bishop, D
Hampton Bishop, D
Hereford, D
Holmer, D
Huntington, D

Kingstone, D
Madley, D
Mardon, D
Moreton Jeffreys, D 3
Norton Canon, D 4
Pipe, D
Preston upon Wye, D
Preston Wynne, D
Putley, D 7
Thruxton, D
Tyberton, D
Withington, D
Woolhope, D 7

58

HEREFORDSHIRE

Herefordshire was in the province of Canterbury and diocese of Hereford, except for eight parishes in the archdeaconry of Brecon, diocese of St. David's. The consistory court of the dean of Hereford (distinct from the episcopal consistory) had jurisdiction over the city of Hereford and 25 parishes in the neighbourhood. There were also 3 peculiars. The records of all these courts are now at the National Library of Wales, and an index to the two Hereford consistories and the peculiars is at present in preparation for eventual publication in the Index Library. It seems possible that these may eventually be transferred back to the county.

The National Library of Wales is a conspicuous building on the eastern outskirts of Aberystwyth, overlooking the town. There is ample car parking. Prior application should be made for a reader's ticket.

Prerogative Court of Canterbury and other courts having general jurisdiction – see page 1.

Episcopal Consistory Court of Hereford (National Library of Wales, Aberystwyth. Tel. Aberystwyth 3816)
   Chronological lists: wills and invs., 1517, 1539-1627; wills, 1628-1657, 1663; invs., 1628-1641, 1660-1661 (calendar); wills and admons., 1662-1857 (act books with index).
   Unindexed: miscellaneous invs., 1662, 1695-1760.

Consistory Court of the Dean of Hereford (National Library of Wales)
   Indexes: wills, 1660-1857, admons., 1670-1857 (in act books).
   Unindexed: admons., 1660-1670, invs., 1660-1857.

Consistory Court of the Archdeaconry of Brecon (*Diocese of St. David's*) (National Library of Wales, page 182)
   Jurisdiction: included eight parishes in Herefordshire, see map.

Peculiar of Little Hereford (*Heref.*) *and Ashford Carbonell* (*Salop.*) (N.L.W.)
   Index: wills, admons. and invs., 1662-1857 (act book).

Peculiar Prebend of Upper Bullinghope or Bullingham (N.L.W.)
   Index: wills, admons. and invs., 1675-1857 (calendar).

Peculiar Prebend of Moreton Magna or Morton-on-Lugg (N.L.W.)
   Index: wills, admons. and invs., 1668-1854.

HERTFORDSHIRE

Hertfordshire was in the province of Canterbury and divided between the dioceses of Lincoln and London. The major part of the county formed the Hitchin division of the archdeaconry of Huntingdon, within the jurisdiction of the commissary court of the bishop of Lincoln; and two parishes (partly in Beds.) were in the archdeaconry of Bedford. The remainder of the county was in the diocese of London, split between the archdeaconry of St. Albans and the Essex and Hertfordshire division of the archdeaconry of Middlesex; with a few parishes in the Essex and Hertfordshire division of the commissary court of London; the consistory court of London had concurrent jurisdiction with these courts. There were three parishes in the peculiar of the dean and chapter of St. Paul's.

The county record office holds the probate records for the two main courts, those of the archdeaconries of St. Albans (throughout from 1415) and Huntingdon (Hitchin division) (original wills from 1557, registered copies from 1607, admons. from 1610), with a card index to all wills, and a 19th century calendar to the admons. in the Huntingdon archdeaconry. The earlier records for the Hitchin division are intermingled with those of the rest of the archdeaconry of Huntingdon, at the Huntingdonshire record office; there is a printed index to wills and admons. there, but there do not appear to be any Herts. entries after about 1580; however there are printed abstracts of Herts. wills there, 1579-1609.

Probate records of 31 parishes on the east of the county, in the Essex and Herts. divisions of the archdeaconry of Middlesex and the commissary court of London, are now at the Essex record office, and there is a printed index to wills for the complete period to 1857. Records of the consistory court of London are at the Greater London Record Office, and for the peculiar of the dean and chapter of St. Paul's at the St. Paul's Cathedral Library; however the Herts. record office has a card index to all Herts. testators to 1811 and 1837 respectively.

The county record office is situated at County Hall, over the county library. County Hall is on the southern outskirts of Hertford, and there is ample car parking. The office issues an excellent guide to *Genealogical Sources* (50p).

Prerogative Court of Canterbury and other courts having general jurisdiction – see page 1.

Archdeaconry of St. Albans (Hertfordshire Record Office, County Hall, Hertford SG13 8DE. Tel. Hertford (09925) 4242, ext. 413)
Formerly the Abbey jurisdiction, and only annexed to the diocese of London in 1550; from that date see also consistory.
Jurisdiction: 22 Hertfordshires parishes; and 4 in Bucks.
Indexes: wills, 1415-1857 (8,000 incl. admons.) (card index); admons., 1540-1857 (calendar); m/f of calendar to 1857 at SG.
Printed abstracts: wills, 1415-1451 (692) (*Herts. Genealogist and Antiquary*, vol. 1, pp. 45, 64, 104, 230, 315, 383; vol. 2, pp. 44, 90, 189, 236; vol. 3, pp. 17, 137, 234, 274).

Archdeaconry of Huntingdon, Hitchin Division (Hertfordshire Record Office)
Jurisdiction: the major part (77 parishes) of the county, in the diocese of Lincoln. Earlier records are at Huntingdon (see below).
Indexes: wills, 1557-1857 (12,500) (registered copies from 1607 only) (card index); admons., 1610-1857 (2,000) (19th cent. calendar).
Unindexed: invs., 1600-1790 (when not filed with wills or admons.).
Printed abstracts: wills, 1579-1609 (303) (*Herts. Genealogist and Antiquary*, vol. 2, pp. 29, 72, 155, 227, 310; vol. 3, pp. 25, 112, 218, 350).
Printed index: wills and admons in act books, 1566-1573, 1596-1599 (Index Lib., vol. 42, pp. 210-16).

Commissary Court of the Bishop of Lincoln and the Archdeacon in the Archdeaconry of Huntingdon (Huntingdonshire Record Office, County Buildings, Huntingdon, page 65)
Jurisdiction: before the late 16th century, the major part of the county, as above, in addition to the county of Huntingdon. Records of the two divisions of Hitchin (Herts.) and Huntingdonshire are intermingled.
Printed index: wills, 1479-c.1576 (Index Library, vol. 42, pp. 1-125); admons., 1559-c.1580 (vol. 42, pp. 126-152).
Printed abstracts: see above.

Archdeaconry Court of Middlesex and Commissary Court of London (Essex and Herts. Divisions) (Essex Record Office, County Hall, Chelmsford, page 46)
Jurisdiction: 31 parishes in Hertfordshire. See also consistory of London.
Printed indexes: wills, 1431-1857 (archdeaconry from 1538) (Index Lib., vols. 78, 79 and 84).
Other indexes: admons. (commissary), 1619-1857; (archdeaconry), 1660-1857.
Printed abstracts: wills (archdeaconry of Middlesex), 1557, 1564-1590 (311) (*Herts. Genealogist and Antiquary*, vol. 1, pp. 33, 69, 132, 237, 332, 369; vol. 2, pp. 37, 84, 119, 179, 215, 318).

CAMBS.

BEDS.

Hitchin

ARCHDEACONRY
OF HUNTINGDON
(HITCHIN
DIVISION)

P

ARCHDY.
OF
MIDDLESEX

ESSEX

Hertford

9

7

4

2

1

3

St. Albans

5

6

8

H

ARCHDY.

OF

ST. ALBANS

MIDDLESEX

10

11

12

Tring

BUCKS.

HERTS.

HERTFORDSHIRE

A = Archdeaconry of St. Albans (diocese of London); B = Archdeaconry of Bedford (diocese of Lincoln); H = Archdeaconry of Huntingdon (Hitchin Division) (diocese of Lincoln); M = Archdeaconry of Middlesex and Commissary Court of London (Essex and Herts. Divisions) (diocese of London); P = Peculiar Court of the Dean and Chapter of St. Pauls.

Albury, P
Aldbury, H
Aldenham, H 11
Great Amwell, M
Little Amwell, H
Anstey, M
Ardeley, H
Ashwell, H
Aspenden, H
Aston, H
Ayot St. Lawrence, H
Ayot St. Peter, H
Baldock, H
Barkway, M
Barley, M
(Chipping) Barnet, A
East Barnet, A
Bayford, H
Bengeo, H
Benington, H
Berkhamsted, H
Little Berkhamsted, H
Bovingdon, H
Bramfield, H
Braughing, M
Brent Pelham, P
Brickendon, H
Broadfield, H
Broxbourne, M
Buckland, M
Bushey, A
Bygrave, H
Caddington, B 6
Caldecote, H
Chesfield, H
Cheshunt, M
Clothall, H
Codicote, A 7
Cottered, H
Datchworth, H
Digswell, H
Eastwick, M
Elstree, A
Essendon, H
Flamstead, H
Flaundon, H

Furneux Pelham, P
Great and Little
  Gaddesden, H
Gilston, M
Graveley, H
Much and Little
  Hadham, M
Harpenden, H
Hatfield, H
Hemel Hempstead, H
Hertford, H
Hertingfordbury, H
Hexton, A 3
Hinxworth, H
Hitchin, H
Hoddesden, M
Great Hormead, M
Little Hormead, M
Hunsdon, M
Ickleford, H
Ippollitts, H
Kelshall, H
Kensworth, H 5
Kimpton, H
Knebworth, H
Abbots Langley, A
Kings Langley, H
Layston, M
Letchworth, H
Lilley, H
Long Marston, H
Meesden, M
North Mimms, H
Minsden, H
Great and Little
  Munden, H
Newnham, A 1
Northaw, A 9
Northchurch, H
Norton, A 2
Offley, H
St. Pauls Walden, A 4
Pirton, H
Puttenham, H
Radwell, H
Redbourn, A

Reed, M
Rickmansworth, A
Ridge, A
Royston, M
Rushden, H
Sacombe, H
St. Albans, A
Sandon, H
Sandridge, A
Sarratt, A
Sawbridgeworth, M
Shenley, H 10
Shephall, A 7
Standon, M
Stanstead Abbots, M
Stanstead
  St. Margarets, M
Stapleford, H
Stevenage, H
Stocking Pelham, M
Bishops Stortford, M
Studham, B 8
Tewin, H
Therfield, H
Thorley, M
Throcking, H
Thundridge, M
Totteridge, H 12
Tring, H
Kings Walden, H
Walkern, H
Wallington, H
Ware, M
Watford, A
Watton-at-Stone, H
Welwyn, H
Westmill, H
Weston, H
Wheathampstead, H
Widford, M
Wigginton, H
Willian, H
Wormley, M
Wyddial, M
Great and Little
  Wymondley, H

Consistory Court of London (Greater London Record Office, County Hall, Westminster Bridge, London, page 86)
> Jurisdiction: concurrent with the archdeaconries of St. Albans and Middlesex and the commissary of London; and during inhibition.
> Index to Herts. testators: wills, 1514-1811 (card index, at Herts. R.O.)
> Other indexes: wills, 1811-1857, admons., 1540-1857 (calendars, chronological).
> Printed abstracts: wills, 1514-1547 (London Record Soc., vol. 3), 1586-1628 (145) (*Herts. Genealogist and Antiquary*, vol. 2, pp. 9, 62, 102; vol. 3, pp. 81, 208).

Diocese of Lincoln, Episcopal Registers (Lincolnshire Archives Office, page 81)
> The diocese included the archdeaconry of Huntingdon, and a very few wills for the county are to be found.
> Printed index: wills, 1320-1547 (Index Lib., vol. 28, pp. 1-17).
> Printed abstracts: all the above (*Early Lincoln Wills*, A. Gibbons, 1888).

Consistory Court of Lincoln (Lincolnshire Archives Office)
> Records of this court refer mainly to Lincolnshire, as court records of the bishop's commissary generally were kept with archdeaconry records, but some Hertfordshire testators occur.
> Printed indexes: wills, 1506-1652 (Index Lib., vols. 28 and 41); admons., 1540-1659 (vol. 52); also 'miscellaneous' wills, 1549-1730 (vol. 57, pp. 430-56).
> Abstracts: wills, 1601-1652 (m/f at SG).

Peculiar of the Dean and Chapter of St. Paul's (The Library, St. Paul's Cathedral, London, page 87)
> Jurisdiction: over the Herts. parishes of Albury, Brent Pelham and Furneux Pelham. Never inhibited.
> Index to Herts. testators: wills, 1560-1837 (card index at Herts. R.O.)
> Other indexes: admons., 1646-1649, 1660-1837 (calendar; m/f to 1837 at SG).

Archdeaconry of Bedford (Bedfordshire Record Office)
> Jurisdiction: Caddington and Studham (partly in Beds.)
> For records and indexes see page 7.

HUNTINGDONSHIRE

Huntingdonshire was in the province of Canterbury and in the diocese of Lincoln until 1837, when it was transferred to the diocese of Ely. The county of Huntingdon formed an archdeaconry (except for peculiars), and probate matters were effectively delegated to the archdeaconry court, very few wills at Lincoln (or at Ely, after 1837) referring to Huntingdonshire. The records of the archdeaconry and of the peculiars are now at the county record office. There is a printed index to pre-Commonwealth wills and admons.

The county record office is situated in part of the county council buildings, in the centre of Huntingdon, and there is no public car park.

Prerogative Court of Canterbury and other courts having general jurisdiction – see page 1.
   Inventories, 1650-1660 (TS at SG).

Commissary Court of the Bishop of Lincoln and of the Archdeacon in the Archdeaconry of Huntingdon (Huntingdonshire Record Office, County Buildings, Huntingdon. Tel. Huntingdon (0480) 52181, ext. 136)
   Jurisdiction: Huntingdonshire except for the peculiars. From 1479 to 1609 also 77 parishes in the Hitchin division of Hertfordshire (see page 61); and Everton in Bedfordshire (page 8) for the whole period Some wills and admons. are also to be found for the four Huntingdonshire peculiars, and for the peculiars of Nassington (N'hants., page 98), Empingham (Rutland, page 97), Isleham (Cambs., page 20) with Freckenham (Suffolk, page 125), and Thorney (Cambs., page 20) These are separately calendared.
   Printed indexes: wills, 1479-1652, admons., 1559-1614 (Index Library, vol. 42); wills and admons. in act books, 1578-1587, 1591-1595 (vol. 42, pp. 204-09).
   Other indexes: wills, 1661-1857 (calendar), admons., 1662-1688 (MS, modern), 1691-1857 (calendar) (30,000 in all); m/f of calendar to 1857 at SG.

Peculiar of Brampton (Huntingdonshire Record Office)
   Printed indexes: wills, 1549-1855, admons., 1738-1854 (Trans. Cambs. and Hunts. Arch. Soc., vol. 6, pt. 3, pp. 79-96); wills, 1549, 1658, 1659 (3 only) (Index Library, vol. 42, p. 217).

Peculiar of Buckden (Huntingdonshire Record Office)
   Printed indexes: wills, 1661-1853, and admons., 1668-1855 (Trans. Cambs. and Hunts. Arch. Soc., vol. 6, pt. 3); wills, 1691-1741 (TS) (Index Library, vol. 57 pp. 368-69) .

Prebend of Long Stow (Huntingdonshire Record Office)
Printed indexes: wills, 1661-1857, and admons., 1737-1837 (Trans. Cambs. and Hunts. Arch. Soc., vol. 6, pt. 3); wills, 1736-1744 (14) (Index Library, vol. 57, p. 429).

Prebend of Leighton Bromswold (Huntingdonshire Record Office)
Printed index: wills and admons., 1738-1838 (Trans. Cambs. and Hunts. Arch. Soc., vol. 6, pt. 3).

Peculiar Court of the Dean and Chapter of Lincoln (Lincolnshire Archives Office, page 81)
Jurisdiction included the peculiars of Long Stow and Leighton Bromswold during inhibition; Brampton and Buckden are likely to have been administered separately.
Printed index: wills and admons., 1534-1834 (Index Library, vol. 57).

Diocese of Lincoln, Episcopal Registers (Lincolnshire Archives Office)
The diocese included Huntingdonshire, and a very few wills for the county are to be found, 1320-1547 (Index Library, vol. 28, pp. 1-17; abstracts in *Early Lincoln Wills* by A. Gibbons, 1888).

Consistory Court of Lincoln (Lincolnshire Archives Office)
Records in this court appear to refer mainly to Lincolnshire, as court records of the Bishop's Commissary generally were kept with the archdeaconry records, but some Hunts. testators occur.
Printed index: wills, 1506-1652 (Index Library, vols. 28 and 41), admons., 1540-1659 (vol. 52); also, miscellaneous wills, 1549-1730 (vol. 57, pp. 430-56).

Consistory Court of Ely (Cambridge University Library, page 18)
Replaced the consistory court of Lincoln in 1837, but Huntingdonshire material is unlikely to be found, any more than at Lincoln.

Consistory Court of Peterborough (Northamptonshire Record Office, page 97)
Jurisdiction: included the Hunts. parish of Washingley.

Huntingdonshire parishes outside the jurisdiction of the archdeaconry court:

Peculiar of Brampton, 4

Peculiar of Buckden, 5

Prebend of Leighton Bromswold, 2

Prebend of Long Stow, 3, with
Barham
Little Catworth
Easton
Spaldwick

Consistory Court of Peterborough, 1
Washingley

CAMBS.

NORTHANTS.

ARCHDEACONRY
OF
HUNTINGDON

Huntingdon

Kimbolton

CAMBS.

St. Neots

BEDS.

HUNTS.

KENT

Kent was in the province of Canterbury and comprised the two dioceses of Canterbury and Rochester, consisting of the eastern and western parts of the county respectively. The records of both and of the peculiars are now at the Kent Archives Office.

The diocese of Canterbury formed the single archdeaconry of Canterbury. The formation of the archdeaconry of Maidstone in 1841 did not affect the probate records; and no probate records appear to have survived for the deanery of Malling and parts of the deaneries of Dartford and Shoreham, formerly in the diocese of Rochester, after the transfer date of 1846. In 1547 the college of Wingham was suppressed and the 5 parishes in which its provost had exercised probate jurisdiction were added to 52 parishes already within the direct jurisdiction of the consistory court of Canterbury diocese. The archdeaconry court had jurisdiction over the remainder of the parishes in the diocese. There are printed indexes to pre-1577 wills and admons. The Archbishop of Canterbury delegated his 'prerogative' throughout the diocese to his commissary-general, and thus there are few wills from this part of Kent in the Prerogative Court of Canterbury.

The diocese of Rochester also formed a single archdeaconry, of Rochester, including, geographically but with exempt jurisdiction, the Archbishop's peculiar of the deanery of Shoreham (administered with the deaneries of the Arches and Croydon). The diocese also included the parish of Lamberhurst in East Sussex. The consistory and archdeaconry courts had concurrent jurisdiction. There are printed indexes to the pre-1561 wills and admons., and a card index to original wills in the consistory court is in course of compilation (at present to about 1766). In 1846 the diocese was reduced to the deanery of Rochester only (with the transfers mentioned above; the parishes of Charlton, Deptford, Eltham, Greenwich, Lee, Lewisham, Plumstead and Woolwich being transferred to the diocese of London), but at the same time the parishes of Gillingham, Northfleet and Meopham (formerly in the deanery of Shoreham), and the peculiar of Cliffe, were attached. From around 1750 there was a considerable decline in the number of wills and admons.

The peculiar deanery of Shoreham comprised 38 parishes. Apart from the three parishes attached to the archdeaconry of Rochester (see above), no probate records survive after 1846 when the remainder of the parishes were attached to the archdeaconry of Maidstone. Its boundary may have varied at times.

The Kent Archives Office is situated in the main County Council building in Maidstone, close to the centre of the town; there is no public car park, but limited meter space. The office issues a leaflet *Notes on Records: Sources of genealogical information*, which summarises the testamentary records held.

Prerogative Court of Canterbury and other courts having general jurisdiction – see page 1 (but also see note above).

Printed index: 1384-1599 (2,000) (*A Calendar of Wills relating to the County of Kent . . .*, by L. L. Duncan, Lewisham Antiquarian Society, 1890 – but the P.C.C. indexes in the Index Library are likely to be more reliable).

Invs., 1650-1660 (TS at SG).

Consistory Court of Canterbury (Kent Archives Office, County Hall, Maidstone, Kent ME14 1XH. Tel. Maidstone 54321, ext. 320)

Jurisdiction: 57 (52 before 1547) parishes exempt from the archdeaconry court.

Printed indexes: wills and admons., 1396-1558 (28,000) (Index Lib., vol. 50, and Kent Arch. Soc., Records Branch, vol. 6, pp. 1-531); admons., 1539-1545 (148) (omitted from the above) (Index Lib., vol. 65, pp. 147-49), wills and admons., 1558-1577 (7,250) (vol. 65, pp. 1-146); wills and admons., 1640-1650 (3,000) (Index Lib., vol. 50, and Kent Arch. Soc., vol. 6, pp. 541-603).

All these include the archdeaconry court as well as the consistory.

Other indexes: wills and admons., 1577-1857 (calendars); m/f of calendars to 1857 at SG; invs., 1566-1638 (calendars), 1685-1748 (TS, by year) (with gaps).

Printed abstracts: wills, 1498-1596 (a selection only, in *Kentish Wills: genealogical abstracts . . .*, ed. A. W. Hughes Clarke, 1929, from an MS by Clement Taylor Smythe); and 15th and 16th century wills relating to church building and topography (*Testamenta Cantiana*, Archaeologia Cantiana, extra volume, 1907).

Archdeaconry Court of Canterbury (Kent Archives Office)

Jurisdiction: those parishes in the diocese not exempt (for which see consistory court, above).

Printed indexes: as for consistory court, above.

Other indexes: wills, 1577-1857, admons. 1586-1645, 1663-1857 (calendars); m/f of calendars at SG; invs., 1565-1638 (calendars).

Unindexed: invs., to 1842 (with gaps).

Exempt Jurisdiction of Wingham (Kent Archives Office)

Jurisdiction: until 1547 only (afterwards in the consistory court of Canterbury) the Provost of the College at Wingham had jurisdiction in Wingham, Ash, Goodneston, Nonington and Womenswould.

Printed index: wills, 1471-1546 (Index Lib., vol. 50, and Kent Arch. Soc. Records Branch, vol. 6).

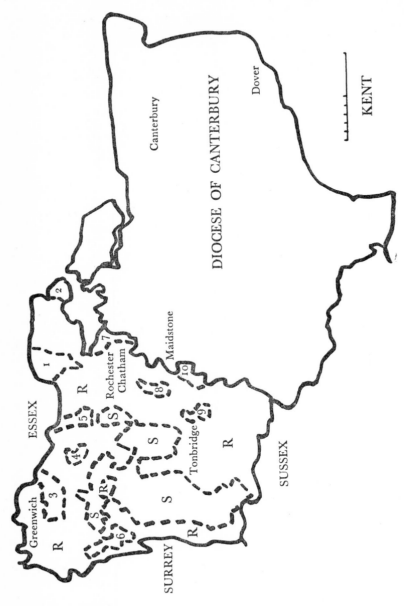

R = Diocese of Rochester

KENT

Peculiar Deanery of
Shoreham (S)

Diocese of Canterbury —
parishes exempt from the jurisdiction
of the archdeacon

Bexley, 3
Brasted
Chevening
Chiddingstone
St. Mary Cray
Crayford, 3
Darenth, 4
Downe, 6
Eynsford
East Farleigh, 10
Farningham
Gillingham, 7
Grain, 2
Halstead
Hayes, 6
Hever
Hunton, 10
Ide Hill
Ifield
Ightham
Keston, 6
Knockholt
Lidsing
East Malling, 8
Meopham
Northfleet, 5
Orpington
Otford
East Peckham, 9
Penshurst
Plaxtol
Sevenoaks
Shoreham
Stansted
Sundridge
Wrotham

Peculiar of Cliffe
(at Hoo), 1

Acol *or* Wood
Adisham
Aldington
Ash-next-Sandwich*
Birchington
Boughton-under-Blean
Bredhurst
Buckland-by-Dover
Canterbury
 St. Alphage
 St. Martin
 Precincts, liberties
Challock
Charing
Deal
Detling
Dover, St. James
Dover, St. Mary
Dunkirk
Eastry
Egerton
Fairfield
Godmersham
Goodneston-next
 -Wingham*
Guston
Harbledown,
 St. Michael's
 Hospital
Herne
Hernhill
Hoath
Hollingbourne

Hucking
Hythe
Ickham
Ivychurch
Loose
Lydd
Lyminge
Maidstone
Monkton
Newchurch
Nonington*
Paddlesworth
Reculver
New Romney
St. Margaret's at
 Cliffe
St. Nicholas at Wade
Saltwood
Sandwich,
 St. Bartholomew's
 Hospital
Sarre
Smeeth
Stanford
Staple
Westwell
Wingham*
Wittersham
Woodchurch
Worth
Womenswould*
Wood *or* Acol

Note. * these parishes were in the
exempt jurisdiction of Wingham until
1546.

Consistory Court of Rochester (Kent Archives Office)
  Jurisdiction: the diocese, concurrently with the archdeaconry court, and
    excluding the peculiar deanery of Shoreham and the peculiar of
    Cliffe; see introductory note. There are also occasional occurrences of
    wills for the bishop of Rochester's peculiar of Isleham (Cambs.,
    page 20) and Freckenham (Suffolk, page 125).
  Printed index: wills and admons., 1440-1561 (8,000) (Kent Arch. Soc.,
    Records Branch, vol. 9).
  Other indexes: (original) wills, 1498-1766 (and in progress) (card index);
    wills and admons., 1561-1652, 1660-1857 (calendars, with gaps: these
    are in a rather confusing series of partly overlapping volumes, also
    including archdeaconry wills and admons. between 1635 and 1679.
    Advice should be requested at the Archives Office on which to use for
    any particular period. M/f of calendars at SG).
  Lists: invs. (before 1719 also including those for the archdeaconry),
    1662, 1667-1669, 1686-1784 (TS, alphabetical by year).

Archdeaconry Court of Rochester (Kent Archives Office)
  Jurisdiction: the diocese, concurrently with the consistory court, and
    excluding the peculiar deanery of Shoreham and the peculiar of
    Cliffe; see introductory note.
  Indexes: wills and admons., 1635-1642, 1671-1857 (calendars; see note
    under consistory court above).
  Lists: invs., 1719-1782 (TS, alphabetical by year); before 1719 these
    were kept with the consistory invs., above.

*Peculiar Jurisdiction of the Archbishop of Canterbury in the Deanery of
Shoreham* (Kent Archives Office)
  The records deposited at Maidstone relate to the Deanery of Shoreham
    only. Further records are at Lambeth Palace Library (page 87).
  Jurisdiction: 38 parishes in Kent. In 1846 these parishes (apart from
    Gillingham, Northfleet and Meopham which were attached to the
    diocese of Rochester) were attached to the archdeaconry of Maidstone,
    but post-1846 probate records do not appear to survive.
  Indexes: wills and admons., 1614-1821, 1841 (calendar, 19th cent.; also
    a TS index, by S. W. Prentis, at SG); invs., 1621-1738.

Peculiar of the Rector of Cliffe (Kent Archives Office)
  Jurisdiction: the parish of Cliffe; exempt from the jurisdiction of the
    diocese of Rochester until 1846, when it was attached to that diocese.
  Index: wills, admons. and invs., 1671-1845.

Consistory Court of London (Greater London Record Office)
  Jurisdiction: from 1846 only, in the parishes of Charlton, Deptford,
    Eltham, Greenwich, Lee, Lewisham, Plumstead and Woolwich.
  For indexes and records, see page 86.

Court of the Prior (or Dean) and Chapter of Canterbury – see page 4.

LANCASHIRE

Lancashire was in the diocese of Chester from its creation in 1541, in the province of York. Before that the southern part, south of the River Ribble, was in the diocese of Lichfield and Coventry, province of Canterbury; the remainder, part of the archdeaconry of Richmond, was in the diocese and province of York.

The records of the archdeaconry of Chester in the consistory court of Chester, which in addition to the southern part of Lancashire included all Cheshire, in England, and parts of Flint and Denbigh, in Wales, have been divided : the Welsh records are now at the National Library of Wales; those for Cheshire are at the Cheshire Record Office; and the remainder are at the Lancashire Record Office. The court was divided into two, estates below £40 being an 'infra jurisdiction', clergy and esquires excepted. There are printed indexes to all wills and admons. to 1830 – the 'infra' wills are separately indexed before 1665, are included as appendices with the main series 1665-1800, and jointly indexed thereafter. There is a modern card index for the remaining period, 1831-1857, and a TS index to wills transcribed in the Bishop's Registers, 1492-1829 (printed to 1650). There are no surviving pre-1541 records relating to the county in the consistory court of Lichfield.

The records of the consistory court of the commissary of the archdeacon of Richmond, Yorks., Western Deaneries, which was attached to the diocese of Chester on its creation in 1541, have suffered considerable vicissitudes in the past, in which much was lost, partiuclarly for the deanery of Amounderness. They are now also in the Lancashire Record Office. There are printed indexes to wills and admons. for the whole period, 1457-1857. Wills relating to the western deaneries but found in the records of the eastern deaneries (at Leeds) have mostly been transferred to Preston.

The county record office is at present in the centre of Preston, adjacent to the town hall; there is a multi-storey car-park nearby. From the autumn of 1974 it will be at Bow Lane, Preston, near the railway station, adjacent to County Hall and with its own car-park.

Prerogative Court of Canterbury and other courts having general jurisdiction – see page 1.

Printed index: (Lancs.) wills, 1650-1660 (Lancs. and Ches. Record Soc., vol. 4, pp. 250-80) and admons., 1650-1660 (vol. 4, pp. 281-300).

Prerogative Court of York and other courts having jurisdiction in the province – see page 150.

Consistory Court of Chester in the Archdeaconry of Chester (Lancashire Record Office, Sessions House, Lancaster Road, Preston PR1 2RE. Tel. Preston (0772) 51905).

Jurisdiction: the county south of the River Ribble; see introductory note. Also the archdeaconry of Richmond during (very occasional) inhibition.

Printed indexes: wills and admons., 1545-1650 (main series) (Lancs. and Ches. Record Soc., vols. 2 and 4), 1590-1665 ('infra' series) (vol. 52), 1660-1800 (main series, with 'infra' series as appendices) (vols. 15, 18, 20, 22, 25, 37, 38, 44 and 45), additional wills and admons., 1670 (vol. 63, pp. 183-87), and additional 'infra' wills and admons., 1693 (vol. 63, pp. 193-99), wills and admons., 1801-1820 (consolidated) (vols. 62, 63 and 78), 1821-1830 (Lancs. separate) (vol. 107, pp. 1-157, and 113, pp. 1-141) (190,000 in all). Wills 'formerly in the diocesan registry', 1487-1800 (9,500) (vols. 33, 43 and 52); wills in the enrolment books, 1512-1635, wills printed in Chetham Soc., vols. 33, 51 and 54 (see below), and wills in Piccope MSS. (abstracts in Chetham Library, Manchester, and not now in consistory court records), 1477-1620 (450) (vol. 2, pp. xi-xxiv).

Other indexes: wills and admons., 1831-1857 (50,000) (card index); m/f of calendar to 1849 at SG.

Printed abstracts: selected wills and invs., 1525-1544 (54) (Chetham Soc., vol. 33), 1483-1589 (106) (vol. 51), 1596-1639 (67) (vol. 54), 1477-1746 (200, incl. admons.) (N.S., vol. 3; included in Part 2, p. 198, 220 wills now lost), 1572-1696 (180) (vol. 28, with an appendix of Lancs. wills proved at York or Richmond, 1542-1649), 1563-1807 (63) (vol. 37); 1301-1752 (123) ('not now found in any probate registry', Lancs. and Ches. Record Soc., vol. 30).

Consistory Court of the Commissary of the Archdeaconry of Richmond (Yorks.), Western Deaneries (Lancashire Record Office)

Jurisdiction: the county north of the River Ribble; also part of Cumberland lying in the deanery of Copeland; parts of Westmorland lying in the deaneries of Kendal and Lonsdale; and part of the West Riding of Yorkshire lying in the deanery of Lonsdale. See also the consistory court of Chester during inhibition.

Printed indexes: wills, admons. and invs. (Lancashire only), 1457-1857 (52,500) (Lancs. and Ches. Record Soc., vols. 10, 13, 23, 66, 99 and 105; these include the Lancashire wills proved in the Eastern Deaneries, but *not* non-Lancashire wills in the western deaneries; they do include an index to a collection of abstracts, 1531-1652, relating mainly to Amounderness, of wills (the originals of which are now lost) in British Museum Add. MS. 32115, m/f at Lancs. Record Office).

Printed abstracts: selected wills and invs. 1442-1579 (208) (Surtees Soc., vol. 26).

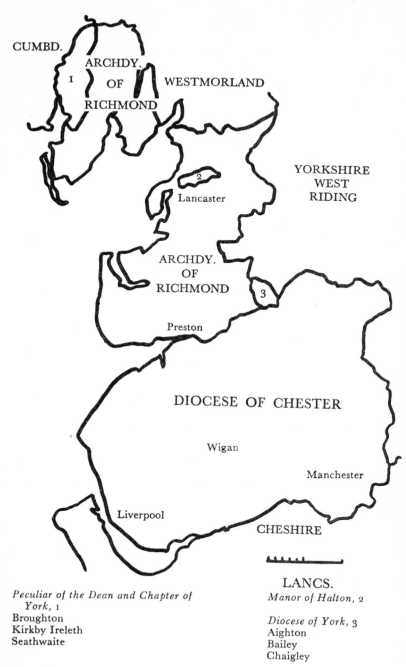

CUMBD.

ARCHDY.
OF
RICHMOND

I

WESTMORLAND

YORKSHIRE
WEST
RIDING

2

Lancaster

ARCHDY.
OF
RICHMOND

3

Preston

DIOCESE OF CHESTER

Wigan

Manchester

Liverpool

CHESHIRE

LANCS.
Manor of Halton, 2

Peculiar of the Dean and Chapter of
York, 1
Broughton
Kirkby Ireleth
Seathwaite

Diocese of York, 3
Aighton
Bailey
Chaigley

Exchequer Court of York (Borthwick Institute, York, page 155)
  Jurisdiction: included Aighton, Chaigley and Bailey (in the Yorkshire West Riding parish of Great Mitton) in Lancashire.

Peculiar Court of the Dean and Chapter of York (Borthwick Institute, York, page 161)
  Jurisdiction: included Broughton, Kirkby Ireleth and Seathwaite in Lancashire; and jurisdiction in the *Chancery Court of York* during inhibition.

Manorial Court of Halton (Lancashire Record Office)
  Jurisdiction: the parish of Halton. Never inhibited.
  Printed indexes: wills and admons., 1615-1815 (262) (Lancs. and Ches. Record Soc., vol. 23, pp. 139-44, vol. 66, p. 106, and vol. 99, in main index).

Diocese of Chester, Episcopal Registers (Chester Record Office)
  Printed index: wills, 1492-1650 (Lancs. and Ches. Record Soc., vol. 2, pp. xi-xix).
  Other index: wills, 1492-1829 (TS).

Rochdale Wills (Rochdale Public Library)
  Wills and admons., 1553-1810, relating to Rochdale people, abstracts (2,400), by Dr. Henry Brierley.

Roman Catholics (Lancashire Record Office)
  Index: wills, 1718-1820 (enrolments in Quarter Sessions) (TS).
  Printed list: wills, 1359-1857 (1,700) (together with other wills relating to Lancashire not recorded in the printed indexes to Chester and Richmond wills, now to be found in the record office) (Lancs. and Ches. Record Soc., vol. 105, pp. 126-143).

Lancashire Wills (Lancashire Record Office)
  Index: to printed abstracts of Lancashire wills (TS).

The Lancashire Record Office also holds registered copies of post-1857 wills for the Lancaster and Liverpool probate registries.

LEICESTERSHIRE

Leicestershire was in the province of Canterbury and diocese of Lincoln. The county formed an archdeaconry, and probate matters were effectively delegated to the archdeaconry court, very few wills at Lincoln referring to Leicestershire. The probate records of the archdeaconry and of the peculiars (together covering the whole county) are now all at the county record office. There are printed indexes to wills and admons. to 1750 (1800 for the peculiars), and a consolidated card index for the remaining period to 1857.

The record office is slightly out of the centre of the city, to the south-east, quite close to the station. There is a small car park for users of the office.

Prerogative Court of Canterbury and other courts having general jurisdiction – see page 1.

Commissary of the Bishop of Lincoln in the Archdeaconry of Leicester, and the Courts (including Vicar General) of the Archdeacon of Leicester (Leicestershire Record Office, 57 New Walk, Leicester LE1 7JB. Tel. Leicester (0533) 57121)
   Jurisdiction: the whole county except peculiars.
   Printed indexes: wills, 1495-1649 (17,500) (Index Lib., vol. 27, pp. 1-151), admons., 1556-1649 (6,000) (vol. 27, pp. 152-204, calendar with index), wills and admons., 1660-1750 (23,000) (gaps in admons. to 1700) (vol. 51, pp. 1-372); 'uncompleted' wills and admons., 1576-1800 (350) (vol. 27, pp. 237-40).
   Other indexes: wills and admons., 1750-1857 (25,000) (card index) (m/f of calendar to 1857 at SG); invs., 1514-1710 (card index, in progress; from 1711 invs. are filed with wills, as are some before then).

Leicestershire District Probate Registry (Leicestershire Record Office)
   Wills, 1858-1940 (card index, in progress)

Prebend of St. Margaret in Leicester (Leicestershire Record Office)
   Jurisdiction: the parish of St. Margaret, Leicester, and the chapelry of Knighton.
   Printed indexes: wills, 1543-1800, admons., 1662-1664, 1724-1800 (700) (vol. 27, pp. 205-17), 1642-1720 (90) (vol. 51, pp. 386-88).
   Other index: wills and admons., 1801-1857 (card index).
   Inventories: 1669-1724 (and with wills and admons.)

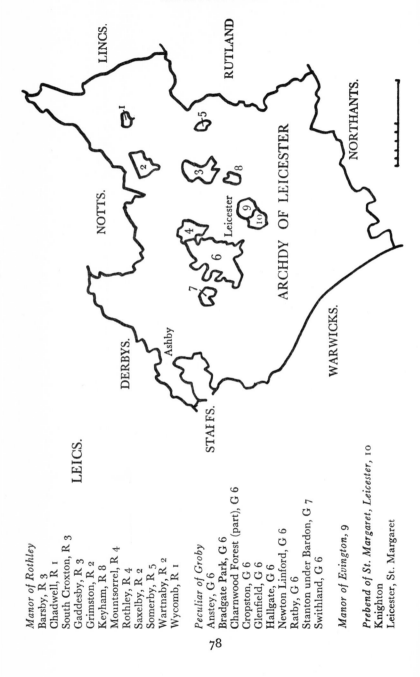

LINCS.

RUTLAND

NORTHANTS.

NOTTS.

ARCHDY OF LEICESTER

Leicester

DERBYS.

Ashby

STAFFS.

WARWICKS.

LEICS.

Manor of Rothley
Barsby, R 3
Chadwell, R 1
South Croxton, R 3
Gaddesby, R 3
Grimston, R 2
Keyham, R 8
Mountsorrel, R 4
Rothley, R 4
Saxelby, R 2
Somerby, R 5
Wartnaby, R 2
Wycomb, R 1

Peculiar of Groby
Anstey, G 6
Bradgate Park, G 6
Charnwood Forest (part), G 6
Cropston, G 6
Glenfield, G 6
Hallgate, G 6
Newton Linford, G 6
Ratby, G 6
Stanton under Bardon, G 7
Swithland, G 6

Manor of Evington, 9

Prebend of *St. Margaret, Leicester*, 10
Knighton
Leicester, St. Margaret

78

Manor of Rothley (Leicestershire Record Office)
Jurisdiction: the parishes of Barsby, South Croxton, Gaddesby, Grimston, Keyham, Mountsorrel, Rothley, Saxelby, part of Somerby, Wartnaby, Wycomb and Chadwell.
Printed index: wills and admons., 1575-1800 (600) (Index Lib., vol. 27 pp. 217-27), additional wills, 1626-1633 (26) (vol. 51, p. 388).
Other index: wills and admons., 1800-1857 (card index).
Inventories: 1577-1781 (and with wills and admons.)

Manor of Evington (Leicestershire Record Office)
Jurisdiction: the parish of Evington.
Printed index: wills and admons., 1581-1800 (100) (Index Lib., vol. 27, pp. 235-37)
Other index: wills and admons., 1801-1857 (card index).
Inventories: 1613-1749 (and with wills and admons.)

Peculiar of Groby (Leicestershire Record Office)
Jurisdiction: Anstey, Bradgate Park and Hallgate, part of Charnwood Forest, Cropston, Glenfield, Newton Linford, Ratby, Stanton under Bardon, and Swithland.
Printed index: wills and admons. 1580, 1636-1637, 1670-1800 (400) (Index Lib., vol. 27, pp. 227-35).
Other index: wills and admons., 1801-1857 (card index).

Diocese of Lincoln, Episcopal Registers (Lincolnshire Archives Office, page 81)
The diocese included Leicestershire, and a very few wills for the county are to be found, 1320-1547 (Index Lib., vol. 28, pp. 1-17; abstracts in *Early Lincoln Wills*, by A. Gibbons, 1888).

Consistory Court of Lincoln (Lincolnshire Archives Office)
Records of this court appear to refer mainly to Lincolnshire, as court records of the bishop's commissary generally were kept with the arch-deaconry records, but some Leicestershire testators occur.
Printed indexes: wills, 1506-1652 (Index Lib., vols. 28 and 41); admons., 1540-1659 (vol. 52); and 'miscellaneous' wills, 1549-1730 (vol. 57, pp. 430-56).

Peculiar Court of the Dean and Chapter of Lincoln (Lincolnshire Archives Office)
Includes some Leicestershire wills.
Printed index: wills, admons. and invs., 1534-1834 (Index Lib., vol. 57, pp. 265-366).

Archdeaconry of Stow (*Lincs.*) (Lincolnshire Archives Office)
Includes some Leicestershire wills.
For records and indexes, see page 81.

There is a large collection of Leicester will abstracts in 48 volumes, 1563-1800, at the county record office.

LINCOLNSHIRE

Lincolnshire was in the province of Canterbury and diocese of Lincoln. Apart from 78 parishes in the north-west quarter of the county, in the archdeaconry of Stow, and for peculiars, the whole county was in the direct jurisdiction of the consistory court. Although the diocese also included all or part of several other counties, most wills in this court relate to Lincolnshire.

There are printed indexes to the consistory court to 1653, to the archdeaconry court of Stow to 1699 and to the peculiars for the whole period (these were mainly merged with the consistory in 1834). The records of all these courts are now at the Lincolnshire Archives Office, which is situated in the castle at Lincoln, close to the cathedral. There is a car-park at the Castle entrance, and others nearby.

Prerogative Court of Canterbury and other courts having general jurisdiction – see page 1.

Consistory Court of Lincoln (Lincolnshire Archives Office, The Castle, Lincoln LN1 3AB. Tel. Lincoln (0522) 25158)

> Jurisdiction: the county apart from the archdeaconry of Stow and the peculiars. From 1834 the whole county. A few wills for other counties in the diocese.
>
> Printed indexes: wills (main series), 1506-1653 (57,000) (Index Lib., vol. 28, pp. 29-349, and vol. 41); admons., 1540-1659 (40,000) (vol. 52); other wills (miscellaneous, relating to places throughout the diocese, including peculiars), 1542-1730 (vol. 57, pp. 430-456); wills and admons. ('sundry', relating to Lincs.), 1508-1608 (400) (vol. 57, pp. 457-465).
>
> Other indexes: wills (main series), 1660-1700 (17,000) (MS, 19th cent.), 1700-1857 (45,000) (calendars, partly 19th cent., by year); admons., 1660-1699 (9,000) (calendar), 1700-1857 (20,000) (calendar, by year); invs., 1508-1831 (MS lists, indexed for place and occupation; n.b., further invs. are filed with admons.); other wills (miscellaneous, probably relating to places throughout the diocese, including peculiars, additional to the printed index above), 1542-1730 (MS); m/f of calendar to 1857 at SG.
>
> Printed abstracts: wills, 1504-1532 (with 8 earlier) (1,000) (Lincoln Record Soc., vols. 5, 10 and 24; *Lincolnshire Wills*, 2 vols., by A. R. Maddison, 1888, 1891).

Diocese of Lincoln, Episcopal Registers (Lincolnshire Archives Office)
Printed index: wills, 1320-1547 (650, relating to the whole pre-Reformation diocese) (Index Lib., vol. 28, pp. 1-17); other wills ('miscellaneous', in portfolio 'Aylmer', mainly relating to Lincs.), 1489-1588 (400) (vol. 28, pp. 18-28).
Printed abstracts: wills, 1320-1547 (as above) (*Early Lincoln Wills, 1280-1547*, by A. Gibbons, 1888).

Archdeaconry Court of Stow (Lincolnshire Archives Office)
Jurisdiction: 78 parishes in the north-west of the county. Records merged with those of the consistory from 1834.
Printed index: wills, 1530-1699 (12,000) (Index Lib., vol. 57, pp. 1-203), admons., 1580-1699 (3,500) (vol. 57, pp. 205-264).
Other indexes: wills, 1700-1834 (6,000), admons., 1700-1834 (2,000) (MS, 19th cent., by year); m/f of calendars to 1834 at SG; after 1834, with consistory; invs., 1616-1787 (MS lists, indexed for place and occupation; n.b., further invs. are filed with admons., others for Stow are included in the consistory court series).
Printed abstracts: wills, 1525-1577 (16) (*Lincolnshire Wills*, vol. 1, pp. 135-43, by A. R. Maddison, 1888).

Peculiar Court of the Dean and Chapter of Lincoln (Lincolnshire Archives Office)
Jurisdiction: 23 parishes in the county (see map); wills for all the peculiars and prebends (during inhibition) may also be found in the records of this court.
Printed index: wills, admons. and invs., 1534-1834 (6,000) (Index Lib., vol. 57, pp. 265-366).

Prebendary of Caistor (Lincolnshire Archives Office)
Printed index: wills, admons. and invs., 1636-1833 (235) (vol. 57, pp. 370-73).

Prebendary of Corringham (Lincolnshire Archives Office)
Printed index: wills, admons. and invs., 1632-1833 (156) (vol. 57, pp. 374-76).

Prebendary of Heydour (Lincolnshire Archives Office)
Printed index: wills, admons. and invs., 1669-1836 (123) (vol. 57, pp. 382-84).

Peculiar of the Sub-Dean of Kirton in Lindsey (Lincolnshire Archives Office)
Printed index: wills, admons. and invs., 1566-1834 (400) (vol. 57, pp. 382-48).

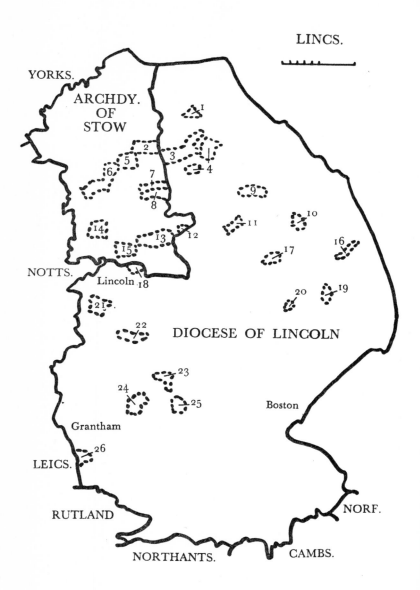

Parishes and places not in the direct jurisdiction of the consistory court, i.e., in the archdeaconry of Stow or in one of the following peculiars: Dean and Chapter of Lincoln (D); Caistor (CA); Corringham (CO); Heydour (H); Kirton in Lindsey (K); Louth (L); Bishop Norton (BN); Sleaford or Lafford (SL); and Stow in Lindsey (ST).

Aisby in
 Corringham, CO 6
Aisby in
 Heydour, H 24
Aisthorpe
Alkborough
Althorpe
Appleby
Asgarby, D 20
Atterby, BN 7
Audleby, CA 4
Barlings
Belton in Axholme
Binbrook, D 9
Blyborough
Blyton
Bottesford
Bransby, ST 14
Brattleby
Broughton
Broxholme
Burton by Lincoln
Burton on Stather
Buslingthorpe
Caenby
Caistor, CA 4
Cammeringham
North Carlton, D 15
South Carlton, D 15
Cherry Willingham
Clixby, CA 4
Coates
Cold Hanworth
Corringham, CO 6
Crowle
Culverthorpe, H 24
Dalby, D 19
Dunholme, D 13
Dunstall, CO 6
Epworth
Faldingworth
Fenton
Fillingham
East Firsby
Fiskerton
Flixborough
Fonaby, CA 4

Friesthorpe, D 12
Frodingham
Gainsborough
Glentham, D 8
Glentworth
Grayingham
Greetwell
Hackthorne
Hainton, D 11
West Halton
Harpswell
Haxey
Heapham
Hemswell
Heydour, H 24
Hibaldstow, D 2
Holdingham, SL 23
Holton le Moor, CA 4
Huckerby, CO 6
Hundon, CA 4
Ingham
Kelby, H 24
North Kelsey, D 3
Kettlethorpe
Kirton in Lindsey, K 5
Knaith
Laughton
Lea
Lincoln
 St. Margaret, D 18
Lincoln
 St. Mary Magd., D 18
Lincoln
 St. Nicholas, D 18
Louth, L 10
Luddington
Manton
Marton
Melton Ross, D 1
Messingham
Nettleham
Newton on Trent
Normanby
Normanby
 by Stow, ST 14
Northorpe, CO 6

Bishop Norton, BN 7
Oasby, H 24
Owmby by Spital
Owston
Redbourne
Reepham
Roxby with Risby
Saxby St. Helen
Saxilby
Scamblesby, D 17
Scampton
Scawby
Scothorne
Scotter
Scotton
Scredington, D 25
Searby cum Owmby,
 D 3
Skillington, D 26
Sleaford, SL 23
Old Sleaford, SL 23
Snarford
Snitterby
Somerby, CO 6
Spital in the Street,
 BN 7
Spridlington
Springthorpe
Stow in Lindsey, ST 14
Strubby, D 16
Sturton, ST 14
Sudbrooke
Thurlby, D 21
Torksey
Upton
Waddingham
Wellingore, D 22
Welton by Lincoln,
 D 13
Whitton
Willingham
Willoughton
Winteringham
Winterton
Wroot
Yawthorpe, CO 6

Prebendary of Louth (Lincolnshire Archives Office)
Printed index: wills, admons. and invs., 1612-1857 (1,000), 1879 (1) (vol. 57, pp. 394-407).

Prebendary of Bishops Norton (Lincolnshire Archives Office)
Printed index: wills, admons. and invs., 1613-1814 (100) (vol. 57, pp. 413-14).

Prebendary of Sleaford (Lincolnshire Archives Office)
Printed index: wills, admons. and invs., 1610-1834 (600) (vol. 57, pp. 415-24).

Prebendary of Stow in Lindsey (Lincolnshire Archives Office)
Printed index: wills, admons. and invs., 1610-1833 (180) (vol. 57, pp. 425-28).

Lincoln City (Lincolnshire Archives Office)
Wills, 1492-1610 (few), in a miscellaneous register, Lincoln City Muniments (L.1/3/1) – (Hist. MSS. Comm. Rept. 14, App. 8, pp. 23-24).

Lincoln Wills (Lincoln Cathedral Library)
Wills, 1309-1376, Burwarmote Book, MS 169 (C.1.14).

LONDON AND MIDDLESEX

The city of London and the county of Middlesex were in the province of Canterbury and diocese of London. The various jurisdictions are probably more complicated than anywhere else in the country and the searcher is advised to examine all major courts, split though they are between several record offices.

1. *Consistory court of London* (Greater London Record Office, County Hall). The superior court, with jurisdiction over the whole city and county except for peculiars, concurrently with the next four courts. An index is in preparation for publication, and there are printed abstracts to 1547.

2. *Court of Husting* (Corporation of London Records Office, Guildhall) – the court of the corporation of the city of London, with jurisdiction in the city and liberties, to 1688 only. Printed index with abstracts of all wills.

3. *Commissary court of London (London Division)* Guildhall Library) – about half the parishes both in the city and in the county. Printed index, 1374-1570, with further volumes to be published shortly.

4. *Archdeaconry of London* (Guildhall Library) – about 40 parishes in the city and 3 populous parishes bordering it. Index to 1649 to be published shortly.

5. *Archdeaconry of Middlesex (Middlesex Division)* (Greater London Record Office (Middlesex Records), Dartmouth Street, SW1) – 26 parishes in the county.

In addition to these courts, there were the following peculiars :

6. *Deaneries of the Arches and Croydon* (Lambeth Palace Library) – 13 parishes in the city (the Arches) and 2 in Middlesex (Croydon). Good MS index, to be published in due course.

7. *Dean and chapter of St. Paul's* (St. Paul's Cathedral Library) – 4 parishes in the city and 5 in the county.

8. *Dean and chapter of Westminster* (City of Westminster Archives Dept., Buckingham Palace Road) – 3 parishes in the county and parts of 2 in the city. Printed index to 1700.

9. *St. Katherine by the Tower* (Guildhall Library).

The Greater London Record Office is in Room B21 in the basement of County Hall; nearest tube stations : Waterloo and Westminster; public car park nearby. The Middlesex Records branch of this record office is in Dartmouth Street; nearest tube station, St. James's Park; a leaflet on *Middlesex Wills* is issued. The Guildhall

Library is on the east of the Guildhall in the City; nearest tube station : Bank. St. Paul's Cathedral Library is above the south-west chapel of the cathedral, reached by the entrance to the dome in the cathedral; nearest tube station : St. Paul's. Lambeth Palace Library is in Lambeth Palace; nearest tube stations : Vauxhall and Westminster. The City of Westminster Archives Department is in the public library close to the air terminal, near Victoria Station.

Prerogative Court of Canterbury and other courts having general jurisdiction – see page 1.

Consistory Court of London (Greater London Record Office, Room B21, County Hall, Westminster Bridge, London SE1 7PB. Tel. 01-633 6851)
>   Jurisdiction: concurrent with the commissary and archidiaconal courts over the whole of the city and of Middlesex except the peculiars.
>   Printed indexes: wills, 1492-1719 (Index Lib., in preparation).
>   Other indexes: wills and admons., 1492, 1508, 1514-1857 (calendars, part 19th cent.); m/f of calendar, 1514-1559 at SG.
>   Printed abstracts: wills, 1492, 1508, 1514-1547 (245) (London Record Soc., vol. 3, 1967).
>   See also *Episcopal Registers*, below.

Court of Husting (Corporation of London Record Office, Guildhall, London EC2P 2EJ).
>   Jurisdiction: the city and liberties of London, to 1688.
>   Printed index and abstracts: wills, 1258-1688 (5,000) (*Calendar of Wills . . . in the Court of Husting*, by R. R. Sharpe, 2 vols., 1888-9).

Commissary Court of London (London Division) (The Guildhall Library, Basinghall Street, London EC2P 2EJ. Tel. 01-606 3030)
>   Printed indexes: wills and admons., 1374-1570 (Index Lib., vols. 82 and 86; 1571-1625 in press, 1626-1700, waiting publication).
>   Other indexes: wills and admons., 1571-1629 (modern MS, in short periods); 1629-1857 (calendar; m/f at SG).

Archdeaconry of London (The Guildhall Library, London)
>   Printed indexes: wills, 1393-1421, 1524-1649, admons. 1564-1649 (Index Lib., in press).
>   Other indexes: wills and admons., 1660-1781 (and a few to 1807) (19th cent. calendar).

Archdeaconry of Middlesex (Middlesex Division) (Greater London Record Office (Middlesex Records) 1 Queen Anne's Gate Buildings, Dartmouth Street, London SW1H 9BS. Tel. 01-633 4431/4430)
>   Indexes: wills, 1608-1612, 1662-1794, 1799, admons., 1667-1760 (12,000) (19th cent. MS calendar); invs., 1667-1773 (card index). There are several small gaps throughout the series of admons. and invs., and probate records of the court become very sparse after 1780.

Peculiar Jurisdiction of the Archbishop of Canterbury in the Deanery of the Arches (Lambeth Palace Library, London SE1 7JU. Tel. 01-928 6222)
Indexes: wills, admons. and invs., 1620-1780, 1832 (3,500) (MS, 19th cent.); admons. and invs., 1664-1738 (TS at SG).

Peculiar Jurisdiction of the Archbishop of Canterbury in the Deanery of Croydon (Lambeth Palace Library)
Indexes: wills, admons. and invs., 1602, 1614-1821, 1841 (MS, 19th cent.); (also TS at Public Record Office and SG).

Peculiar of the Dean and Chapter of St. Paul's (The Library, St. Paul's Cathedral, London EC4)
Indexes: wills, 1535-1672 (MS, 19th cent.), 1672-1840, admons., 1646-1837 (calendars; m/f at SG).
Printed list: selected wills, 1226-1642 (79) (Hist. MSS. Comm. 9th Report, Appx., pp. 45-48).

Royal Peculiar of the Dean and Chapter of Westminster (City of Westminster Archives Department, Public Library, Buckingham Palace Road, London SW1. Tel. 01-730 0446)
Jurisdiction: Precincts of the Abbey, St. Margaret's Westminster, Paddington – from c.1700 see under consistory, and archdeaconry of Middlesex; precincts of St. Martin le Grand, and parts of the parishes of St. Leonard Foster Lane, and St. Anne and St. Agnes.
Printed index: wills and admons., 1504-1540, 1550-1641, 1660-1700, (*Indexes to the Ancient Testamentary Records of Westminster*, A. M. Burke, 1913); also, wills, 1540-1556 (from the consistory court of London, Westminster entries, when the jurisdiction of the dean and chapter was suspended during the short-lived existence of the see of Westminster) (pp. 90-102); and miscellaneous testamentary records in Westminster Abbey muniments, 1228-1700 (pp. 103-104).
Other index: wills and admons., as above, and to 1820/30 (very few in later period) (calendar, printed by HMSO, 1864, for probate use only, never published; another copy on open shelves at P.R.O., but very few other copies known to exist).

Royal Peculiar of St. Katherine by the Tower (Guildhall Library, London)
Indexes: wills, 1689-1772, 1818, admons., 1688-1740 (TS lists), 1741-1793 (original act book) (also 19th cent. MS calendar to all records, but incomplete).

Diocese of London, Episcopal Registers (Guildhall Library, London)
Wills and admons., 1313-1548 (TS).
Wills and admons. in the episcopal registers, 1514-1559, are also indexed in the calendar to the consistory court wills at the Greater London Record Office.

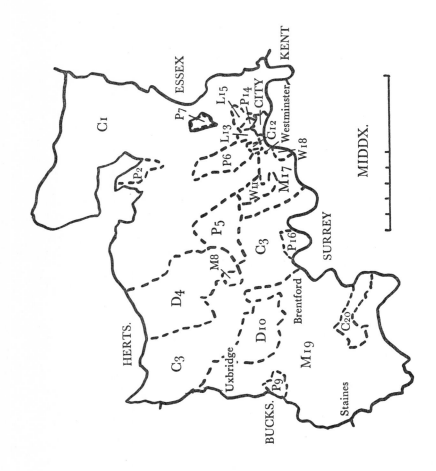

The parishes and chapelries in the City of London and county of Middlesex are listed below, with the jurisdiction(s) into which they fell indicated as follows:

C=Commissary of London (London division); L=Archdeaconry of London; M=Archdeaconry of Middlesex; A=Peculiar Deanery of the Arches; D= Peculiar Deanery of Croydon; P=Peculiar of the Dean and Chapter of St. Paul's; K=Peculiar of St. Katherine-by-the-Tower; W=Peculiar of the Dean and Chapter of Westminster; S=Archdeaconry Court of Surrey (diocese of Winchester) – parishes in Southwark before 1858 were still in that county – see page 129. Numbers refer to map.

This list is based, for the City, on that in Lewis's *Topographical Dictionary* published in 1831, and includes places that may have been chapelries within other parishes and subsequently became parishes in their own right. Parishes were in the City or its immediate vicinity unless otherwise stated.

Acton, C 3
St. Alban Wood Street, C
Allhallows Barking, C
Allhallows Bread Street, C
Allhallows the Great, L
Allhallows Honey Lane, C
Allhallows the Less, L
Allhallows Lombard Street, A
Allhallows Staining, C
Allhallows London Wall and
 St. Augustin Papey, L
St. Alphage London Wall, L
St. Andrew Holborn, L 13
St. Andrew Hubbard, C
St. Andrew Undershaft with
 St. Mary-Axe, C
St. Andrew-by-the-Wardrobe, L
St. Anne and St. Agnes
 Aldersgate with
 St. John Zachary, W & L
St. Anne Blackfriars, C
St. Anne (Soho) Westminster, M
St. Antholin, C
Ashford, M 19
St. Augustine Watling Street, L
Friern Barnet, P 2
St. Bartholomew by the
 Exchange, L
St. Bartholomew the Great, L
St. Bartholomew the Less, L
Bedfont, M 19
St. Benet Fink, C
St. Benet Gracechurch, C
St. Benet Paul's Wharf, C
St. Benet Sherehog, C
Bethnal Green, St. Matthew, C 1

St. Botolph Aldersgate, L
St. Botolph Aldgate, L
St. Botolph Billingsgate, C
St. Botolph without Bishopsgate, C
Bow, C
Brentford, M 19
St. Bride, Fleet Street, C
Bromley, St. Leonard, C 1
Chelsea, M 17
Chiswick, P 16
Christchurch Greyfriars
 Newgate Street, L
Christchurch Southwark, S
Christchurch Spitalfields, C 1
St. Christopher le Stocks, C
St. Clement Danes, M
St. Clement Eastcheap, C
Cowley, M 19
Cranford, M 19
St. Dionis Backchurch, A
West Drayton, P 9
St. Dunstan in the East, A
St. Dunstan in the West, C
Ealing, C 3
Edgware, C 1
Edmonton, C 1
St. Edmund the King, C
Enfield, C 1
St. Ethelburga, L
St. Faith, P
Feltham, M 19
Finchley, C 1
Fulham, C 3
St. Gabriel Fenchurch, C
St. George Bloomsbury, C 12
St. George Botolph Lane, C

St. George in the East, C 1
St. George Hanover Square, M 17
St. George the Martyr and
  St. Andrew above Bars, L 13
St. George Southwark, S
St. Giles Cripplegate, P
St. Giles in the Fields, C 12
St. Gregory by St. Paul's, P
Greenford, C 3
Hackney, C 1
Monken Hadley or Hadleigh, C 1
Hammersmith, C 3
Hampstead, C 1
Hampton, M 19
Hanwell, M 19
Hanworth, C 20
Harefield, C 3
Harlington, M 19
Harmondsworth, M 19
Harrow, D 4
Hayes, D 10
St. Helen Bishopsgate, P
Hendon, C 1
Heston, M 19
Highgate, P 6
Hillingdon, M 19
Hornsey, C 1
Hounslow, M 19
Hoxton (Shoreditch), P
Ickenham, C 3
Isleworth, M 19
Islington, C 1
St. James Clerkenwell, L 13
St. James Duke's Place, C
St. James (Piccadilly)
  Westminster, M
St. John Baptist, L
St. John Baptist Savoy, L
St. John Clerkenwell, L 13
St. John Evangelist,
  Watling Street, A
St. John Evangelist
  Westminster, M 18
St. John Horsleydown, S
St. John Millbank (Smith Square), C
St. John Zachary, L
St. Katherine Coleman, L
St. Katherine Creechurch, C
St. Katherine by the Tower, K
Kensington, M 17
Kingsbury, C 1
Laleham, M 19

St. Lawrence Jewry, C
St. Lawrence Pountney, C
St. Leonard Eastcheap, A
St. Leonard Foster, W & C
St. Leonard Shoreditch, L 15
Limehouse, C 1
Littleton, M 19
St. Luke Old Street, P 14
St. Magnus the Martyr, L
St. Margaret New Fish Street, C
St. Margaret Lothbury, L
St. Margaret Moses, L
St. Margaret Pattens, C
St. Margaret Westminster,
  M & W 18
St. Martin in the Fields, W & L
Precincts of St. Martin-le-Grand, W
St. Martin Ironmonger Lane, C
St. Martin Ludgate, L
St. Martin Orgar, C
St. Martin Outwich, C
St. Martin Vintry, C
St. Mary Abchurch, L
St. Mary Aldermanbury, C
St. Mary Aldermary, A
St. Mary-le-Bone, C 1
St. Mary Bothaw, A
St. Mary le Bow, A
St. Mary Colechurch, L
St. Mary at Hill, L
St. Mary Magdalene
  Old Fish Street, L
St. Mary Magdalene Milk Street, C
St. Mary Mounthaw, L
St. Mary Somerset, L
St. Mary Staining, L
St. Mary-le-Strand, M
St. Mary Woolchurch Haw, C
St. Mary Woolnoth, L
St. Matthew Friday Street, C
St. Michael Bassishaw, L
St. Michael Cornhill, C
St. Michael Crooked Lane, A
St. Michael Queenhithe, L
St. Michael le Quern, L
St. Michael Royal, A
St. Michael Wood Street, C
St. Mildred Bread Street, C
St. Mildred Poultry, C
South Mimms, C 1
St. Nicholas Acons, C
St. Nicholas Cole Abbey, C

St. Nicholas Olave, C
Northolt, C 3
Norwood, D 10
St. Olave Hart Street, L
St. Olave Old Jewry, C
St. Olave Silver Street, L
St. Olave Southwark, S
Paddington, M & W 11
St. Pancras (Middx.), P 6
St. Pancras Soper Lane, A
St. Paul Covent Garden, M
St. Peter Cornhill, L
St. Peter near Paul's Wharf, C
St. Peter le Poer, C
St. Peter ad Vincula, Tower*
St. Peter Westcheap, L
Pinner, D 4
Poplar, C 1
Precinct of Portpool, P
Ruislip, C 3
St. Saviour Southwark, S
St. Sepulchre, C
Shadwell, St. Paul, C
Shepperton, M 19

Shoreditch, P
Staines, M 19
Stanmore, C 1
Stanwell, M 19
St. Stephen Coleman Street, C
St. Stephen Walbrook, L
Stepney, C 1
Stoke Newington, P 7
Sunbury, M 19
St. Swithin London Stone, C
Teddington, C 20
St. Saviour Southwark, S
St. Thomas the Apostle, L
Tottenham, C 1
Trinity the Less, L
Trinity in the Minories, L
Twickenham, M 19
Uxbridge, M 19
St. Vedast Foster Lane, A
Wapping, St. John, C
Precincts of Westminster Abbey, W
Whitechapel, St. Mary, C 1
Willesden, P 5

* It is not clear into which court's jurisdiction St. Peter ad Vincula fell.

NORFOLK

Norfolk was in the province of Canterbury and diocese of Norwich, except for one parish in the diocese of Ely. Probate records are divided between the archdeaconries of Norfolk and Norwich, mainly the southern and northern parts of the county respectively, and the consistory court of Norwich, all of which, together with the peculiars, are now at Norwich. There are printed indexes to wills in the consistory to 1818 and to the Norfolk archdeaconry to 1560.

The county record office is in the library building in the centre of Norwich. Its booklet *Notes for the Assistance of Genealogists* gives excellent guidance to the probate material there. There are public car-parks nearby, but car parking generally is difficult.

Prerogative Court of Canterbury and other courts having general jurisdiction – see page 1. Some 1653-1660 copy wills relating to the county are in the record office.
    Inventories, 1650-1660 (TS at SG).

Consistory Court of Norwich (Norfolk Record Office, Central Library, Bethel Street, Norwich NOR 57E. Tel. Norwich (0603) 22233, ext. 509)
    Jurisdiction: Norfolk, Suffolk and part of Cambridgeshire.
    Printed indexes: wills, 1370-1603 (30,000) (Norf. Record Soc., vols. 16 and 21, and Index Lib., vols 69 and 73), 1604-1818 (33,000) (Norf. Record Soc., vols. 28, 34 and 38; further vols. in preparation).
    'Sede vacante' admons. granted by the *Court of the Prior and Chapter of Christ Church, Canterbury* (page 4), 1500 (60) (Kent Arch. Soc., Records Branch, vol. 3, pp. 47-48).
    Other indexes: wills, 1818-1857 (calendar, by year); admons., 1549-1555 (calendar by year); 1555-1646 (TS), 1666-1668, 1673-1688, 1690-1857 (calendar, by year); invs., 1584-1846 (with gaps); m/f of calendars to 1857 at SG.
    Unindexed: admons., 1370-1499, 1549-1555.

Archdeaconry of Norfolk (Norfolk Record Office)
    Jurisdiction: southern Norfolk, and parts of north-eastern and north-western Norfolk; see also the consistory.
    Printed indexes: wills, 1453-1560 (Norfolk and Norwich Genealogical Soc., vols. 3 and 5; further vols. in preparation).
    Other indexes: wills, 1560-1784 (calendar); 1795-1857 (calendar, by year); admons., 1541-1618, 1672-1676, 1678-1682, 1687-1857 (calendar); invs., 1728-1774 (TS); m/f of calendars at SG.
    Unindexed: admons., 1677, 1683-1685.

Archdeaconry of Norwich (Norfolk Record Office)
Jurisdiction: most of northern Norfolk, and the deaneries of Breccles
and Thetford in southern Norfolk; see also the consistory.
Indexes: wills, 1469-1603 (calendar, by year); 1604-1652 (TS); 1660-
1857 (calendar, by year); admons., 1624-1626, 1632-1637, 1660-1688
(with gaps), 1700-1857 (calendar); invs., 1674-1701 (with gaps), 1703-
1825 (TS); m/f of calendars to 1857 at SG.
Unindexed: admons., 1590-1609.

Peculiar Court of the Dean and Chapter of Norwich (Norfolk Record
Office)
Indexes: wills, 1416-1559 (with gaps), 1572, 1589-1600 (TS); 1600-1857.
(MS); admons., 1500-1530 (TS), 1737-1857 (calendar); invs., 1678-
1686, 1737-1782 (calendar).
Unindexed: admons., 1613-1680, 1706-1736; invs., 1685-1737.

Peculiar of Castle Rising (Norfolk Record Office)
Indexes: wills, 1639-1692; wills, admons. and invs., 1703-1720 (MS)

Peculiar of Great Cressingham (Norfolk Record Office)
Unindexed: wills, 1675-1749, admons., 1702-1751, invs. 1707-1720.

Court of the City of Norwich (Norfolk Record Office)
Printed index: copy wills, 1298-1340, 1377-1405, 1413-1508 (Norf.
Record Soc., vol. 16, and Index Lib., vol. 69, pp. 413-423).
Printed abstracts: copy wills, 1298-1340, 1377-1405, 1413-1854
(*Calendar of Norwich Deeds Enrolled, etc.,* an 'inaccurate and in-
complete list and index').

Consistory Court of Ely (Cambridge University Library, page 18)
Jurisdiction: included the Norfolk parish of Emneth, a peculiar of the
bishop of Ely.

Wills at King's Lynn (Town Hall, King's Lynn)
Wills, 1276-1751, relating to property in the town, registered in the
Guildhall. Also a few 'enrolled wills', 1307-1399, and extracts, 1597-
1840 (29 only) in town records.

Norwich District Probate Registry (Norfolk Record Office)
Index: wills, 1858-1941 (yearly MS).

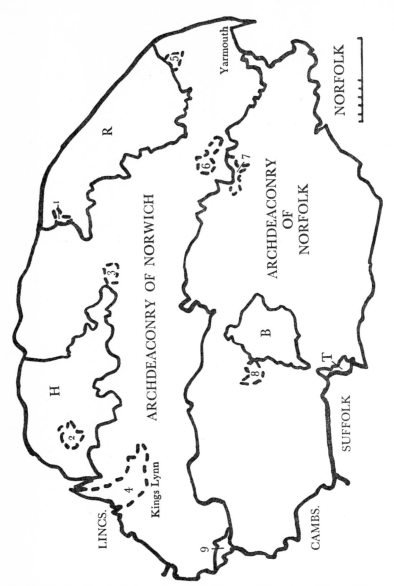

Parishes in the detached deaneries of Heacham and Burnham (H), and Repps and Waxham (R), in the archdeaconry of Norfolk; and in the detached deaneries of Breccles (B) and Thetford (T) in the archdeaconry of Norwich; parishes in the peculiars of the Dean and Chapter of Norwich (DC), Castle Rising (CR), and Great Cressingham (GC); and the parish of Emneth in the diocese of Ely (E).

Aldborough, R
Antingham, R
Arminghall, DC 7
Ashill, B
Ashmanhaugh, R
Aylmerton, R
Bacton, R
Bagthorpe, H
Barmer, H
Barningham Norwood, R
Barningham Town, R
East Barsham, H
North Barsham, H
West Barsham, H
Barton Turf, R
Barwick, H
West Beckham, DC 1
Beeston Regis, R
Beeston St. Lawrence, R
Bessingham, R
Great Bircham, H
Newton Bircham, H
Bircham Tofts, H
Bradfield, R
Brancaster, H
Breckles, B
Brumstead, R
Burnham Deepdale, H
Burnham Norton, H
Burnham Overy, H
Burnham Thorpe, H
Burnham Ulpe, H
Burnham Westgate, H
Carbrooke, B
Castle Rising, CR 4
Caston, B
Catfield, R
Catton, DC 6
Great Cressingham,
GC 8
Cromer, R
Crostwight, R
Croxton, H
Dilham, R
Docking, H
Dunton, H
Eaton, DC 7
Eccles, R
Edingthorpe, R
Emneth, E 9
Fakenham, H
Felbrigg, R
Felmingham, R

Fring, H
Fulmodeston, H
Gatesend, H
Gimingham, R
Gresham, R
Griston, B
Gunton, R
Hanworth, R
Happisburgh, R
Heacham, H
Hempstead, R
Hickling, R
Hindolveston, DC 3
Holme next the Sea, H
Honing, R
Horning, R
Horsey, R
Houghton (next
Harpley), H
Hoveton St. John, R
Hoveton St. Peter, R
Hunstanton, H
Ingham, R
Ingoldisthorpe, H
Irstead, R
Kettlestone, H
Knapton, R
Lakenham, DC 7
Lessingham, R
Ludham, R
Martham, DC 5
Matlask, R
Merton, B
Metton, R
Mundesley, R
Neatishead, R
Northrepps, R
Norwich, DC 7
(Cathedral,
St. Helen,
St. James,
St. Paul)
Overstrand, R
Ovington, B
Palling, R
Paston, R
Plumstead, R
Great Plumstead, DC 6
Potter Heigham, R
Ridlington, R
Ringstead, H
Roughton, R

Roydon near
Lynn, CR 4
Runton, R
East Ruston, R
Little Ryburgh, H
Saham Toney, B
Sco Ruston, R
Scoulton, B
Sculthorpe, H
Sedgeford, DC 2
Sheringham, R
Shernborne, H
Sidestrand, R
Sloley, R
Smallburgh, R
Snettisham, H
Little Snoring, H
Southrepps, R
Sprowston, DC 6
Stalham, R
Stanhoe, H
Stow Bedon, B
Suffield, R
Sustead, R
Sutton, R
Swafield, R
Syderstone, H
Tatterford, H
Tattersett, H
Thetford, T
Thompson, B
Thornham, H
Thorpe Market, R
Threxton, B
Thurgarton, R
Titchwell, H
Tottington, B
Trimingham, R
Trowse Newton, DC 7
Trunch, R
Tunstead, R
Walcott, R
North Walsham, R
Waterden, H
Watton, B
Waxham, R
Westwick, R
Witton (nr.
North Walsham), R
North Wootton, CR 4
South Wootton, CR 4
Worstead, R

NORTHAMPTONSHIRE AND RUTLAND

Northamptonshire and Rutland were in the province of Canterbury, and formed the diocese of Peterborough from its creation in 1541; before this the counties were in the diocese of Lincoln. The archdeaconry of Northampton covered the two counties (except for peculiars) and was coterminous with the diocese of Peterborough.

The records of consistory and archdeaconry courts are now at the Northamptonshire Record Office. Until between 1590 and 1598, when there appears to have been an administrative reorganisation, wills from all deaneries were proved either at Northampton in the archdeaconry court or, after 1541, in the consistory court at Peterborough (pre-1541 wills in the consistory court of Lincoln are rare). The two courts had concurrent jurisdiction, but even in the 16th century the bulk of the wills appear to have been proved before the archdeacon of Northampton. After 1598 wills from the seven western deaneries of Brackley, Daventry, Haddon, Higham, Northampton, Preston and Rothwell were proved at Northampton, and those of the four eastern deaneries of Oundle, Peterborough, Rutland and Weldon at Peterborough.

There is a printed index to wills in the archdeaconry court, 1510-1652, and a TS index to wills in the consistory court, 1604-1719. There are also printed calendars to 17th century admons. in the archdeaconry court, by the Rev. H. I. Longden. Mr. Longden also compiled several MS calendars to wills and admons. which though not fully alphabetical are sometimes easier to use than the alternative contemporary calendars.

The county record office is in a country house set in a park on the outskirts of Northampton, and there is ample free parking space. There is a leaflet detailing the wills and other probate records in the office.

Prerogative Court of Canterbury and other courts having general jurisdiction – see page 1.

Archdeaconry Court of Northampton (Northamptonshire Record Office, Delapré Abbey, Northampton NN4 9AW. Tel. Northampton (0604) 62129)
   Jurisdiction: see introductory note above.
   Printed indexes: wills, 1510-1652 (18,000) (Index Library, vol. 1); admons., 1545-1546, 1638-1641, 1660-1676 (700), by H. I. Longden (1939); 1677-1710 (4,000), (Index Library, vol. 70) (these are in the form of an alphabetical calendar, by year, but with a full index to the book).

Archdeaconry of Northampton, contd.

Other indexes: wills, 1469-1504 (650) (TS, by H. I. Longden; also copy at SG), 1660-1751 (MS, by H. I. Longden), 1752-1820 (calendar); wills and admons., 1821-1857 (calendar); admons., 1711-1820 (MS, by year, by H. I. Longden); m/f of calendar to 1724 at SG.

Consistory Court of Peterborough (Northamptonshire Record Office)

Jurisdiction: see introductory note above.

Indexes: wills, 1541-1646 (gaps 1576-1584 and 1592-1597) (MS, by H. I. Longden); 1604-1719 (TS, copies at SG and with Phillimore and Co. Ltd., Shopwyke Hall, Chichester, Sussex); wills and admons., 1720-1857 (calendar); admons., 1598-1719 (calendars, partly modern MS); m/f of calendar to 1724 at SG.

Unindexed: admons., 1547-1582.

Peculiar of Banbury (Oxon.) (Bodleian Library, Oxford, page 105)

A peculiar of the dean and chapter of Lincoln.

Jurisdiction included the parish of Kings Sutton and parts of the hamlets of Astrop, Charlton and Purston, partly in the parish of Newbottle, and Grimsbury in the parish of Banbury (Oxon.), all in Northamptonshire.

Printed index: wills and admons., 1547-1856 (Oxfordshire Record Society, vol. 40, and Banbury Historical Society, vol. 1).

Peculiar of Empingham (Rutland) (Lincolnshire Archives Office, page 80)

A peculiar of the dean and chapter of Lincoln, see below; and see also the archdeaconry of Stow (Lincs.), below.

Printed index: wills, admons. and invs., 1669-1744 (100) (Index Lib., vol. 57, pp. 377-78).

M/f of documents at Northampton.

Wills and admons., 1745-1835, are also to be found in the records of the *Archdeaconry of Huntingdon* (page 65); and there is a TS list at Northampton to original documents at Lincoln.

Peculiar of Gretton (Northants.) (Lincolnshire Archives Office)

A peculiar of the dean and chapter of Lincoln; see also that court, below.

Printed index: wills, admons. and invs., 1657-1832 (173) (Index Lib., vol. 57, pp. 379-81).

M/f of documents at Northampton.

Peculiar Court of Ketton (Rutland) (Lincolnshire Archives Office)

A peculiar of the dean and chapter of Lincoln; see also that court, below.

Printed index: wills, 1666-1677 (12) (Index Library, vol. 57, pp. 385).

Microfilm of documents at Northampton.

See also below.

Peculiar Court of Liddington (Rutland) (Lincolnshire Archives Office)
A peculiar of the dean and chapter of Lincoln; see also that court, below.
Printed index: wills, 1668-1676 (20), 1810 (1) (Index Library, vol. 57, p. 393).
Microfilm of documents at Northampton.
See also below.

Prebends of Caldecott, Ketton with Tixover, and Liddington (Rutland) (Leicestershire Record Office, page 77)
Printed index: wills and admons., Caldecott: 1669-1820; Ketton with Tixover: 1574, 1722-1820; Liddington: 1723-1819 (Index Lib., vol. 51, pp. 389-91).
Other indexes: wills and admons., Caldecott: 1812-1830; Ketton with Tixover: 1812-1834; Liddington: 1820-1832 (card index).

Peculiar of Nassington (Northants.) (Lincolnshire Archives Office)
A peculiar of the dean and chapter of Lincoln; see also that court, below.
Printed index: wills, admons. and invs., 1660-1753 (200), 1788 (1) (Index Lib., vol. 57, pp. 408-12).
Unindexed: wills, admons. and invs., 1746-1844 (200).
Wills, 1748-1844, and admons., 1753-1838, are also to be found in the records of the *Archdeaconry of Huntingdon* (page 65); and there is a TS list at Northampton to original documents at Lincoln.

Dean and Chapter of Lincoln (Lincolnshire Archives Office)
Jurisdiction: over places in the peculiars on occasion.
Printed index: wills, admons. and invs., 1534-1834 (Index Lib., vol. 57, pp. 265-366).

Archdeaconry of Stow (Lincs.) (Lincolnshire Archives Office)
Jurisdiction: at times (mid 16th cent.) over Empingham.
Printed index: wills, 1530-1699 (Index Lib., vol. 57, pp. 1-203); admons., 1580-1699 (vol. 57, pp. 205-64).

Diocese of Lincoln, Episcopal Registers (Lincolnshire Archives Office)
The pre-1541 diocese included Northamptonshire and Rutland, and a few wills for the counties are to be found.
Printed index: wills, 1320-1547 (Index Lib., vol. 28, pp. 1-17).

Burgess Court of Higham Ferrers (Northamptonshire Record Office)
The rolls of the Burgess Court of Higham Ferrers contain the text of many wills which were registered in respect of property there.
See *Historical Manuscripts Commission Report* 12, Appendix Part 9, p. 530.

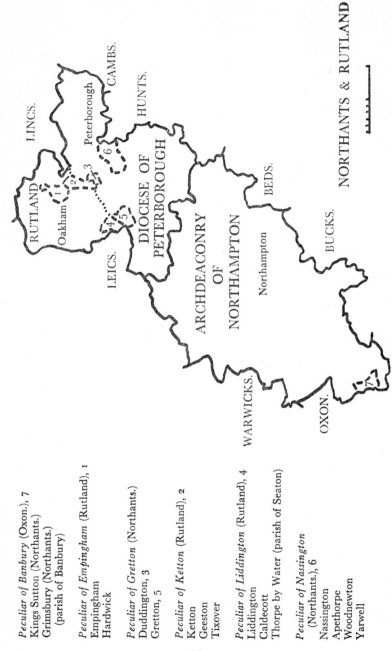

Peculiar of *Banbury* (Oxon.), 7
Kings Sutton (Northants.)
Grimsbury (Northants.)
(parish of Banbury)

Peculiar of *Empingham* (Rutland), 1
Empingham
Hardwick

Peculiar of *Gretton* (Northants.)
Duddington, 3
Gretton, 5

Peculiar of *Ketton* (Rutland), 2
Ketton
Geeston
Tixover

Peculiar of *Liddington* (Rutland), 4
Liddington
Caldecott
Thorpe by Water (parish of Seaton)

Peculiar of *Nassington*
(Northants.), 6
Nassington
Apethorpe
Woodnewton
Yarwell

99

NOTTINGHAMSHIRE

Nottinghamshire was in the province and diocese of York. The county lay entirely (peculiars excepted) in the archdeaconry of Nottingham. In 1837 this was transferred ecclesiastically to the diocese of Lincoln, but this does not appear to have affected probate matters which continued in the same jurisdictions to 1857.

The original probate records of the archdeaconry are now at the county record office, having been separated from those of the rest of the exchequer court of York, which remain at York. The printed indexes to the prerogative and exchequer courts of York, to 1688, include the Nottinghamshire archdeaconry; and there is a modern typed index (based on probate act books at York, not the original records) to the period 1688-1731 (available at the record office and at the Borthwick Institute, York). A card index (based on the original records) is in preparation, and at present covers the periods c.1500-1630 and 1701-1748. This will eventually supersede the 19th century calendar (arranged by deanery) for the remaining period to 1857. The act books at Nottingham list all wills whether proved in the exchequer or the prerogative court. Only the original wills of the archdeaconry are at Nottingham, many of which have not survived. There will usually be a registered copy at the Borthwick Institute bound in with all the other exchequer and prerogative copy wills, within the period 1389-1857, whilst those at Nottingham do not represent a complete set.

Also at the county record office are the records of the important peculiar of Southwell and of several other peculiars – these are all in a consolidated card index for the whole period.

The Borthwick Institute at York holds the records of the chancery court of the archbishop of York, which had jurisdiction during archiepiscopal visitations, over beneficed clergy, and in appeals from lower courts; and those of the court of the dean and chapter of York, which had jurisdiction in all courts (apart from peculiars) during archiepiscopal vacancy. There are printed indexes to 1658 for the chancery court and (partially) to 1724 for the court of the dean and chapter.

The Nottinghamshire Record Office is situated in a handsome town house in the older part of the city, just to the west of the inner ring road and not far from the station. Car parking in Nottingham is extremely difficult, but there are multi-storey car parks at some distance from the office.

Prerogative Court of Canterbury and other courts having general juris-diction – see page 1.

Prerogative Court of York and other courts with jurisdiction in the province – see page 150.

Exchequer Court of the Archbishop of York in the Archdeaconry of Nottingham (Nottinghamshire Record Office, County House, High Pave-ment, Nottingham NG1 1HR. Tel. Nottingham (0602) 54524)
  Jurisdiction: the county except for peculiars.
  Printed indexes (prerogative and exchequer courts jointly): wills, 1389-1636, and admons., 1389-1652 (Yorks. Arch. Soc. Record Series, vols. 6, 11, 14, 19, 22, 24, 26, 28, 32, and 35 – the admons. are indexed separately in appendices in each volume); wills, 1636-1652 (vol. 4); wills and admons., 1660-1684 (vols. 49, 60, 68 and 89, pp. 1-145), vacancies, 1683, 1686-1688 (vol. 89, pp. 146-210); (Notts.) wills and admons. (extracted from the above volumes), 1568-1619 (9,500).
  Other indexes (Nottingham archdeaconry only): wills and admons., 1688-1731 (TS); c.1500-1630, 1700-1748 (card indexes, and in pro-gress); 1749-1858 (50,000) (MS, 19th cent. calendar, by deanery).
  See also under Yorkshire, page 155, for registered copies at Borthwick Institute.

Nottinghamshire Peculiars (Nottinghamshire Record Office)
  For places within the various jurisdictions, see map. See also exchequer court.
  Index: wills, admons. and invs., 1506-1857 (20,000) (consolidated card index); m/f of calendars to Southwell, Mansfield, Gringley and Kinoulton peculiars at SG.
  Printed index (to Manor of Edwinstowe only): of some records, 1521-1801 (180) (*Northern Genealogist*, vol. 1, pp. 20-24).
  Printed abstracts (for peculiar of Southwell only): wills, 1470-1542 (34) Camden Soc., N.S., vol. 48, pp. 96-145, 1891); invs., 1512-1586 (118) (Thoroton Soc. Record Series, vol. 22).
  Other abstracts: wills, admons. and invs. (in manor of Mansfield only), 1640-1695 (TS, at SG).

Court of the Dean and Chapter of York (Borthwick Institute, York)
  Jurisdiction included 6 places in Notts. – see map.
  For records and indexes, see page 161.

Prebend of Apesthorpe (Borthwick Institute, York)
  Now known as Habblesthorpe.
  Wills, admons. and invs., 1557-1844 (few).

Prebend of Bole (Borthwick Institute, York)
  Wills, admons. and invs., 1546-1847 (few).

Manor of Skegby and Teversal (Nottinghamshire Record Office)
  Wills, 1721-1858 in Skegby court rolls.

YORKS.

1

2   3

4

B

5

6

7   8

Y

9

LINCS.

DERBYS.

10

E

T   M   R

11

S

Newark

ARCHDY. OF NOTTINGHAM

Nottingham

12

K

LEICS.

NOTTS.

102

NOTTINGHAMSHIRE

A=Prebend of Apesthorpe; B=Prebend of Bole; E=Manor of Edwinstowe; G=Manor of Gringley-on-the-Hill; J=Manor of St. John of Jerusalem or Shelford St. Johns; K=Peculiar of Kinoulton; M=Manor of Mansfield; R=Manor of Rufford Abbey; S=Peculiar of Southwell; T=Manor of Skegby and Teversal; Y=Peculiar of the Dean and Chapter of York.

Note. Most of the following places are also likely to be in the exchequer (archdeaconry) court records. The manorial court of St. John of Jerusalem (J) had jurisdiction over tenants of the manor only, in a number of places in the south of the county – these are not marked on the map.

Apesthorpe, A 6
Askham, Y
Aslockton, J
Barnby-in-the-Willows, J
Beckingham, S & G 4
Bleasby, S
Blidworth, S
Budby, M 10
Calverton, S
Carburton, E
Car Colston, J
Carlton in Gedling, J
Carlton on Trent, S 11
Caunton, S 11
Cotgrave, J
Cropwell Bishop, S 12
Darlton, S 9
East Drayton, Y
Dunham, S 9
Eaton, S 7
Edingley, S
Edwinstowe, E
Farnsfield, S
Flintham, J
Gedling, J
Gringley-on-the-Hill, G 2
Halam, S
Halloughton, S
Hickling, J
Holme, S 11
Hoveringham, J
Hucknall under Huthwaite, M
Kilton (Worksop), M
Kinoulton, K
Kirklington, S
Kneeton, J
Laneham, Y

North Leverton, S 6
Mansfield, M
Mansfield Woodhouse, M
Misterton, G & Y 1
Morton, S
North Muskham, S 11
South Muskham, S 11
Normanton-on-Soar, J
Normanton-on-the-Wolds, J
Norwell, S 11
Owthorpe, J
Oxton, S
Plumtree, J
Radcliffe-on-Trent, J
Ragnall, S 9
Rampton, S 8
Rempstone, J
Ruddington, J
Rufford, R
Scarrington, J
Scofton (Worksop), M
Skegby, T
Southwell, S
Stanford-on-Soar, J
West Stockwith, G & Y 1
Stokeham, Y
Sutton-in-Ashfield, M
Teversal, T
Tollerton, J
Treswell, Y 8*
Upton, S
Walkeringham, G 3
Warsop, M
South Wheatley, S 5
Willoughby-on-the-Wolds, J
Woodborough, S
Worksop, M

* Treswell was only in the jurisdiction of the court of the dean and chapter of York at an early period.

OXFORDSHIRE

Oxfordshire was in the province of Canterbury and formed the diocese of Oxford from its foundation in 1542; before this, the archdeaconry of Oxford, which was almost coterminous with the county, was in the diocese of Lincoln. In 1836 the archdeaconry of Berkshire was transferred from the diocese of Salisbury to that of Oxford, while in 1845 the archdeaconry of Buckinghamshire was transferred from Lincoln. There are however very few Berkshire and Buckinghamshire wills in the records of the consistory.

The probate records of the consistory and archdeaconry are intermingled and jointly indexed to 1732 (a good 19th century index, in preparation for publication); with separate 19th century indexes thereafter. There is also a good 19th century index to all the Oxfordshire and Buckinghamshire peculiars (and some for Berkshire), consolidated, for the whole period; and a printed index to the peculiar court of Banbury and Cropredy, and the manorial court of Sibford, extracted from this. All these records are in the custody of the Department of Western MSS., Bodleian Library. There is also a printed index to the records of the court of the Chancellor of the University of Oxford, which are in the University Archives, c/o Bodleian Library.

The Bodleian Library is in the centre of Oxford, and the headquarters of the Department of Western Manuscripts is Duke Humfrey's Reading Room. The department issues a leaflet on *Genealogical Sources within the Diocese of Oxford*. Prior application for a reader's ticket should be made. Long delays are likely unless documents are ordered in advance. There are no public car parks nearby, and car parking in Oxford generally is very difficult.

Prerogative Court of Canterbury and other courts having general jurisdiction – see page 1.
    Printed abstracts: wills, 1393-1510 (Oxon. Record Soc., vol. 39).

Consistory and Archdeaconry Courts of Oxford (Department of Western MSS., Bodleian Library, Oxford OX1 3BG. Tel. Oxford (0865) 44675)
    Jurisdiction: concurrent throughout the county except in the peculiars; some mid 16th century records of the peculiars are filed with these records.
    Indexes: wills, admons. and invs., 1528-1732 (MS, 19th century, to be published in due course in Index Library); 1733-1857 (MS, 19th century, consistory and archdeaconry separately).
    Printed abstracts: invs., 1550-1590 (Oxon. Record Soc., vol. 44).

Court of Chancellor of the University of Oxford (The University Archives c/o Bodleian Library, Oxford)

> Application to see these should be made to the Deputy Keeper of the University Archives. They are not administered by the Bodleian Library.
>
> Jurisdiction: over resident members of the University and some other 'privileged' persons within the precincts.
>
> Printed index: wills and admons., 1436-1814, invs., 1443-1740 (2,000) (*An Index to Wills Proved in the Court of the Chancellor,* John Griffiths, 1862).

Peculiar for Banbury and Cropredy (Dept. of Western MSS., Bodleian Library)

> Jurisdiction: Banbury and its hamlets; Cropredy and its hamlets, Claydon, Mollington and Wardington; Horley and Hornton, all in Oxfordshire; and Kings Sutton in Northamptonshire. These are sometimes described as four separate peculiars, but appear to have been jointly administered so far as testamentary records are concerned, at least after 1574. Before 1574 some records of the peculiars are indexed with the consistory and archdeaconry records.
>
> Printed index: wills, admons. and invs., 1542-1857 (3,750) (including pre-1574 entries in consistory and archdeaconry court index) (Oxon. Record Soc., vol. 40, and Banbury Hist. Soc., vol. 1).
>
> Printed abstracts: invs., 1550-1590 (Oxon. Record Soc., vol. 44); wills, admons. and invs., 1590-1650 (400) (Banbury only) (Banbury Hist. Soc., vol. 12, in press).
>
> This was a peculiar of the dean and chapter of Lincoln; see also that peculiar court, below.

Peculiars of Dorchester, Langford, Monks Risborough (Bucks.) and Thame (Dept. of Western MSS., Bodleian Library)

> Jurisdiction in Oxfordshire: *Dorchester*, Benson (Bensington), Chiselhampton, Clifton Hampden, Drayton St. Leonard, Marsh Baldon, Nettlebed, Pishill, Stadhampton, Toot Baldon and Warborough; *Langford* (partly in Berks.); *Monks Risborough* (Bucks): Newington with Britwell Prior; *Thame* and its hamlets, Great Milton, Sydenham and Tetsworth.
>
> Index: wills, admons. and invs., 1547-1857 (MS, 19th cent., consolidated for all peculiars, with Bucks. and Berks. peculiars. Some 16th and early 17th cent. records are with the consistory and archdeaconry records, above. Records of the individual peculiars commence: Dorchester, 1553 (to 1835 only); Langford, 1560-1576, 1590, 1607-1833 only; Monks Risborough, 1605; Thame, 1547 (very incomplete before 1660).
>
> Thame was part of the peculiar of the dean and chapter of Lincoln, though separately administered; and Langford was a Lincoln prebend; see below. Dorchester was a private jurisdiction derived from Dorchester Abbey and Monks Risborough was a peculiar of the archbishop of Canterbury, never inhibited.

Manorial Court of Sibford (Dept. of Western MSS., Bodleian Library)

Jurisdiction: Sibford Gower and Sibford Ferris, hamlets in the parish of Swalcliffe.

Printed index: wills and admons., 1733-1829 (Oxon. Record Soc., vol. 40, and Banbury Hist. Soc., vol. 1).

Peculiar Court of the Dean and Chapter of Lincoln (Lincolnshire Archives Office, page 81)

Very occasional records of the peculiars are found in the records of this court at Lincoln.

Printed index: wills, admons. and invs., 1534-1834 (Index Library, vol. 57, pp. 265-366: Banbury (3), 1573, 1632, 1673, Gt. Milton (1), 1638); also under 'miscellaneous' wills, 1542-1730 (vol. 57, pp. 430-56; Banbury (2), 1660, 1672; Hornton (1), 1580; Wardington (1), 1671).

See also Oxon. Arch. Soc. Report for 1909, p. 33, for a list of a few Oxon. wills 'preserved at Lincoln'.

Diocese of Lincoln, Episcopal Registers (Lincolnshire Archives Office)

Before 1542 the diocese included Oxfordshire, and a few wills are to be found.

Printed index: wills, 1320-1547 (Index Library, vol. 28, pp. 1-17).

Printed abstracts: all the above (*Early Lincoln Wills*, A. Gibbons, 1888).

Pre-1542 Oxfordshire testators are unlikely to be found in the Consistory Court of Lincoln (Index Library, vols. 28 and 52).

NOTE: For Shenington and Widford, formerly in Glos., see under that county (page 50). Caversfield, formerly a detached part of Bucks., was within the archdeaconry of Oxford for probate purposes.

Places in Oxfordshire outside the jurisdiction of the consistory and archdeaconry courts.

OXON.

Banbury, 1
Benson (Bensington), 9
Britwell Prior, 9

NORTHANTS.

WARWICKS.

Banbury

Chipping Norton

GLOS.

Bicester

DIOCESE OF OXFORD

BUCKS.

Witney

Oxford

BERKSHIRE

DIOCESE
OF
OXFORD

Henley

Caversfield (Bucks.), 5
Chiselhampton, 9
Clifton Hampden, 9
Claydon, 1
Cropredy, 1
Dorchester, 9
Drayton St. Leonard, 9
Horley, 2
Hornton, 2
Langford, 7
Marsh Baldon, 9
Great Milton, 9
Mollington, 1
Nettlebed, 11
Newington, 9
Pishill, 10
Shenington (Glos.), 3
Sibford (parish of Swalcliffe), 4
Stadhampton, 9

Sydenham, 8
Tetsworth, 8
Thame, 8
Toot Baldon, 9
Warborough, 9
Wardington, 1
Widford (Glos.), 6

107

SHROPSHIRE

Shropshire was in the province of Canterbury, the south-western half lying in the diocese of Hereford and north-eastern in the diocese of Lichfield (and Coventry); with a few extreme north-western parishes in the diocese of St. Asaph; and Halesowen in the diocese of Worcester. There are also several peculiars.

The records of the episcopal consistory courts of Hereford and St. Asaph, and of the peculiars of Bridgnorth, Buildwas, Ellesmere, Longdon-on-Tern, Shrewsbury St. Mary, Wombridge and Ashford Carbonell are all at the National Library of Wales, Aberystwyth. Those of the diocese of Lichfield, and of the peculiar of Prees, are at Lichfield; and those of Worcester, at Worcester; there are printed indexes to pre-Commonwealth wills and admons. and good modern indexes to the remaining period in both these dioceses.

The Lichfield Joint Record Office is in the same building as the library, in the centre of Lichfield; there are public car-parks nearby. The office issues a *Handlist to the Diocesan, Probate and Church Commissioners' Records* (1970) (35p), which summarises the probate records there. The National Library of Wales is a conspicuous building on the eastern outskirts of Aberystwyth, overlooking the town. There is ample car parking. Prior application should be made for a reader's ticket.

Prerogative Court of Canterbury and other courts having general jurisdiction – see page 1.

    Printed index: (Salop.) wills, 1700-1749 (1,150) (*Shropshire Probates*, by G. F. Mathews, 1929); and, 1750-1770 (MS, at SG).

Consistory Court of Lichfield (Lichfield Joint Record Office, Public Library, Bird Street, Lichfield WS13 6PN. Tel. Lichfield (05432) 22177)

    Jurisdiction: the north-eastern half of Shropshire.

    Index: wills and admons., 1516-1857 (MS, 19th cent., calendar – this is considered more accurate that the printed index below; m/f of calendar at SG).

    Printed index: wills and admons., 1516-1652 (Index Lib., vol. 7, pp. 1-516 – this calendar with index was compiled direct from the contemporary calendars and has been found incomplete and unreliable – if possible the MS index above should be consulted).

Consistory Court of St. Asaph (National Library of Wales)

    Jurisdiction: 9 parishes in north-western Shropshire.

    For records and indexes see page 177.

Episcopal Consistory Court of Hereford (National Library of Wales,
Aberystwyth. Tel. Aberystwyth 3816)
Jurisdiction: the south-western half of Shropshire.
Chronological lists: wills and invs., 1517, 1539-1627; wills, 1628-1657,
1663; invs., 1628-1641, 1660-1661 (calendar); wills and admons., 1662-
1857 (act books with index).
Unindexed: miscellaneous invs., 1662, 1695-1760.
An index to all these records is in preparation for eventual publication
in the Index Library.

Consistory Court of Worcester (Worcestershire Record Office)
Jurisdiction: Halesowen, formerly a detached part of Shropshire.
Printed indexes: wills, 1451-1495, 1509-1652, admons. and invs., 1520-
1652 (Index Lib. vols. 31 and 39).
Other indexes: wills, admons. and invs., 1660-1857 (TS); m/f of
calendar to 1857 at SG.

Royal Free Chapel of Shrewsbury St. Mary (National Library of Wales)
Jurisdiction: Albrighton, Astley, Clive and St. Mary Shrewsbury.
Index: wills, admons. and invs., 1661-1857.

*Peculiar Deanery of Bridgnorth and the Royal Free Chapelry of St. Mary
Magdalen* (N.L.W.)
Jurisdiction: Bridgnorth, Alveley, Bobbington, Claverley and Quatford.
Index: wills, admons. and invs., 1635-1857; m/f of calendar to 1857 at
SG.

Peculiar of Buildwas Abbey (National Library of Wales)
Wills and admons., 1799-1819 (5) (as above)

*Manors of Ellesmere, Colemere, Hampton and Lineal, with the Court of
the Town and Liberty of Ellesmere* (National Library of Wales)
Jurisdiction: Ellesmere with Colemere, Lyneal and Welshhampton.
Index: wills and admons., 17th cent.-1857; m/f of calendar to 1857
at SG; see also the Bridgewater Collection in Shropshire Record
Office.

Manor of Longdon-on-Tern (National Library of Wales)
Wills and admons., 1777-1857 (11 only).

Peculiar of Wombridge Abbey (National Library of Wales)
Index: wills, admons., and invs., 1787-1854

Peculiar of Little Hereford (Heref.) and Ashford Carbonell (Salop.)
(N.L.W.)
Index: wills, admons. and invs., 1662-1857 (calendar).

Peculiar of Prees or Pipe Minor (Lichfield Joint Record Office)
Jurisdiction: Calverhall, Darliston, Press, and Whixhall.
Index: wills, 1697-1857 (MS, 19th century, calendar, consolidated with
other Lichfield peculiars); m/f of calendar to 1857 at SG.

Wills at William Salt Library, Stafford
Miscellaneous wills, including a few for Prees and Worfield (see page 121).

Corporation of Ludlow (Shropshire Record Office, Shirehall, Abbey Foregate, Shrewsbury)
Wills, 1336-1500.

Corporation of Shrewsbury (The Guildhall, Dogpole, Shrewsbury)
Wills, 1336-1404 (very few) (Hist. MSS. Comm. Rept. 15, App. Pt. 10, 1899).

Manor of Ruyton-of-the-Eleven-Towns (Shrewsbury Public Library, Castle Gates, Shrewsbury)
Printed index: wills, 1665-1709 (64) (Salop. Arch. Soc. Trans. vol. 52, pp. 116-18)
Unindexed: wills, 1709-1816. See also *A List of Wills and Marriage Settlements in the Local History Collection of the Shrewsbury Public Library*, comp. R. E. James (Shrewsbury Library Committee, 1958) (mainly probate copies).

Diocese of St. Asaph
Kinnerley
Knockin
Llanyblodwel
Llanmynech
Melverley
Oswestry
St. Martins
Selattyn
Whittington

Royal Free Chapel of Shrewsbury St. Mary
Albrighton, 5
Astley, 6
Clive, 4
Shrewsbury St. Mary, 7

Peculiar Court Longdon-on-Tern, 8

Peculiar Court of Wombridge Abbey, 9

Peculiar of Ashford Carbonell, 13

Peculiar Deanery of Bridgnorth
Bridgnorth, 10
Alveley, 11
Bobbington, 11
Claverley, 11
Quatford, 10

Manor Court of Ellesmere, 1
Ellesmere
Colemeare
Lyneal
Welshampton

Peculiar Court of Prees
Calverhall, 3
Darliston, 3
Prees, 3
Whixall, 2

Consistory Court of Worcester
Halesowen, 12

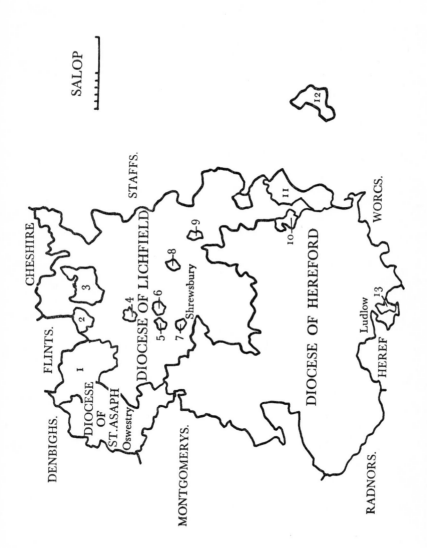

SALOP

CHESHIRE

STAFFS.

DIOCESE OF LICHFIELD

DENBIGHS.

FLINTS.

DIOCESE
OF
ST. ASAPH

Oswestry

MONTGOMERYS.

1

2

3

4

5

6

7

Shrewsbury

8

9

10

11

12

DIOCESE OF HEREFORD

WORCS.

HEREF

Ludlow

13

RADNORS.

SOMERSET

Somerset was in the province of Canterbury and diocese of Bath and Wells.

All probate records for the diocese of Bath and Wells deposited in the probate registry at Exeter were destroyed by enemy action in 1942. The records included those of the episcopal consistory court of Bath and Wells, the archdeaconry courts of Wells and Taunton, the consistory courts of the dean and chapter and of the dean, the peculiar courts of the precentor, the chancellor and the sub-dean of Wells, the royal peculiar court of Ilminster, and the various prebendary courts. There are printed indexes to the lost wills and admons. for the archdeaconry of Taunton to 1799, and for the peculiar of Ilminster to 1857; and there are MS copies of most calendars at the Society of Genealogists.

From 1812 copies of wills, whatever the court, had to be deposited with the Estate (or Stamp) Duty Office in London. Copies of most Somerset wills from this collection have now been deposited in the Somerset Record Office (it appears that not all the peculiar court wills were received), so there should still be a virtually complete record for the period 1812-1857, enhanced by the inclusion of P.C.C. wills for the county. There is a card index to them. From 1805 abstracts of wills and admons. had similarly to be sent to this Office. These abstracts remain in the Public Record Office, London, and continue after 1811 (at present, under a 150-year rule, they are available to 1823). Unlike the complete copies, which were indexed in one series, these abstracts are still arranged by courts.

The parish of Abbots Leigh was within the jurisdiction of the consistory court of Bristol, whose records survive at Bristol.

Some original probate records, relevant material in act books, inventories and admon. bonds – much of them in bad condition and unfit for production – do survive in the Somerset Record Office. The Somerset Record Society has published two volumes of abstracts of surviving wills, and further material accumulated by the Society has been deposited at the record office. The record office keeps a card index to 'stray' wills formerly in private custody and now deposited amongst family, estate and solicitors' records, and any similar collections.

The Somerset Record Office is on the north-eastern outskirts of Taunton. There is a small car-park.

Prerogative Court of Canterbury and other courts having general jurisdiction – see page 1.

Printed abstracts: wills (P.C.C.), 1383-1558 (Som. Record Soc., vols. 16, 19 and 21); wills ('at Lambeth'), 1363-1491 (vol. 19, pp. 286-356). Selected wills, from the MS collection of Rev. F. Brown (*Abstracts of Somerset Wills* . . ., printed by F. A. Crisp, 6 vols., 1887-1890). The complete MS collection of 32 vols. is now at the Somerset Record Office.

Estate (or Stamp) Duty Office Wills (Somerset Record Office, Obridge Road, Taunton TA2 7PU. Tel. Taunton (0823) 87600)

See introductory note; should include wills from all Somerset courts, apart from men who died on active service and who were exempt from duty. It appears that not all peculiar court wills were received.

Index: copy wills, 1812-1857 (card index).

Estate (or Stamp) Duty Office Abstracts (Public Record Office, Chancery Lane, London WC2A 1LR. Tel. 01-405 0741)

See introductory note; should include abstracts of all wills and admons. from all courts, arranged by court.

Indexes: wills and admons., 1805-1811 (refs. IR 26/289-293), 1812-1857 (from 1824 the indexes only are available, under a 150-year rule, but more abstracts will become available gradually).

These copies and abstracts of wills and admons. are described in two articles in the *Genealogists' Magazine* (vol. 15, no. 11, Sept. 1967, pp. 393-97, by A. J. Camp, and vol. 16, no. 6, June 1970, pp. 269-73, by D. T. Hawkings – the latter relates specifically to Somerset).

Episcopal Consistory Court of Bath and Wells (Somerset Record Office)

Virtually all the records of this court were destroyed in 1942.

Jurisdiction: over the whole diocese at most times, and solely (apart from peculiars) in the archdeaconry of Bath.

Printed index (to the destroyed records): wills, 1528-1600 (from a MS copy calendar to all the courts at Wells, at SG) (Som. Record Soc., vol. 62).

Printed abstracts: wills (complete), 1528-1536 (600) (*Wells Wills, arranged in parishes*, by F. W. Weaver, 1890); 1539-1542 (Som. Arch. and Nat. Hist. Soc. Proc., vol. 61 (1916), pp. 54-104); miscellaneous wills (in this and other courts), pre-1600 (350) (Som. Record Soc., vol. 62, pp. 121-39).

Other indexes (to surviving records): wills, c.1575-1640 (1,750) (TS), 1558-1559 (35), 1590-1591 (2), 1618-1619 (65), 1626 (3) (TS), invs., c. 1575-1640 (and a few to 1682) (325) (TS); (to the destroyed records): wills, 1601-1648 (MS copy calendar to all the courts at Wells, at SG); wills, 1660-1829 (6 vols. MS copy calendar, at SG).

Unindexed surviving records: admons., c.1570-c.1680 (some thousands); probate and admon. books, 1680-1716, admon. act books, 1558-1578, 1595-1603, 1610-1612, 1631-1633, 1636-1637, 1663-1665, office day

Episcopal Consistory Court of Bath and Wells, contd.
books including probate and admons. acts, 1570-1737 (incomplete series). All the foregoing are in bad condition and generally not available for searching. Visitation act books, 1531-1534, 1555-1556. Probate and admon. act books, 1817-1823, 1827-1835, 1837 (Jan.-May), 1842-1850 (Sep.).

Consistory Court of the Archdeaconry of Wells (Somerset Record Office)
Virtually all the records of this court were destroyed in 1942.
Jurisdiction: all the archdeaconry except the peculiars.
Printed abstracts: wills (complete), 1543-1546, 1554-1556 (531) (Som. Record Soc., vol. 40).
Printed index (to the destroyed records): wills, 1528-1600, as for consistory court, above.
Other indexes (to the destroyed records): wills, 1601-1648, as for consistory court, above; wills, 1660-1799 (3 vols. MS copy calendar, at SG).
Unindexed surviving records: admons., 1623-1649, 1671, 1686-1703; probate and admon. act books, 1817-1850, as for consistory court, above.

Consistory Court of the Archdeaconry of Taunton (Somerset Record Office)
Virtually all the records of this court were destroyed in 1942.
Jurisdiction: all the archdeaconry except the peculiars.
Printed index (to the destroyed records): wills and admons., 1537-1593 (Index Lib., vol. 45, pp. 1-88), wills (only), 1597-1799 (pp. 89-437) (25,000 in all); admons., 1596-1799 (6,800) (Index Lib., vol. 45a or 53); wills (omitted from vol. 45 above) (373) (*The Genealogists' Magazine,* vol. 5, pp. 328-336). The Record Office has an annotated version of vol. 45 showing all known surviving wills or abstracts. These include about 200 wills, mainly 1634-1756, and 75 admon. accounts. There are also about 3,000 invs., index in preparation.
Abstracts: wills, 1561-1731 (760) (TS, at SG – these include the 373 mentioned above; also index with Som. Arch. Soc.); wills, 1538-1782 (640) (at Record Office).

Consistory Court of the Dean of Wells (Somerset Record Office)
Virtually all the records of this court were destroyed in 1942.
Jurisdiction: 15 parishes throughout the county.
Printed index (to the destroyed records): wills, 1528-1600, as for consistory court, above.
Other indexes (to the destroyed records): wills, 1601-1648, as for consistory court, above; wills and admons., 1660-1804 (2 vols. MS copy calendars, at SG).
Unindexed surviving records: probate and admon. act books, 1662-1771, 1812-1846.

Consistory Court of the Dean and Chapter of Wells (Somerset Record Office)

Virtually all the records of this court were destroyed in 1942.

Jurisdiction: 10 parishes throughout the county, and the Liberty of St. Andrew in Wells.

Printed index (to the destroyed records): wills, 1528-1600, as for consistory court, above.

Other indexes (to the destroyed records): wills, 1601-1648, as for consistory court, above; wills, 1660-1720, admons. and invs., 1660-1837, wills and admons., 1837-1857 (MS copy calendar, at SG).

Unindexed surviving records: probate and admon. act books, 1662-1665.

Wells Peculiars (Somerset Record Office)

Virtually all the records of these courts were destroyed in 1942.

21 parishes throughout the county, wills and admons. generally from the mid-17th century on; apart from Witham Friary for which the peculiar jurisdiction was extinguished in 1827, thereafter in the archdeaconry of Wells. Pre-Commonwealth entries may be found in the indexes to destroyed records listed under the consistory court.

Indexes (to the destroyed records): wills and admons., c.1660-1857 (MS copy calendar, by individual peculiars, at SG).

Unindexed surviving records: probate and admon. act books, 1662-1741.

Royal Peculiar of Ilminster

Printed index (to destroyed records): wills, 1690-1857 (250), admons., 1838-1857 (20) (Index Lib., vol. 53, pp. 127-31).

Consistory Court of the Bishop of Bristol in the Deanery of Bristol (Bristol Archives Office, page 51)

Jurisdiction included the Somerset parish of Abbots Leigh.

Wills in deposited collections (Somerset Record Office)

A card index is maintained to miscellaneous wills and other testamentary material in deposited collections. This includes the MS collection of Thomas Serel, made before 1879.

Chew Magna, Chew Stoke, Dundry and Stowey

Printed abstracts: wills, 1530-1599 (225) (Som. Record Soc., vol. 62, pp. 75-120).

Other abstracts: wills (Som. Arch. Soc. and Weston-super-Mare libraries).

Other printed indexes

Somerset Parishes: a handbook of historical reference to all places in the county, by A. L. Humphreys, 1905, indexes many wills by parish.

Wills of Wellington and West Buckland, 1372-1811, by A. L. Humphreys, 1908.

The Municipal Records of Bath, 1189-1604, by A. J. King and B. H. Watts, 1885, Appx. A, Part II.

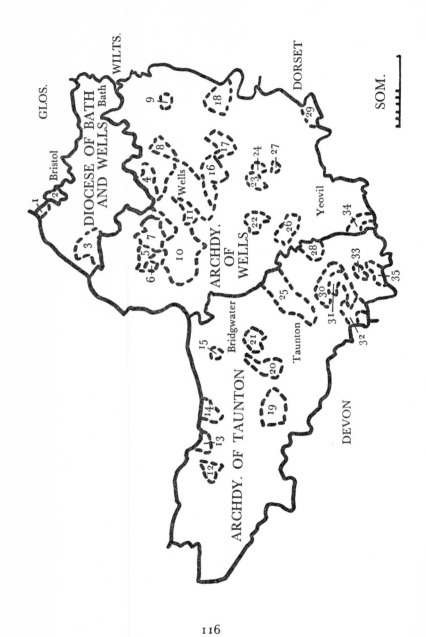

Somerset parishes outside archdeaconry jurisdiction.

B=Consistory court of Bristol; C=Consistory court of the Dean and Chapter of Wells; D=Consistory court of the Dean of Wells; I=Royal peculiar court of Ilminster; P=other Wells peculiar and prebendal courts.

Abbots Leigh, B 2
(Chapel) Allerton, D 10
Ashill, P 30
South Barrow, C 27
Biddisham, D 6
Binegar, D 8
Bishop's Lydeard, C 20
Broomfield, D 21
Buckland Dinham, P 9
Carhampton, D 13
Cheddar, C 7
Chesterblade, D 17
Chilcompton, D 8
Combe St. Nicholas, C 32
Compton Bishop, P 5
Compton Dundon, P 22
Cudworth, P 33
North Curry, C 25
St. Decumans, P 14
Dinder, D 10
Easton in Gordano, P 1
Evercreech, D 17
Fitzhead (pec. of
    Wiveliscombe), P 19
East Harptree, P 4
Haselbury Plucknett, P 34
West Hatch, C 25
Henstridge, P 29
Ilminster, I 31
Ilton, P 30

Kenn (pec. of Yatton), P 3
Kingsbury, P 28
Knowle (pec. of Cudworth), P 33
East Lambrook (pec. of
    Kingsbury), P 28
Litton, P 4
Lovington, C 24
Bishop's Lydeard, C 20
West Lydford, P 23
Mark, D 10
Pilton, P 16
Priddy, D 10
St. Decumans, P 14
Stoke St. Gregory, C 25
Nether Stowey, D 15
Long Sutton, C 26
Timberscombe, P 12
Wedmore, D 10
Wells (St. Cuthbert), D 10
Wells (Liberty of
    St. Andrew's), C
Westbury, D 10
Whitelackington, P 30
Winsham, C 35
Witham Friary, P 18
Wiveliscombe, P 19
Wookey, P 11
North Wootton, P 16
Yatton, P 3

Parishes and other places in Derbyshire in peculiars; they are likely also to appear in the consistory court. Records of all except Dale Abbey are at Lichfield.

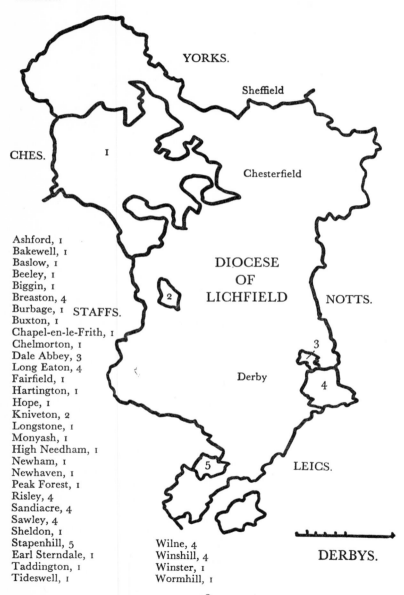

YORKS.

Sheffield

CHES.

1

Chesterfield

DIOCESE
OF
LICHFIELD

NOTTS.

Ashford, 1
Bakewell, 1
Baslow, 1
Beeley, 1
Biggin, 1
Breaston, 4
Burbage, 1 STAFFS.
Buxton, 1
Chapel-en-le-Frith, 1
Chelmorton, 1
Dale Abbey, 3
Long Eaton, 4
Fairfield, 1
Hartington, 1
Hope, 1
Kniveton, 2
Longstone, 1
Monyash, 1
High Needham, 1
Newham, 1
Newhaven, 1
Peak Forest, 1
Risley, 4
Sandiacre, 4
Sawley, 4
Sheldon, 1
Stapenhill, 5
Earl Sterndale, 1
Taddington, 1
Tideswell, 1

2

3

Derby

4

5

Wilne, 4
Winshill, 4
Winster, 1
Wormhill, 1

LEICS.

DERBYS.

118

STAFFORDSHIRE AND
DERBYSHIRE

Staffordshire and Derbyshire were in the province of Canterbury and in the diocese of Lichfield (and Coventry). After the creation of the diocese of Chester in 1540 the diocese of Lichfield still included all of both counties, and parts of Shropshire and Warwickshire. Probate matters (except for the peculiars) were wholly in the jurisdiction of the consistory court.

The records of the consistory court and of almost all the peculiars are now in the Lichfield Joint Record Office. There is a good 19th century MS index there to the complete consistory court series, wills and admons., 1516-1857; and a similar separate one to all the peculiars, in one consolidated index; these are more accurate than the printed index to pre-Commonwealth wills and admons.

The record office is in the same building as the library, in the centre of the city; there are public car-parks nearby. The office issues a *Handlist to the Diocesan, Probate and Church Commissioners' Records* (1970) (35p) which summarises the testamentary records.

Prerogative Court of Canterbury and other courts having general jurisdiction – see page 1.

Consistory Court of Lichfield (Lichfield Joint Record Office, Public Library, Bird Street, Lichfield WS13 6PN. Tel. Lichfield (05432) 22177)
 Jurisdiction: the whole of both counties, except for peculiars.
 Index: wills and admons., 1516-1857 (225,000) (MS, 19th cent. calendar (m/f at SG) – this is considered more accurate than the printed index below).
 Printed index: wills and admons., 1516-1652 (50,000) (Index Lib., vol. 7, pp. 1-516 – this calendar with index was compiled direct from the contemporary calendars and has been found incomplete and unreliable – if possible the MS index above should be consulted).

Staffordshire and Derbyshire Peculiars (Lichfield Joint Record Office)
In addition to the court of the dean and chapter of Lichfield, and of the dean alone, which had jurisdiction over a number of places, there were fifteen individual peculiars in Staffordshire and four with jurisdiction in Derbyshire. In general, apart from the dean and chapter, records do not start before the late 17th century. The wills and admons. of all these peculiars are jointly indexed (together with others in the diocese). The indexes to the consistory court should always be consulted as well, as places theoretically in peculiars frequently appear in the consistory records.

Index: wills and admons., 1536-1857 (25,000) (MS, 19th cent. calendar (m/f at SG), consolidated for all peculiars; pre-Commonwealth entries mainly relate to the court of the dean and chapter; the peculiars are included in the printed index, below, but the MS index is considered more accurate). There is also an index to wills, 1461-1626 (MS), which no longer exist.

Printed index: wills and admons., 1536-1652 (1,300) (Index Lib., vol. 7, pp. 517-30, calendar – see remarks under consistory court above; many wills for the peculiar of Wolverhampton, 1618-1652, listed here, are now missing).

Printed abstracts: invs., 1568-1680 (190) (in city and close of Lichfield, Burntwood, Ediall, Elmhurst, Farewell, Hammerwich, Pipe Hill, Streethay, Wall, Whittington and Woodhouses only) (Staffs. Record Soc., 4th series, vol. 5).

Peculiar of Alrewas and Weeford (Staffordshire County Record Office, Eastgate Street, Stafford)
Wills and admons., 1558-1601 (75).
Later records are with other peculiars at the Lichfield J.R.O., and are included in that index.

Peculiar of Dale Abbey (Derbys.) (Nottinghamshire Record Office, page 100)
Printed index: wills, 1753-1790 (19 only) (Index Lib., vol. 7, p. 537).
Other index: wills, 1791-1856 (36 only).

Manor of Sedgley (Central Public Library, St. James's Road, Dudley)
Index: wills and admons., 1614-1803 (TS, with abstracts, by N. W. Tildesley, at SG).

Manor of Tyrley (National Library of Wales, page 176)
Jurisdiction: that part of the parish of Drayton in Hales (Market Drayton) that lies in Staffordshire.
Index: wills and admons., 1695-1841 (calendar; m/f at SG).
Earlier records are with other peculiars at the Lichfield J.R.O., and are included in that index. There are also printed abstracts to wills and inventories, 1553-1563 (Staffs. Record Soc., vol. 68, 1945/6).

Consistory Court of Worcester (Worcestershire Record Office, page 146)
Jurisdiction: the parish of Clent in Staffordshire.

Consistory Court of Chester (Cheshire Record Office, page 23)
Jurisdiction: Balterley in Staffordshire.

Wills at William Salt Library, Stafford
Jurisdiction uncertain, but register includes parishes in Stafford, Eccleshall and Gnosall, with a few for Baswich, Blithfield, Castle Church, Church Eaton, Gratwood, Hartwell, Leek, Lichfield, High Offley, Penkridge, Penn, Seighford, Stone, Swinnerton, Trentham, and Wolstanton, all in Staffordshire, and Prees and Worfield in Shropshire.
Printed abstracts: wills, c.1537-1558, 1571, 1576-1578, after 1583 (80) (William Salt Arch. Soc., vol. 50, 1926).

Wills from the Earl of Dudley's archives (Dudley Central Library)
Wills, 1578-1885 (120) mainly relating to Dudley, Sedgley and Kingswinford.

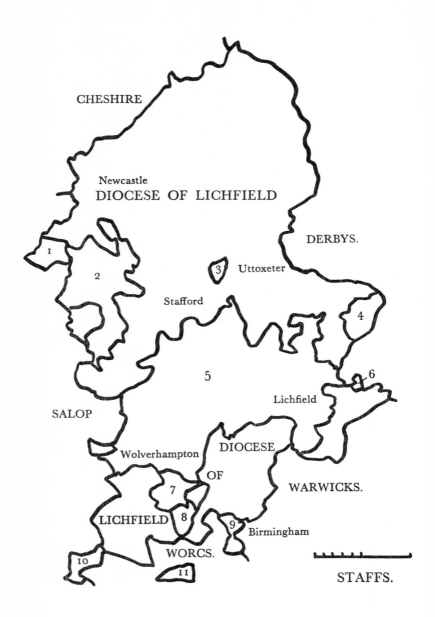

CHESHIRE

Newcastle
DIOCESE OF LICHFIELD

DERBYS.

1

2

3 Uttoxeter

Stafford

4

5

6

Lichfield

SALOP

Wolverhampton   DIOCESE
OF

WARWICKS.

7

LICHFIELD 8

9 Birmingham

10

WORCS.

11

STAFFS.

Staffordshire parishes in the jurisdiction of courts other than the consistory court of Lichfield. Clent and Dudley were in the diocese of Worcester. Records of all peculiars except the manors of Sedgley and Tyrley (Drayton in Hales or Market Drayton) are at the Lichfield Joint Record Office; but there are a few for the peculiar of Alrewas and Weeford also at Staffordshire Record Office. Places in this peculiar are asterisked. All places in peculiars are likely to appear in the consistory court records too, and some places not actually in peculiars may still nevertheless be found in records of peculiars.

Acton Trussell, 5	Eccleshall, 2	Rodbaston, 5
Adbaston, 2	Edingale,* 6	Rugeley, 5
Alrewas,* 5	Farewell, 5	Saredon, 5
Upper Arley, 10	Fradley,* 5	Sedgley, 7
Armitage, 5	Fradswell, 3	Shareshill, 5
Baswich, 5	Gnosall, 2	Shobnall, 4
Bednall, 5	Hammerwich, 5	Shugborough, 5
Bentley, 5	Handsacre, 5	Slindon, 2
Bilbrook, 5	Harborne, 9	Smethwick, 9
Bilston, 5	Haselour, 5	Stafford St. Chad
Blithbury,* 5	Hatherton, 5	Streethay, 5
Branstone, 4	Great Haywood, 5	Stretton in Burton, 4
Brewood, 5	Hilton in	Stretton in Penkridge, 5
Bromley Regis,* 5	Wolverhampton, 5	Sugnall, 2
Broughton, 2	Hints,* 5	Swinfen,* 5
Brownhills, 5	Horninglow, 4	Tettenhall, 5
Burton upon Trent, 4	Kings Bromley, *5	Tipton, 5
Bushbury, 5	Kinvaston, 5	Trescott, 5
Cannock, 5	Levedale, 5	Tyrley, 1
Charnes, 2	Lichfield, 5	Wall, 5
Chorlton, 2	Longdon, 5	Walton, 2
Clent, 11	Mavesyn Ridware,* 5	Water Eaton, 5
Codsall, 5	Norton Canes, 5	Wednesfield, 5
Colwich, 5	Oaken, 5	Weeford,* 5
Compton in	High Offley, 2	The Wergs, 5
Tettenhall, 5	Ogley Hay, 5	Wetmore, 4
Congreve, 5	Packington,* 5	Whittington, 5
Coppenhall, 5	Pattingham, 5	Willenhall, 5
Cotes, 2	Pelsall, 5	Wolverhampton, 5
Drayton in Hales, 1	Penkridge, 5	Wrottesley, 5
Dudley (Worcs.), 8	Perton, 5	Wyrley, 5
Dunston, 5	Pipe Ridware,* 5	Yoxall, 5

SUFFOLK

Suffolk was in the province of Canterbury and diocese of Norwich. The eastern part formed the archdeaconry of Suffolk, whose records are now at Ipswich, with a modern card index to wills and admons., 1444-1857. The western part comprised most of the archdeaconry of Sudbury, records now at Bury St. Edmunds, with a modern card index to wills and admons., 1354-1700, 1800-1857, and the period 1700-1800 also available in a modern index. The parishes in the north-east of the archdeaconry of Sudbury (constituting the deaneries of Stow and Hartismere), which were in the civil division of East Suffolk, were transferred ecclesiastically to the archdeaconry of Suffolk in 1837, but probate jurisdiction appears to have remained unchanged. The records of the consistory court of Norwich are at the Norfolk Record Office, and there are printed indexes to wills to 1818.

The record office at Ipswich is in County Hall, near the centre of the town; there is a large public car-park nearby. The office issues a booklet *A Short Guide for Genealogists* (1969) (30p), which describes the probate records there. The record office at Bury St. Edmunds is close to the Shire Hall, where there are car-parks for visitors; it is about half a mile from the main shopping area and bus station, and a mile from the railway station. A leaflet of *Notes on Genealogical Sources* is issued.

Prerogative Court of Canterbury and other courts having general jurisdiction – see page 1.
> Printed index: (Suffolk) wills, 1383-1604 (*Calendar*, by T. W. Oswald-Hicks, 1913).
> Other index: (Suffolk) wills, 1700-1769 (MS, Phillimore and Co. Ltd., Shopwyke Hall, Chichester, Sussex).
> Invs., 1650-1660 (TS at SG).

Archdeaconry of Suffolk (Suffolk Record Office (Ipswich), County Hall, Ipswich IP4 2JS. Tel. Ipswich (0473) 55801, ext. 235)
> Jurisdiction: East Suffolk, except for the deaneries of Stow and Hartismere. See also consistory court.
> Printed indexes: wills and admons., 1444-1702 (40,000) (Index Lib., in press; this will supersede the *Calendar*, 1444-1600, by F. A. Crisp (1895) (incomplete in many respects but still a sound guide); 1751-1793 (*Calendar*, by W. Gandy (1929), 'found wanting in many respects', in preference to which the card index below should be consulted).

Archdeaconry of Suffolk, contd.

Other indexes: wills and admons., 1702-1857 (consolidated card index); m/f of admons., 1609-1699, invs., 1582-1702, at SG.

Archdeaconry of Sudbury (Suffolk Record Office (Bury St. Edmunds), School Hall Street, Bury St. Edmunds, IP33 1RX. Tel. Bury St. Edmunds (0284) 63141)

The records of this court incorporate those of the *Episcopal Commissary Court for Bury St. Edmunds* (before 1539 the *Court of the Sacrist of St. Edmund's Abbey* for the peculiar of Bury St. Edmunds), which was not officially merged with the archdeaconry until 1844, but shared registers from 1566.

Jurisdiction: West Suffolk with the addition of the deaneries of Stow and Hartismere in East Suffolk. See also consistory court.

Printed index: wills, 1354-1538 (8,000) (*Proceedings of the Suffolk Institute of Archaeology*, vol. 12 (1904-06), 'often incorrect re spellings and dates'). This will in due course be superseded by

Other indexes: wills and admons., 1354-1700 (card index, to be published shortly in Index Library); 1700-1800 (MS, by T. W. Crosfield, in Ipswich Public Library, and microfilm at S.R.O., Bury St Edmunds); 1800-1857 (card index); m/f of calendar to 1857 at SG.

Consistory Court of Norwich (Norfolk Record Office)

Jurisdiction: Norfolk, Suffolk, and part of Cambridgeshire.

Printed indexes: wills, 1370-1603 (Norfolk Record Society, vols. 16 and 21, and Index Library, vols. 29 and 73), 1604-1818 (Norfolk Record Society, vols. 28, 34 and 38; further volumes in preparation).

For other indexes see page 92.

Archdeaconries of Norfolk and Norwich (Norfolk Record Office, pages 92-93)

Jurisdiction included Rushford and Thetford respectively (both partly in Norfolk).

Peculiar of Isleham (Cambs.) *and Freckenham* (Suffolk) (Suffolk Record Office, Bury St. Edmunds)

Isleham in the diocese of Ely and Freckenham in the diocese of Norwich were a peculiar of the bishop of Rochester. There are a few wills for both in the consistory court of Norwich, this court claiming jurisdiction during visitations by the bishop of Norwich (see above and page 92). There are also some wills in the *Consistory Court of Rochester* (see page 72) and post-1649 wills and admons. in the records of the *Archdeaconry of Huntingdon* (see page 65).

Indexes (Freckenham): wills, 1556-1856, admons. 1665-1817 (card index, by Rev. J. A. Humphries).

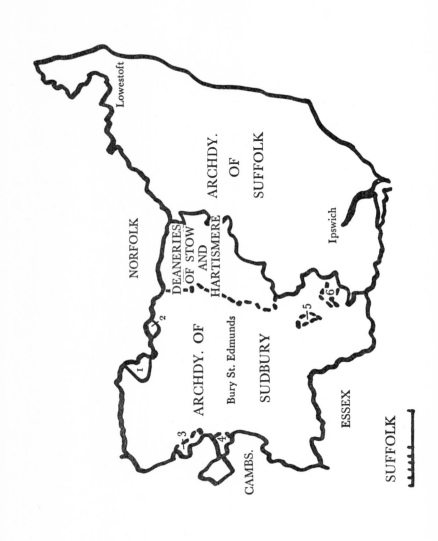

SUFFOLK

Lowestoft

NORFOLK

ARCHDY.
OF
SUFFOLK

DEANERIES
OF STOW
AND
HARTISMERE

Ipswich

ARCHDY. OF

Bury St. Edmunds

SUDBURY

ESSEX

CAMBS.

Deaneries of Stow and Hartismere
in the Archdeaconry of Sudbury
Aspall
Bacton
Botesdale
Braiseworth
Brockford
Brome
Burgate
Buxhall
Combs
Cotton
Creeting All SS.
Creeting St. Peter
Eye
Great Finborough
Little Finborough
Finningham
Gislingham
Harleston
Haughley
Mellis
Mendlesham
Old Newton
Oakley
Occold
Onehouse
Palgrave
Redgrave
Redlingfield
Riccinghall Inferior
Riccinghall Superior
Rishangles
Shelland

Stoke Ash
Stowmarket
Stowupland
Stuston
Thorndon
Thornham Magna
Thornham Parva
Thrandeston
Thwaite
Westhorpe
Wetherden
Wetheringsett
Wickham Skeith
Wortham
Wyverstone
Yaxley

Archdeaconry of Norfolk
Rushford, 2

Archdeaconry of Norwich
Thetford, 1

Peculiar of Freckenham, 3

Peculiar of the Archbishop of
Canterbury
Monks Eleigh, 5
Hadleigh, 6
Moulton, 4

Peculiar of the Archbishop of Canterbury in the Deanery of Bocking
(Essex Record Office, page 47)
Jurisdiction included Monks Eleigh, Hadleigh and Moulton in Suffolk.
Printed indexes: wills, 1627-1857 (Index Library, vols. 79 and 84).
Abstracts: wills, 1627-1857, wills from P.C.C., 1649-1660; admons.,
1665-1683, 1722-1738, 1756-1853 (TS, by S. W. Prentis, at Essex
Record Office and SG).

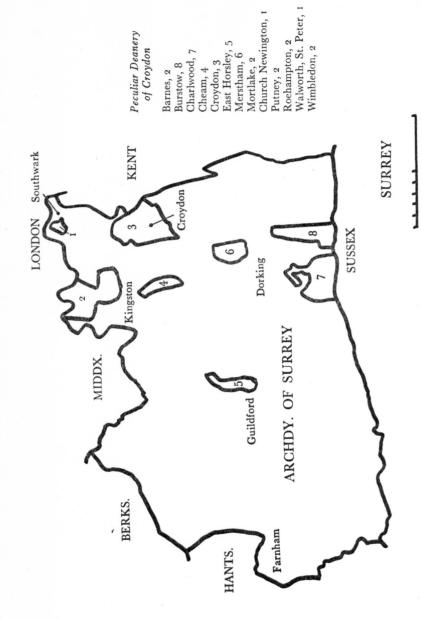

SURREY

Surrey was in the province of Canterbury, and in the diocese of Winchester except for the exempt deanery of Croydon, a peculiar in the jurisdiction of the archbishop of Canterbury.

The county formed the archdeaconry of Surrey in the diocese of Winchester. Apart from the peculiar deanery of Croydon, wills and admons. for the county are to be found either in the commissary court of the bishop of Winchester in the archdeaconry of Surrey, or in the archdeaconry court of Surrey itself. The records of both these courts are now at the Greater London Record Office in County Hall. Until the early 17th century a few Surrey wills are to be found in the consistory court of Winchester; there is a TS index to these.

Eleven Surrey parishes were in the peculiar deanery of Croydon. The records of the deanery are now at the Lambeth Palace Library, where there is a good 19th century MS index.

The Greater London Record Office is in Room B21 in the basement of County Hall; nearest tube stations: Waterloo and Westminster; public car park nearby. Lambeth Palace Library is in Lambeth Palace; nearest tube stations: Vauxhall and Westminster.

Prerogative Court of Canterbury and other courts having general jurisdiction – see page 1.

Commissary Court of the Bishop of Winchester in the Archdeaconry of Surrey (Greater London Record Office, Room B21, County Hall, Westminster Bridge, London SE1 7PB. Tel. 01-633 6851)
Indexes: wills and admons., 1662-1857 (calendar).

Archdeaconry Court of Surrey (Greater London Record Office)
Very few admons. were granted by this court.
Indexes: wills and admons., 1480-1524, 1529-1649, 1660-1857 (calendar, partly 19th cent.).
Printed abstracts: wills, 1480-1490, 1595-1607 (Surrey Record Soc., vols. 17, 3, 7 and 15).

Peculiar Jurisdiction of the Archbishop of Canterbury in the Deanery of Croydon (Lambeth Palace Library, London SE1 7JU. Tel. 01-928 6222)
Jurisdiction: see map.
Indexes: wills, admons. and invs., 1602, 1614-1821, 1841 (2,943) (MS, 19th cent.); (also TS at Public Record Office and SG).

Consistory Court of Winchester (Hampshire Record Office, page 54)
Index: wills (Surrey only), 1606-1645 (TS, also copy at SG).

SUSSEX

Sussex was in the province of Canterbury and was co-extensive with the diocese of Chichester, divided into the two archdeaconries of Chichester and Lewes, corresponding approximately to the civil divisions of West and East Sussex.

Probate was in the hands of the bishop's consistory courts in the two archdeaconries; that at Lewes was sometimes known as the archdeaconry court, and covered the whole of East Sussex together with eleven parishes bordering the division but in West Sussex; and excluding the peculiars of South Malling and Battle, and the parish of Lamberhurst which was in the diocese of Rochester. The records of this court and of the peculiars, to which there are printed indexes to the pre-Commonwealth wills and admons., and a typescript index to the rest (recently compiled by Mr. M. Burchall of the Sussex Family History Group), are now at the East Sussex Record Office at Lewes. The office is in a pleasant house in the centre of the town (shared with other county council offices); there is no public car park. A booklet *How to Trace the History of your Family* (20p) summarises the testamentary records in the office, and there is also available *Your County Record Office* (free) which describes services and facilities.

The whole of West Sussex, apart from the parishes mentioned above, and excluding the peculiars of Chichester and of Pagham and Tarring, was in the archdeaconry of Chichester. The records of the bishop's consistory court in the archdeaconry, and of the peculiars, to which there are printed indexes to wills and admons. to 1800, are now at the West Sussex Record Office at Chichester. This is a handsome town house adjacent to the County Hall and in the centre of the city; there are public car-parks nearby.

Prerogative Court of Canterbury and other courts having general jurisdiction – see page 1.
    Printed index: wills, 1614-1639, 1658-1662, 1667-1670 (115 only, in West Sussex Record Office, of Sussex testators – ostensibly in the peculiar of the archbishop, proved in London, but not apparently included in the records of P.C.C.) (Index Lib., vol. 64, pp. 215-217).
    Other index: wills, 1652-1668 (TS) (not apparently in the records of P.C.C.).

Consistory Court of the Bishop of Chichester for the Archdeaconry of Chichester (West Sussex Record Office, John Edes House, West Street, Chichester PO19 1RN. Tel. Chichester (0243) 85100, ext. 351)

Jurisdiction: see introductory note. The whole of West Sussex (except peculiars and some parishes in the Archdeaconry of Lewes, see below). Vacancy jurisdiction lay in the Archbishop of Canterbury and was exercised by the Dean of Pagham and Tarring as his Commissary (so occasional wills are to be found in that peculiar court), although there are some wills in the Archiepiscopal Registers at Lambeth (page 3).

Printed indexes: wills, 1482-1800 (23,500) (Index Lib., vol. 49); admons. 1555-1800 (10,500) (Index Lib., vol. 64, pp. 1-187 – this omits some admons. between 1586 and 1684, detailed below); 1675-1676 (omitted from the above) (*Sussex Notes and Queries*, vol. 12, pp. 37-39).

Other indexes: wills and admons., 1801-1857 (calendar; m/f at SG).

Unindexed: admons., 1586-1592, 1599-1602, 1623-1626, 1679-1684 (omitted from printed index above).

Note: all testamentary documents at West Sussex Record Office are also now available on microfilm at East Sussex Record Office.

Consistory Court of the Bishop of Chichester for the Archdeaconry of Lewes (also known as the *Archdeaconry Court of Lewes*) (East Sussex Record Office, Pelham House, Lewes. Tel. Lewes (07916) 5400)

Jurisdiction: see introductory note. The whole of East Sussex (except peculiars, and the parish of Lamberhurst, in the diocese of Rochester), and the parishes of Beeding, Crawley, Cowfold, Henfield, Kingston, Ifield, Shermanbury, Old and New Shoreham, Southwick and Woodmancote in West Sussex. See also the consistory (archdeaconry) of Chichester, above.

Printed index: wills and admons., 1518-1652 (26,400) (calendar with index) (Index Lib., vol. 24, pp. 1-440 – the spine misleadingly gives 1541 as the starting date, but see pp. 238-240).

Other index: wills and admons., 1660-1857 (TS) (publication by the Sussex Family History Group probable); m/f of calendar to 1857 at SG.

Peculiar Court of the Dean of Chichester (West Sussex Record Office)

Jurisdiction: Chichester (St. Andrew, St. Bartholomew, St. Martin, St. Olave, St. Pancras, St. Peter the Great otherwise Sub-deanery, St. Peter the Less, and the Close), New Fishbourne and Rumboldswyke. See also the consistory, above.

Printed index: wills, 1553-1643, 1660-1800, admons., 1577-1626, 1660-1768 (Index Lib., vol. 64, pp. 231-269).

Other indexes: wills, 1801-1857 (calendar); admons., 1626-1652 (TS); 1781-1857 (calendar); m/f of calendar to 1857 at SG.

Unindexed: admons., 1768-1781.

Note: all these documents are also available on microfilm at East Sussex Record Office.

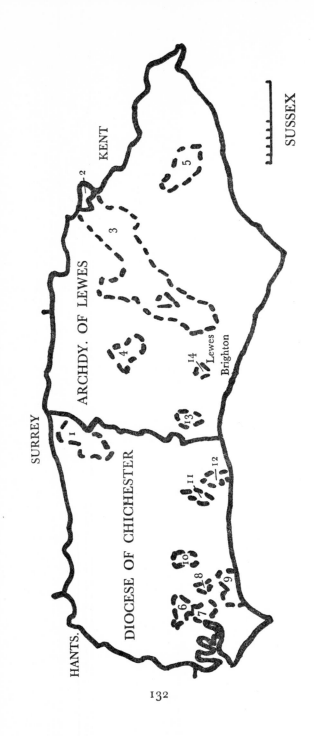

SUSSEX

KENT

SURREY

HANTS.

ARCHDY. OF LEWES

DIOCESE OF CHICHESTER

Lewes

Brighton

Peculiar Court of the Archbishop of Canterbury for the Exempt Deaneries of Pagham and Tarring (West Sussex Record Office)
> Printed index: wills, 1516-1541, 1553-1648 (1,300) (Index Lib., vol. 64, pp. 189-213), admons., 1560-1670 (2,850) (vol. 64, 219-269).
> Other indexes: wills, 1678-1857, admons., 1805-1857 (calendar).
> Unindexed: wills, 1661-1678, admons., 1690-1803.
> Note, all these documents are also available on m/f at East Sussex Record Office.

Peculiar of the Archbishop of Canterbury for Exempt Deanery of South Malling (East and West Sussex Record Offices)
> Printed indexes: wills and admons., 1559-1567 (Index Lib., vol. 64, pp. 189-213, and Sussex Arch. Soc. Collections, vol. 50, pp. 138-146) (these documents are at West Sussex Record Office; those listed below are at East Sussex Record Office).
> Wills, 1588-1646 (Index Lib., vol. 24, pp. 425-440).
> Other indexes: wills, 1661-1857, admons., 1714-1857, invs., 1731-1836 (calendar; m/f at SG).

Peculiar of the Dean of Battle (East Sussex Record Office)
> Printed index: wills, 1531-1617, admons., 1548, 1572-1617 (350) (Index Library, vol. 24, pp. 441-446).
> Other indexes: wills, 1657-1856, admons., 1716-1856 (calendar and TS in progress).

Consistory and Archdeaconry Courts of Rochester (Kent Archives Office, page 72)
> Jurisdiction: in the parish of Lamberhurst in East Sussex only.

Sussex parishes outside the jurisdiction of the archdeaconries of Chichester and Lewes.

B=Deanery of Battle; C=Peculiar of the Dean of Chichester; M=Deanery of South Malling; P=Deaneries of Pagham and Tarring; R=Diocese of Rochester.

Battle, B 5
South Bersted, P 9
Buxted, M 3
Chichester, All SS., P 7
Chichester (remainder), C 7
(The) Cliff, M 3
Durrington, P 12
Edburton, M 13
(New) Fishbourne, C 7
Framfield, M 3
Glynde, M 3
Heene, P 12
Horsham, P 1
Isfield, M 3
Lamberhurst, R 2

East Lavant, P 6
St. Thomas Lewes, M 3
Lindfield, M 4
South Malling, M 3
Mayfield, M 3
Pagham, P 9
Patching, P 11
Ringmer, M 3
Rumboldswyke, C 7
Slindon, P 10
Stanmer, M 14
Tangmere, P 8
West Tarring, P 12
Uckfield, M 3
Wadhurst, M 3

WARWICKSHIRE

Warwickshire was in the province of Canterbury and split between the dioceses of Lichfield (and Coventry) and Worcester.

The major, north-eastern, part of the county was in the jurisdiction of the consistory court of Lichfield, the records of which, together with those of the peculiars of the dean and chapter of Lichfield (including Arley and Edgbaston), Bishops Itchington, Bishops Tachbrook and Merevale, are at the Lichfield Joint Record Office. There is a good 19th century MS index there to the complete consistory court series, wills and admons., 1516-1857; and a similar separate one to all the peculiars, in one consolidated index; these are more accurate than the printed index to pre-Commonwealth records. The record office is in the same building as the library, in the centre of the city; there are public car parks nearby. The office issues a *Handlist to the Diocesan, Probate and Church Commissioners' Records* (1970) (35p) which summarises the probate records.

The south-western part of the county (over 70 parishes) was in the jurisdiction of the consistory court of Worcester, the records of which are at the Worcestershire Record Office. There is a printed index to pre-Commonwealth wills and admons., and a TS index to the rest, 1660-1857. Probate records of the diocese of Worcester are deposited in the department of the Worcestershire Record Office situated in St. Helen's church, Fish Street. From the south, this is the first small turning to the left beyond a main road (Deansway) turning off just past the cathedral; there is a small car-park for users of the office, behind the church.

Records of the peculiar courts of Stratford and Hampton Lucy are at the Shakespeare's Birthplace Library (the record office is on the right of the Birthplace, *not* in the main library in the Shakespeare Centre). Records of the peculiars of Baddesley Clinton, Barston, Knowle, Packwood and Temple Balsall are at the Warwickshire Record Office, and there is a consolidated printed index to all these.

Parishes at the southern tip of Warwickshire have changed both county and diocese at different times, and it is wise to consult the records of adjacent jurisdictions if there is any doubt.

Prerogative Court of Canterbury and other courts having general jurisdiction – see page 1.

Consistory Court of Lichfield (Lichfield Joint Record Office, Public Library, Bird Street, Lichfield, WS13 6PN. Tel. Lichfield (05432) 22177)
Jurisdiction: the north-eastern part of the county.
Index: wills and admons., 1516-1857 (MS, 19th cent., calendar (m/f at SG) – this is considered more accurate than the printed index below).
Printed index: wills and admons., 1516-1652 (Index Lib., vol. 7, pp. 1-516, calendar with index – this was compiled direct from the contemporary calendars and has been found incomplete and unreliable – if possible the MS index above should be consulted).

Dean and Chapter of Lichfield (Lichfield Joint Record Office)
Jurisdiction: the Warwickshire parishes of Arley and Edgbaston. See also consistory of Lichfield.
Index: wills and admons., 1536-1857 (MS, 19th cent., calendar (m/f at SG), consolidated with other Lichfield peculiars; these are included in the printed index below, but the MS index is considered more accurate).
Printed index: wills and admons., 1536-1652 (Index Lib., vol. 7, pp. 517-30, calendar).

Consistory Court of Worcester (Worcestershire Record Office, St. Helen's Church, Fish Street, Worcester. Tel. Worcester (0905) 23400, ext. 463)
Jurisdiction: 71 parishes in south-western part of Warwickshire.
Printed indexes: wills, 1451-1495, 1509-1652, admons. and invs., 1520-1652 (calendars with indexes, Index Lib., vols. 31 and 39; there are some omissions).
Other indexes: wills, admons. and invs., 1660-1857 (TS); m/f of calendar to 1857 at SG.

Consistory Court of Gloucester (Gloucestershire Records Office, page 51)
Jurisdiction: the parishes of Welford and Weston upon Avon, partly in Glos.

Peculiar Court of Stratford-upon-Avon (Shakespeare's Birthplace Trust, Stratford-upon-Avon, Warw. Tel. Stratford-upon-Avon (0789) 4016)
Jurisdiction: Stratford (borough) and the hamlets of Bishopton, Bridgetown, Clopton, Dodwell, Drayton, Luddington, Shottery and Welcombe, in the parish of Old Stratford). See also consistory of Worcester.
Index: wills and admons., 1685-1849 (389) (TS).
The office also holds a miscellaneous collection of wills (1,379), abstracts, etc., mostly 18th and 19th cent., relating to Stratford and area (TS index).

Peculiar Court of Hampton Lucy (Shakespeare's Birthplace Trust)
Jurisdiction: Hampton Lucy, Alveston, Charlecote and Wasperton. See also consistory of Worcs.
Index: wills, admons. and invs., 1678-1795 (164) (MS).

Peculiar Courts of Baddesley Clinton, Barston, Knowle, Packwood, and Temple Balsall (Warwickshire Record Office, Shire Hall, Warwick)
See also consistory of Lichfield.
Printed index: wills and admons., 1675-1790 (450) (Index Lib., vol. 7, pp. 531-36. (Baddesley Clinton from 1773, Knowle from 1727, Packwood from 1759, Temple Balsall from 1742); also wills (Knowle only), 1665(1), 1726-1730 (12) (vol. 7, tipped-in page facing p. 530).
Index: post-1790 records for all courts, and 1652-1741 for Temple Balsall only (500). (MS, calendar, consolidated, for all peculiars – also at Worcs. R.O.).

Peculiar Courts of Bishops Itchington, Bishops Tachbrook and Merevale (Lichfield Joint Record Office)
Jurisdictions: the places named and Chadshunt and Gaydon (Bishops Itchington), see also consistory of Lichfield.
Printed indexes: 1701-1790 (Index Lib., vol. 7, pp. 531-36. Bishops Tachbrook from 1731 and Merevale from 1770 (12 only). See also Lichfield Peculiars, 1529-1652).
Other indexes: wills and admons., 1791-1857 (MS, 19th cent., calendar, consolidated with other Lichfield peculiars, which should also if possible be consulted for earlier periods. There are also some Itchington and Tachbrook wills, a separate deposit, listed separately).

Peculiar Court of Banbury and Cropredy (*Oxon.*) (Bodleian Library, Oxford, page 105)
Jurisdiction: included the chapelry of Mollington (partly Oxon.) in the parish of Cropredy (Oxon.).

Diocese of Worcester
Alcester
Great Alne
Alveston
Arrow
Aston Cantlow
Atherstone on Stour
Barcheston
Barford
Barton on the Heath
Bearley
Beaudesert
Bidford
Billesley
Binton
Brailes
Budbrooke
Burmington
Butlers Marston
Charlecote
Cherington
Claverdon
Long Compton
Compton Verney
Compton Wynyates
Coughton
Eatington
Exhall
Halford
Hampton Lucy
Haseley
Haselor
Hatton
Henley in Arden
Honington
Idlicote
Ilmington (detd.), W 8
Ipsley

Kineton
Kinwarton
Lapworth
Lighthorne
Loxley
Moreton Morrell
Morton Bagot
Newbold Pacey
Norton Lindsey
Oxhill
Pillerton Hersey
Pillerton Priors
Preston Bagot
Rowington
Salford
Sherbourne
Snitterfield
Spernall
Stratford-on-Avon
Stretton on the Fosse (detd.), W 8
Studley
Tanworth
Temple Grafton
Tysoe
Ullenhall
Warwick
Wasperton
Weethley
Wellesbourne
Whatcote
Whichford
Whitchurch (detached), W 8
Wixford
Great Wolford
Wolverton
Wootton Wawen
Wroxhall

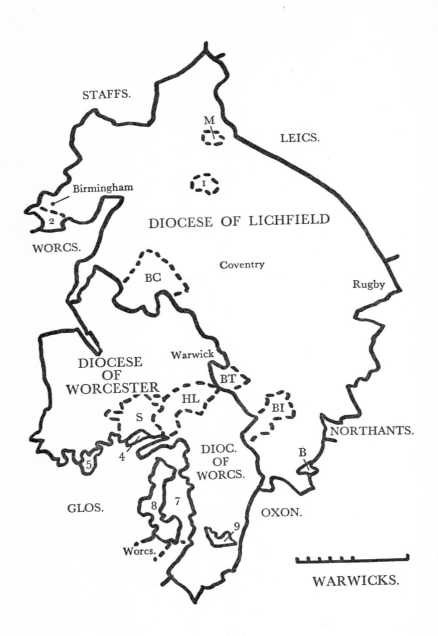

STAFFS.

M

LEICS.

I

Birmingham

2

WORCS.

DIOCESE OF LICHFIELD

Coventry

BC

Rugby

Warwick

DIOCESE
OF
WORCESTER

BT

HL

BI

S

NORTHANTS.

4

5

DIOC.
OF
WORCS.

B

8   7

GLOS.

9

OXON.

Worcs.

WARWICKS.

Peculiar of Stratford-upon-Avon (S)

Stratford-upon-Avon
Bishopton
Bridgetown
Clopton
Dodwell
Drayton
Luddington
Shottery
Welcombe

Peculiar of Hampton Lucy (HL)

Hampton Lucy
Alveston
Charlecote
Wasperton

Peculiar of Banbury and Cropredy (Oxon.) (B)

Mollington

Peculiar of Bishops Itchington (BI)

Bishops Itchington
Chadshunt
Gaydon

Peculiar of Bishops Tachbrook (BT)

Peculiar of the Dean and Chapter of Lichfield (D)

Arley, D 1
Edgbaston, D 2

Diocese of Gloucester (G)
(parishes partly in Glos.)

Welford, G 5
Weston upon Avon, G 4
Sutton-under-Brailes, G 9

Diocese and County of Worcester (W7)
(Worcs. parishes detached)

Alderminster
Shipston on Stour
Tidmington
Tredington

Peculiars of Baddesley Clinton, Barston, Knowle, Packwood, and Temple Balsall (BC)

Peculiar of Merevale (M)

WILTSHIRE

Wiltshire was in the province of Canterbury and diocese of Salisbury (Sarum), except for the parishes of Kingswood and Marston Meysey (diocese of Gloucester), and Whitsbury and West Wellow (diocese of Winchester).

Apart from the many peculiars, the county is divided between the archdeaconries of Salisbury (the southern part), Wiltshire (the northern part), and the Sub-Dean of Salisbury (5 parishes), all inhibited by the consistory court of Salisbury. The consistory court also had jurisdiction over 10 Wiltshire parishes (bishop's peculiars), and all rectors in the diocese. The records of all these courts (except Berkshire) and of the peculiars are all now at the county record office at Trowbridge. The records of the archdeaconry of Berkshire, which also, until 1836, fell within the jurisdiction of the consistory court, are now at the Bodleian Library, Oxford.

The Wiltshire Record Office is part of the County Hall complex on the southern side of Trowbridge, on the opposite side of the road to the actual County Hall. There is ample car-parking, including space specifically reserved for users of the office. A leaflet *Notes on Sources for Genealogical Research* is available (free), there is a recent detailed *Guide* to the diocesan records, and probate material is included in a *Guide to County Council . . . and other Official Records,* 1961.

Prerogative Court of Canterbury and other courts having general jurisdiction – see page 1.

Invs., 1650-1660 (TS at SG).

Archdeaconry of Salisbury (Wiltshire Record Office, County Hall, Trowbridge BA14 8JG. Tel. Trowbridge (02214) 4036)

Jurisdiction: the southern part of the county, except for peculiars and the archdeaconry of the sub-dean. See also the consistory.

Index: wills, 1528-1857, admons. and invs., 1540-1857 (22,000) (MS, 19th cent. calendar with modern additions; m/f to 1799 at SG).

Archdeaconry of Wiltshire (Wiltshire Record Office)

Jurisdiction: the northern part of the county, except for peculiars. See also consistory.

Indexes: wills, 1557-1857, admons. and invs., 1587-1857 (15,500) (MS, 19th cent. calendar with modern additions; m/f to 1857 at SG); the same, to 1799 only (TS, fully alphabetical, also copy at SG).

Episcopal Consistory Court of Salisbury (Wiltshire Record Office)
Jurisdiction: over the archdeaconries of Berkshire, Salisbury, Wiltshire, and the sub-dean of Salisbury, during inhibition; all rectors in the diocese; and 10 Wiltshire parishes which were bishop's peculiars.
Index: wills, 1526-1857, admons. and invs., 1584-1857 (15,000) (MS, 19th cent. calendar with modern additions; m/f to 1799 at SG).

Archdeaconry of the Sub-Dean of Salisbury (Wiltshire Record Office)
Jurisdiction: Salisbury (apart from the Close), Milford and Stratford-sub-Castle. See also the consistory, above, and *Miscellaneous Wills,* below.
Index: wills, 1581-1588, wills, admons. and invs., 1584, 1611-1857 (modern MS calendar).

Peculiar of the Dean of Salisbury (Wiltshire Record Office)
Jurisdiction: included Salisbury Close and 8 parishes in Wilts., 7 Berkshire parishes, and 28 Dorset parishes or chapelries; also during inhibition parishes in jurisdiction of the dean and canons of Windsor, the lord warden of Savernake Forest (Great and Little Bedwyn only) and the prebendal peculiars (including Faringdon in Berks.).
Index: wills, admons. and invs., 1557-1857 (19th cent. calendar with modern additions; m/f to 1857 at SG).
See also *Miscellaneous Wills* below.

Peculiar of the Dean and Chapter of Salisbury (Wiltshire Record Office)
Chronological list: wills, admons. and invs., 1600-1857 (19th cent. MS; m/f to 1801 to SG).

Peculiar of the Precentor of Salisbury (Wiltshire Record Office)
Index: wills, admons. and invs., 1614-1857 (19th cent. calendar; m/f to 1800 at SG).

Peculiar of the Treasurer of Salisbury in the Prebend of Calne (Wiltshire Record Office)
Index: wills, admons. and invs., 1610-1857 (19th cent. calendar; m/f to 1800 at SG).

Peculiar of the Dean and Canons of Windsor in Wantage (Wiltshire Record Office)
See also court of the dean of Salisbury, during inhibition, and after 1840.
Chronological list: wills, admons. and invs., 1669-1840 (19th cent. MS; m/f to 1801 at SG).

Peculiar of Castle Combe (Wiltshire Record Office)
After 1786 see archdeaconry of Wiltshire.
Index: wills, admons. and invs., 1669-1786 (19th cent. calendar; m/f at SG).

Peculiar of the Perpetual Vicar of Corsham (Wiltshire Record Office)
Jurisdiction: Corsham (includes also some Stratton St. Margaret wills); concurrent with the consistory and archdeaconry of Wiltshire.
Chronological list: wills, 1462-1857, admons. and invs., 1720-1857 (19th cent. MS); wills, 1662-1799, admons. and invs., 1720-1799 (TS at SG).

Peculiar of the Lord Warden of Savernake Forest (Wiltshire Record Office)
Jurisdiction: Great and Little Bedwyn (inhibited by the court of the dean of Salisbury, and after 1829 superseded by it) and Collingbourne Ducis (inhibited by the consistory court, and after 1829 superseded by it).
Index: wills, admons. and invs., 1617-1829 (19th cent. calendar; m/f to 1799 at SG).

Prebend of Bishopstone (Wiltshire Record Office)
See also court of the dean of Salisbury.
Index: wills, admons. and invs., 1625-1799, 1800-1854 (19th cent. calendar; m/f to 1799 at SG).

Prebend of Chute and Chisenbury (Wiltshire Record Office)
See also court of the dean of Salisbury.
Index: wills, admons. and invs., 1608-1799, 1800-1855 (19th cent. calendar; m/f to 1799 at SG).

Prebend of Coombe and Harnham (Wiltshire Record Office)
See also court of the dean of Salisbury.
Index: wills, admons. and invs., 1648-1799, 1800-1855 (19th cent. calendar; m/f to 1799 at SG).

Prebend of Durnford (Wiltshire Record Office)
See also court of the dean of Salisbury.
Index: wills, admons. and invs., 1634-1799, 1800-1857 (19th cent. calendar; m/f to 1799 at SG).

Prebend of Highworth (Wiltshire Record Office)
See also court of the dean of Salisbury.
Index: wills, admons. and invs., 1609, 1623-1799, 1800-1857 (19th cent. calendar; m/f to 1799 at SG).

Prebend of Hurstbourne and Burbage (Wiltshire Record Office)
Jurisdiction: Burbage in Wiltshire. There are no wills for Hurstbourne (in Hampshire). See also court of the dean of Salisbury.
Index: wills, admons. and invs., 1635-1799, 1800-1856 (19th cent. calendar; m/f to 1799 at SG).

Prebend of Netheravon (Wiltshire Record Office)
See also court of the dean of Salisbury.
Index: wills, admons. and invs., 1597-1799, 1800-1854 (19th cent. calendar; m/f to 1799 at SG).

Peculiar of Trowbridge (Wiltshire Record Office)
See *Miscellaneous Wills*.

Prebend of Wilsford and Woodford (Wiltshire Record Office)
See also court of the dean of Salisbury.
Index: wills, admons. and invs., 1615-1854 (19th cent. calendar; m/f to 1799 at SG).

Miscellaneous Wills (Wiltshire Record Office)
Many of these relate to the courts of the dean and of the sub-dean of Salisbury.
Index: wills, 1540-1809 (2,000) (TS, superseding printed index below).
Printed index: (Wilts.) wills, 1540-1809 (Wilts. Arch. and Nat. Hist. Mag., vol. 45, pp. 36-67; but is now incomplete).

Consistory Court of Gloucester (Gloucester City Library, page 51)
Jurisdiction included Kingswood (detached) and Marston Meysey in Wiltshire.

Consistory Court of Winchester (Hampshire Record Office, page 54)
Jurisdiction included Whitsbury or Whitchbury and West Wellow in Wiltshire.

Salisbury City Records
Wills, 1361-1434 (TS list at Wiltshire Record Office).

GLOS.

ARCHDY. OF WILTSHIRE

BERKS.

SOM.

Warminster

ARCHDY.
OF
SALISBURY

Wilton /Salisbury

DORSET

HANTS.

WILTS.

144

Parishes in Wiltshire outside the jurisdiction of the archdeaconries of Salisbury and Wiltshire.

B=Prebend of Bishopstone; C=Prebend of Chute and Chisenbury; CB= Prebend of Coombe (Bissett) and Harnham; CC=Peculiar of Castle Combe; CG=Consistory Court of Gloucester; CS=Consistory Court of Salisbury (in Bishop's Peculiars); CW=Consistory and Archdeaconry Courts of Winchester; D=Prebend of Durnford; DC=Peculiar Court of the Dean and Chapter of Salisbury; DS=Peculiar Court of the Dean of Salisbury; H=Prebend of Highworth; HB=Prebend of Hurstbourne and Burbage; N=Prebend of Netheravon; P=Peculiar Court of the Precentor of Salisbury; SD=Archdeaconry of the Sub-Dean of Salisbury; SF=Peculiar of the Lord Warden of Savernake Forest; T=Peculiar of Trowbridge; TC=Peculiar Court of the Treasurer in the Prebend of Calne; VC=Peculiar of the Perpetual Vicar of Corsham; W=Peculiar of the Dean and Canons of Windsor in Wantage; WW=Prebend of Wilsford and Woodford.

Alderbury, TC 38
Baydon, DS 6
Great Bedwyn, SF & DS 15
Little Bedwyn, SF & DS 15
Berwick Bassett, TC 9
Berwick St. James, CS 28
Bishops Canning, DC 13
Bishopstone, B & DS 4
Blackland (Calne), TC 8
Bramshaw, DC 42
Bratton (Westbury), P 20
Britford, DC 37
Broad Blunsden, H & DS 2
South Broom, DC 13
Burbage, HB & DS 14
Calne, TC 8
Castle Combe, CC 5
Cherhill (Calne), TC 8
Chisenbury, C & DS 24
Chute, C & DS 23
Collingbourne Ducis, SF & CS 22
Coombe Bissett, CB & DS 39
Corsham, VC & CS 7 (also archd. of Wilts.)
Devizes, CS 18
Dilton (Westbury), P 20
Durnford, D & DS 30
Farley, TC 34
Figheldean, TC 25
(West) Harnham, CB & DS 35
Heytesbury, DS 26
Highworth, H & DS 2
Hill Deverill, DS 27
Homington, DC 40
Horningsham, DS 27
Hungerford, W & DS 12

Kingswood, CG (detached)
Knook, DS 26
Lake (Wilsford), WW & DS 19
West Lavington, CS 21
Marlborough, CS 11
Marston Meysey, CG 1
South Marston, H & DS 2
Mere, DS 32
Milford, SD & CS 33
Netheravon, N & DS 24
Ogbourne St. Andrew, W & DS 10
Ogbourne, St. George, W & DS 10
Pitton, TC 34
Potterne, CS 18
Preshute, CS 11
Ramsbury, DS 6
Salisbury, SD & CS 33
Salisbury Close, DS 33
Sevenhampton, H & DS 2
Shalbourne, W & DS 16
Southbroom, DC 13
Staverton (Trowbridge), CS 17
Stert, CS 18
Stratford-sub-Castle, SD & CS 33
Stratton St. Margaret, VC & CS 3 (also archd. of Wilts.)
Swallowcliffe, DS 36
Trowbridge, CS & T 17
Tytherington (Heytesbury), DS 26
West Wellow, CW 42
Westbury, P 20
Whitsbury or Whichbury, CW 41
Wilsford, WW & DS 19
Winterbourne Dauntsey, C & DS 31
Woodford, WW & DS 29

WORCESTERSHIRE

Worcestershire was in the province of Canterbury and diocese of Worcester, apart from a few parishes in the dioceses of Hereford and at times in Gloucester.

The major part of the county was in the jurisdiction of the consistory court of Worcester; but the court of the dean and chapter of Worcester exercised jurisdiction over eight parishes which formed separate peculiars; and there were eight other separate peculiars. The records of all these are at the county record office. There is a printed index to pre-Commonwealth wills and admons. in the consistory, and a TS index to the rest, 1660-1857. There is also a duplicated TS index to wills in the Worcester Probate Registry, 1858-1928.

A few parishes in the extreme west of the county were in the diocese of Hereford. The records of the episcopal consistory court are now at the National Library of Wales. An index is in preparation for eventual publication.

Parishes at the south-east tip of Worcestershire, some of them detached, have changed both county and diocese at different times, and it is wise to consult the records of adjacent jurisdictions if there is any doubt.

Probate records of the diocese of Worcester are deposited in the department of the Worcestershire Record Office situated in St. Helen's church, Fish Street. Coming from the south, this is the first small turning to the left beyond a main road (Deansway) turning off just past the cathedral; there is a small car-park for users of the office, behind the church. The office issues leaflets covering probate records in its custody, names and addresses of local searchers, and more general genealogical information.

Prerogative Court of Canterbury and other courts having general jurisdiction – see page 1.

Consistory Court of Worcester (Worcestershire Record Office, St. Helen's Church, Fish Street, Worcester. Tel. Worcester (0905) 23400, ext. 463)
> Jurisdiction: the county of Worcester, apart from parishes in the diocese of Hereford (and, at times, Gloucester) and peculiars.
> Printed indexes: wills, 1451-1495, 1509-1652, admons. and invs., 1520-1652 (36,000) (calendars with indexes, Index Lib., vols. 31 and 39; there are some omissions).
> Other indexes: wills, admons. and invs., 1660-1857 (70,000) (TS); m/f of calendar to 1857 at SG.

Episcopal Consistory Court of Hereford (National Library of Wales, page 59)
Jurisdiction about 15 parishes in Worcestershire.

Court of the Dean and Chapter of Worcester (Worcestershire Record Office)
Jurisdiction: over the peculiars below. See also consistory
Chronological lists. Berrow, 1670-1786 (65); Kempsey, 1668-1779 (138); Norton near Kempsey, 1668-1785 (58); Stoulton, 1668-1787 (54); Tibberton, 1770-1788 (23); Wolverley, 1668-1788 (134); St. Michael in Bedwardine and the College precincts, 1669-1783 (122) (MS, 19th cent.).
Unindexed: late 17th cent. act book (for all peculiars).

Peculiar of the Rector of Alvechurch or Allchurch (Worcs. Record Office)
Calendar: 1718-1773.

Peculiar of the Rector of Bredon with Norton and Cutsdean (Worcs. R.O.)
Calendar: 1718-1773.

Peculiar of the Rector of Fladbury (Worcs. Record Office)
Jurisdiction: Fladbury, with Wyre Piddle, Throckmorton, Stock and Bradley.
Calendar: wills and admons., 1642-1795 (308) (MS, 19th cent.); also act books, 1666-1709, 1721-1775.

Peculiar of Hanbury (Worcestershire Record Office)
Calendar: 1720-1784; also act book, 1647-1762.

Peculiar of Hartlebury (Worcestershire Record Office)
Calendar: 1720-1784.

Peculiar of the Rector of Ripple with Queenhill and Holdfast (Worcs. Record Office)
Calendar: 1663-1727 (act book), 1721-1779.

Peculiar of the Rector of Tredington (Worcestershire Record Office)
Calendar: 1691-1697 (act book), 1717-1788.

Peculiar of Evesham (Worcestershire Record Office)
This jurisdiction appears to have lapsed at the Reformation, after which see the consistory.
Wills, 1528-1537.

Worcester District Probate Registry (Worcestershire Record Office)
Printed index: wills, 1858-1928 (28,000) (2 vols., duplicated TS).

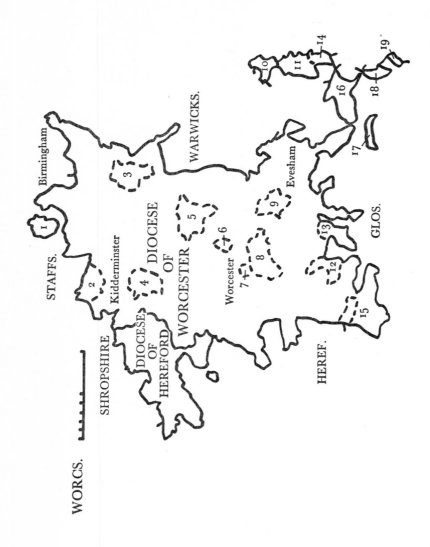

STAFFS.

Birmingham

SHROPSHIRE

Kidderminster

DIOCESE
OF
HEREFORD

WORCESTER

Worcester

DIOCESE
OF

WARWICKS.

Evesham

HEREF.

GLOS.

WORCS.

Worcestershire parishes, detached from the main county, or in peculiars, but still also in the jurisdiction of the consistory court of Worcester; and those in the jurisdiction of the consistory court of Hereford.

Detached parishes in the diocese of Worcester

Alderminster, 10
Blockley, 16
Daylesford, 19
Dudley, 1
Evenlode, 18
Shipston-on-Stour, 14
Tidmington, 14

Peculiars (also subject to the consistory court of Worcester)

Alvechurch, 3
Berrow, 15
Bradbury (Fladbury), 9
Bredon, 13
Bredons Norton, 13
Cutsdean, 17
Fladbury, 9
Hanbury, 5
Hartlebury, 4
Holdfast, 12
Kempsey, 8
Norton (near Bredon), 13
Norton (near Kempsey), 8
Queenhill, 12
Ripple, 12
Stock (Fladbury), 9
Stoulton, 8
Throckmorton (Fladbury), 9
Tibberton, 6
Tredington, 11
Wolverley, 2
Worcester, College Precincts, 7
  St. Michael in Bedwardine, 7
Wyre Piddle (Fladbury), 9

Parishes and chapelries in the diocese of Hereford

Abberley
Bayton
Bockleton
Clifton-on-Teme
Eastham
Edvin Loach
Hanley Child
Hanley William
Knighton-on-Teme
Kyre Magna
Kyre Parva
Lindridge
Mamble
Orleton
Pensax
Rock
Lower Sapey
Stanford-on-Teme
Stockton-on-Teme
Tenbury

THE PROVINCE OF YORK

The Prerogative Court of the Archbishop of York had jurisdiction over the whole province, that is, in addition to the diocese of York itself, the dioceses of Carlisle, Chester, Durham, and Sodor and Man (before 1541, and the creation of the diocese of Chester, the southern half of that diocese, comprising the county of Cheshire and that part of Lancashire south of the River Ribble, formed part of the diocese of Lichfield, in the province of Canterbury). This jurisdiction was over any person having goods either in more than one jurisdiction within the diocese of York, or in more than one diocese in the northern province, or in both northern and southern provinces. Unless there is positive evidence that the person had goods in more than one jurisdiction or diocese, the probate records of the diocese in which the deceased died should first be searched.

During archiepiscopal visitations, jurisdiction lay in the Chancery Court of the Archbishop of York, which also heard appeals from lower courts. During archiepiscopal vacancies, jurisdiction in both these courts was taken over by the court of the dean and chapter of York. The records of all three courts are now at the Borthwick Institute in York. For the Prerogative Court, there are printed indexes to 1688, a modern TS index for the period 1688-1731 (in preparation), and calendars, chronological within letter, for 1731-1857. For the Chancery Court, there is a printed index for the period, 1427-1658, but since its publication further wills and inventories have come to light. Records of the dean and chapter exercising jurisdiction during vacancies are scarce before the 17th century. Indexes to the probate records of the vacancies in 1683 and 1686-1688 are printed; for that of 1724 the contemporary registers must be consulted; while in subsequent vacancies the wills and admons. are included in the main series of probate indexes to the prerogative and exchequer courts.

The Borthwick Institute is on the north-east side of York, just inside the city wall. There are small public car-parks nearby, and a larger one just outside the walls. The Institute issues leaflets on the *Probate Records of the Diocese of York* and on *How to Find a Will*; and there is a *Guide to the Archive Collections* (1973) (£1.90), which gives greater details of all probate records.

Prerogative Court of Canterbury and other courts having general jurisdiction – see page 1.

Prerogative Court of the Archbishop of York (The Borthwick Institute of
Historical Research, St. Anthony's Hall, Peasholme Green, York YO1
2PW. Tel. York (0904) 59861, ext. 274) 642315
   Jurisdiction: the whole province; see introductory note.
   Printed indexes (prerogative and exchequer court jointly): wills, 1389-
      1636, and admons., 1389-1652 (Yorks. Arch. Soc. Record Series, vols.
      6, 11, 14, 19, 22, 24, 26, 28, 32 and 35 – the admons. are indexed
      separately in appendices in each volume); wills, 1636-1652 (vol. 4);
      wills and admons., 1660-1684 (vols. 49, 60, 68 and 89, pp. 1-145),
      vacancies, 1683, 1686-1688 (vol. 89, pp. 146-210) (143, 500 in all).
   Other indexes: wills and admons., 1688-1731 (prerogative court only)
      (TS – in preparation; 1731-1857 (jointly with exchequer court)
      (19th cent. calendar); m/f of calendar, 1688-1857, at SG.
   Printed abstracts: wills, 1316-1551 (Testamenta Eboracensis: wills at
      York illustrative of the history . . . of the province. Surtees Soc.,
      vols. 4, 30, 45, 53, 79, 106; these are a selection only).

Chancery Court of the Archbishop of York (Borthwick Institute, York)
   Jurisdiction: throughout the province during archiepiscopal visitations;
      in appeals from lower courts; and over beneficed clergy in the
      diocese of York.
   Printed indexes: wills, admons. and invs., 1427-1658 (the earliest are
      in fact Exchequer Court wills) (Yorks. Arch. Soc. Record Series, vol.
      73, pp. 1-30, under the erroneous title of Consistory Wills). Since
      this index was published a number of additional Chancery wills and
      invs. have been found. Wills, 1316-1822, in the archbishops' registers
      (4,250) (Y.A.S.R.S., vol. 93).

Court of the Dean and Chapter of York (Borthwick Institute, York)
   Jurisdiction: throughout the province during archiepiscopal vacancies.
   Printed indexes: wills, admons. and invs., 1464-1664 (very few)
      (included in the appropriate vols. of the Yorks. Arch. Soc. Record
      Series, see under Prerogative Court above), 1683, 1686-1688
      (Y.A.S.R.S., vol. 89); wills in Sede Vacante Register, 1336-1343
      (vacancy, 1340-1342) (Y.A.S.R.S., vol. 60).
   Unindexed: wills, admons. and invs., 1724 (contemporary calendars).
   Other indexes. wills, admons. and invs., 1743 and subsequent vacancies,
      in main prerogative and exchequer series (MS, 19th cent., chronologi-
      cal within letter).
   For records and indexes relating to non-vacancy jurisdiction, see page
      161.

For the Court of the Archbishop within the Liberty of Hexham and
Hexhamshire, whose records are at the Borthwick Institute York, see
under Northumberland, page 45.

PROVINCE OF YORK

SCOTLAND

NORTHUMBER
LAND

1

CUMBERLAND 2

DURHAM

3

WESTMOR
LAND

4

NORTH RIDING

5 6 7

8 9

12

10

YORKSHIRE

11

13

14

EAST RIDING

WEST RIDING

LANCASHIRE

LINCOLNS.

FLINT

CHESHIRE

DERBYS.

15

DENBIGH

16

NOTTING
HAMSHIRE

FLINT

SALOP

STAFFS.

LEICS.

152

The Province of York

Apart from the areas listed below
Cheshire was in the diocese of Chester (from 1542)
Cumberland was in the diocese of Carlisle
Durham was in the diocese of Durham
Flintshire (southern detachment) was in the diocese of Chester (from 1542)
Lancashire was in the diocese of Chester (from 1542)
Northumberland was in the diocese of Durham
Nottinghamshire was in the diocese of York
Westmorland was in the diocese of Carlisle
Yorkshire (all Ridings and the Ainsty of York (13)) was in the diocese of
York

In *Cumberland* the deanery of Copeland (3) was in the western division of
the consistory court of the archdeaconry of Richmond (diocese of Chester),
and the parish of Alston (2) was in the diocese of Durham.
In *Denbighshire* the parish of Holt (16) was in the diocese of Chester (from
1542)
In *Flintshire* the peculiar of Hawarden (15) was in the diocese of Chester
(from 1542)
In *Lancashire* that part of the county north of the River Ribble (5 and 10)
was in the western division of the consistory court of the archdeaconry
of Richmond (diocese of Chester); and Aighton, Chaigley and Bailey (14)
were in the diocese of York.
In *Northumberland* the peculiar of Hexham and Hexhamshire (1) was in
the jurisdiction of the archbishop of York; and Tockerington (Throckrington) (1) was a prebend of York.
In *Westmorland* the deaneries of Kendal and Lonsdale (6) were in the
western division of the consistory court of the archdeaconry of Richmond
(diocese of Chester).
In *Yorkshire, North Riding,* the deaneries of Richmond and Catterick (8)
were in the eastern division of the consistory court of the archdeaconry of
Richmond (diocese of Chester), the peculiar of Allerton and Allertonshire
(9) was in the jurisdiction of the bishop of Durham; and the parishes of
Sockburn (4) and Crayke (12) fell within the jurisdiction of the consistory
court of Durham.
In *Yorkshire, West Riding,* the deanery of Lonsdale (7) was in the western
division of the archdeaconry of Richmond (diocese of Chester), the
deanery of Boroughbridge (11) was in the eastern division.

YORKSHIRE

Yorkshire was in the province of York, and mainly in the diocese of York. The only major exception was the western half of the North Riding and a few parishes in the West Riding, which were in the eastern division of the archdeaconry of Richmond, part of the diocese of Chester. The county has long been divided into the civil divisions of the North, East and West Ridings; and the city of York and the Ainsty (the area immediately surrounding the city).

Most probate records relating to the diocese, those of the exchequer court (the equivalent of a consistory court elsewhere), are now at the Borthwick Institute in York. There are printed indexes to wills, admons. and inventories to 1688 (together with the prerogative court); a separate TS index for the period 1688-1731; and calendars (with the prerogative court) for 1731-1857.

The chancery court had probate jurisdiction over beneficed clergy in the diocese, heard appeals from lower courts, and exercised jurisdiction during archiepiscopal visitations. During archiepiscopal vacancies, jurisdiction in both these courts was taken over by the court of the dean and chapter of York. For the chancery court, there is a printed index to 1658, but since its publication further wills and inventories have come to light. The records of the dean and chapter are at present inadequately indexed, and the printed partial index of wills and admons., 1524-1724, is very incomplete.

The records of the eastern division of the archdeaconry of Richmond in the diocese of Chester (and of some peculiars) are now at the Leeds Archives Department. As well as the western half of the North Riding this included the deanery of Boroughbridge in the West Riding, a few parishes just outside the Ainsty of York.

Other parts of the county outside the diocese of York, or with records elsewhere than York or Leeds, were :
North Riding : the parishes of Sockburn and Crayke, in the diocese and consistory of Durham; and the Bishop of Durham's peculiar of Allerton and Allertonshire – records of these are at Durham.
West Riding : the parishes of Sedbergh, Bentham, Clapham and Thornton-in-Lonsdale, in the western division of the archdeaconry of Richmond, diocese of Chester; and the chapelries of Whitewell and Saddleworth (in the Lancashire parishes of Whalley and Rochdale) in the diocese and consistory of Chester – records of these are at the Lancashire Record Office, Preston. The parish of Rossington, and parts of the Nottinghamshire parishes of Blyth and Finningley

which extended into the county, in the archdeaconry of Nottingham, diocese of York – original exchequer court records of which are now at the Nottinghamshire Record Office.

The Borthwick Institute is on the north-east side of York, just inside the city wall. There are small public car-parks nearby, and a larger one just outside the walls. The Institute issues leaflets on the *Probate Records of the Diocese of York* and on *How to Find a Will*; and there is an excellent *Guide to the Archive Collections* (1973) (£1.90), which gives greater detail of all probate records.

Prerogative Court of Canterbury and other courts having general jurisdiction – see page 1.

> Printed index: wills and admons., 1649-1660 (5,000) (Yorks. Arch. Soc. Record Series, vol. 1, pp. 51-259 – calendar, alphabetical by year).
> Printed abstracts: wills, 1648-1660 (251) (Y.A.S.R.S., vol. 9); 1383-1604 (Surtees Soc., vols. 116 and 121).

Prerogative Court of York and other courts having jurisdiction in the province – see page 150.

Exchequer Court of the Archbishop of York (The Borthwick Institute of Historical Research, St. Anthony's Hall, Peasholme Green, York YO1 2PW. Tel. York (0904) 59861, ext. 274)

> Jurisdiction: the whole county except the archdeaconry of Richmond, the chapelries of Saddleworth and Whitewell, the peculiars, and beneficed clergy; see introductory note. Jurisdiction during vacancy lay in the court of the dean and chapter of York (page 151).
> Printed indexes (prerogative and exchequer courts jointly): wills, 1389-1636, and admons., 1389-1652 (Y.A.S.R.S., vols. 6, 11, 14, 19, 22, 24, 26, 28, 32 and 35 – the admons. are indexed separately in appendices in each volume); wills, 1636-1652 (vol. 4); wills and admons., 1660-1684 (vols. 49, 60, 68 and 89, pp. 1-145), vacancies, 1683, 1686-1688 (vol. 89, pp. 146-210).
> Other indexes: wills and admons., 1688-1731 (exchequer court only) (TS); 1731-1857 (jointly with prerogative court) (calendar); m/f of calendar, 1688-1857, at SG.

Chancery Court of the Archbishop of York (Borthwick Institute)

> Jurisdiction: over beneficed clergy in the diocese; in appeals from lower courts; and during archiepiscopal visitations. Jurisdiction during vacancy lay in the court of the dean and chapter of York (page 151).
> Printed indexes: wills, admons. and invs., 1427-1658 (900) (the earliest are in fact exchequer court wills) (Y.A.S.R.S., vol. 73, pp. 1-30, under the erroneous title Consistory Wills). Since this index was published a number of additional chancery wills and invs. have been found.
> Wills, 1316-1822, in the archbishops' registers (Y.A.S.R.S., vol. 93).

The following parishes, chapelries and other places were at some or all of times outside the direct jurisdiction of the exchequer court of York. The civil division of the county into which each fell is shown by the initial letter in brackets following each name:

(A)=Ainsty of York; (E)=East Riding; (N)=North Riding; (W)=West Riding. Details of the exchequer court of York are given under 'Yorkshire' on page 155. Details of all other jurisdictions in the county are given under the Riding sections, and places may be located on the maps of each Riding. The peculiars of the dean and chapter, and of the dean, of York each covered a number of parishes; places in these and those subject to consistory or archdeaconry courts have the following keys:

AN=Archdeaconry of Nottingham (diocese of York); CC=Consistory of Chester; CD=Consistory of Durham; DC=Peculiar of the dean and chapter of York; DY=Peculiar of the dean of York; R=Archdeaconry of Richmond, eastern deaneries (diocese of Chester); RW=Archdeaconry of Richmond, western deaneries (diocese of Chester); SLH=Peculiar of St. Leonard's Hospital, York. The names of all other peculiars are shown in bold type and can be identified from the key letters.

The peculiars of St. Leonard's Hospital, York (SLH) and of Beverley (BG) had concurrent jurisdiction with the exchequer court over a number of parishes, ceasing by the mid-16th century. Likewise the jurisdiction of the dean and chapter of York (DC) over a few parishes faded out, although it continued in many others. In such cases where the exchequer court had later jurisdiction, these places are included in the following alphabetical list but are not shown on the maps.

Acklam, (E), LE 36
Acomb (A), **AC** 46
Airmyn (W), SN 96
Aldborough (N), DC 17
Aldborough (W), DC 70
Aldbrough (in Stanwick St. John) (N), **AD** 1
Allerston (N), DY 11
Allerthorpe (E), DY 52
Allerton and Allertonshire (N), **AE** 8
Allerton Mauleverer (W), R 77
Alne (N), **AH** 21
Altofts (W), **AL** 93
Ampleforth (N), **AM** 14
Anderby Steeple (N), R
Anston (W), LE 104
Appleton Wiske (N), R
Arkendale (W), K 76
Arkengarthdale (N), **AR** 4
Askham Bryan (A), **AS** 48
Askrigg (N), R
Asselby (E), HO 56
Austerfield (W), AN 101
Aysgarth (N), R

Balne (W), SN 96
Barlby (E), HO 56
Barlow (W), SE 90
Barmby Marsh (E), HO 56
Barmby Moor (E), DY & BA 52
Barnby (E), **DY** & **BA** 52
Barnoldswick (W), **BD** 81
Barton (N), R
Batley (W), **BE** 92
Bedale (N), R
Beeford (E), **BF** 43
Beilby (E), DY 52
Beningbrough (N), NO 23
Bentham (W), RW 68
Beverley (E), **BG**
Bielby (E), DY 52
Bilton in Ainsty (A), **BI** 44
Bilton in Holderness (E), BG
Bingley (W), CR 84
Bishop Wilton (E), **BS** 40
Blacktoft (E), HO 56
Blubberhouses (W), K 76
Blyth (W and Notts.), AN 101
Bolton (nr. Pocklington) (E), BS 40
Bolton upon Swale (N), R
Castle Bolton (N), R

Boston (Spa) (W), DC 83
Bowes (N), R
Bramham (W), DC 83
Brandesburton (E), BG
Brantingham (E), HO 62
Brayton (W), SE 90
Brignall (N), R
Brompton (N), AE 8
Brotherton (W), DC 95
Bubwith (E), DC
Bugthorpe (E), BU 39
Burn (W), SE 90
Burneston (N), R & SLH
Burton Leonard (W), DC 76
Burton Pidsea (E), BG & DC 66
Carlton in Snaith (W), SN 96
Carlton Husthwaite (N), HU 16
Carnaby (E), SLH
Castley (W), K 76
Cattal (W), HS 78
Catterick (N), R
North Cave (E), SLH
South Cave (E), CA & SLH 61
Cawood (W), WI 87
Cayton (W), K 76
Chapel le Dale (W), RW 68
Cherry Burton (E), BG
Church Fenton (W), FE 86
Clapham (W), RW 68
Cleasby (N), R
Clint (W), K 76
Coneythorpe (W), K 76
Copgrove (W), R 73
Copmanthorpe (A), DC 49
Cottam (E), LA 34
Cottingley (W), CR 84
Coverham (N), R
Cowick (W), SN 96
East Cowton (N), R
South Cowton (N), R
Crayke (N), CD 19
Croft (N), R
Crossley (W), CR 84
Cundall (N), R 17
South Dalton (E), BG
Dalton on Tees (N), DC
Danby Wiske (N), R
Deighton (N), AE 8
Dent (W), RW 68
Dob Cross (W), CC 98
Downholme (N), R
Driffield (E), DR 38

Drypool (E), BG
Dukeswick (W), K 76
Dunnington (E), DU 51
Dunsforth (W), DC 70
Easby (N), R
Eastrington (E), HO 56
Ebberston (N), DY 11
Ellerburn (N), DY 11
Ellerker (E), HO 62
Elloughton (E), WG 63
Eryholme (N), R
Fangfoss (E), DY 41
Farnham (W), K 76
Fenton (W), FE 86
Fewston (W), K 76
Fimber (E), WG 37
Finghall (N), R
Finningley (W and Notts.) AN 101
Firbeck (W), LE 104
Forcett (N), R
Foston on the Wolds (E), BG
Fridaythorpe (E), FR & WG 37
Garsdale (W), RW 68
Gateforth (W), SE 90
Gate Helmsley (N), BG & O **27**
Gildingwells (W), LE 104
Gilling (N), R
Gisburn (W), SLH
Givendale (E), DY & GI 42
Goathland (N), DY 10
Goldsborough (W), R **77**
Goodmanham (E), DC
Goole (W), SN 96
Gowdall (W), SN 96
North Grimston (E), LA **33**
Grindal (E), GR 32
Grinton (N), R
Hambleton (W), SE 90
Hampsthwaite (W), K 76
Handsworth (W), LE 103
Hardraw (N), R
Harrogate (W), K 76
Hartwith (W), MF 71
Hauxwell (N), R
Haverah Park (W), K 76
Hawes (N), R
Haxby (N), DR & ST 25
Hayton (E), DY 52
Heath (W), WB 94
Heck (W), SN 96
Over Helmsley (N), SLH
Helperby (N), DC 18

West Rounton (N), AE 6
Routh (E), BG
Rufforth (A), SLH
Ruston (E), BG
Saddleworth (in Rochdale, Lancs.)
  (W), CC 98
Salton (N), SA 15
Saxton (W), SLH
Scorborough (E), BG
Scruton (N), R
Sedbergh (W), RW 68
Selby (W), SE 90
Sherburn in Elmet (W), FE 86
Shipton (E), WE 53
Shiptonthorpe (E), WE 53
Sigglesthorne (E), BG
Silsden (W), SI 82
Skelton nr. York (N), AH 24
Skipwith (E), HO 56
Great Smeaton (N), R
Snaith (W), SN 96
Sockburn (N), CD 2
Spennithorne (N), R
Stainburn (W), K 76
South Stainley (W), K 76
Stalling Busk (N), R
Startforth (N), R
Staveley (W), K & R 76
Stillington (N), SO 20
Stockton on the Forest (N), BU 26
Strensall (N), ST 25
Swindon (W), K 76
Swinefleet (W), SN 96
West Tanfield (N), R
Temple Newsam (W), TN 89
Thornton in Lonsdale (W), RW 68
Thornton on Spalding Moor
  (E), DY 52
Thornton Steward (N), R
Thornton Watlass (N), R
Thorpe Salvin (W), LE 104
Thorpe Willoughby (W), SE 90
Throapham St. John (W), LE 104
Tollerton (N), AH 21
Topcliffe (N), DC & SLH
Tunstall (E), TU 67
Ulleskelf (W), U & WG 85
Wadworth (W), WA 100
Wales (W), LE 104

Walkington (E), BG & HO 58
Walshford (W), HS 78
Warmfield (W), WB 94
Warthill (N), WD 28
Wath (N), R
Wawne (E), LE 59
Weaverthorpe (E), DC 31
Weeton (W), K 76
Weighton (E), WE 53
Well (N), R
Welton (E), HO 64
Welwick (E), BG
Wensley (N), R
Westerdale (N), WF 5
Wetwang (E), BG & WG 37
Wharram le Street (E), DC 33
Whitewell (in Whalley, Lancs.)
  (W), CC 79, 80
Whitgift (W), SN 96
Whixley (W), R 77
Wigginton (N), AH 24
Wilton (N), DY 11
  see also Bishop Wilton
Wistow (W), WI 87
Withernwick (E), HA 60
East Witton (N), R
West Witton (N), R
High Worsall (N), AE 3
Wycliffe (N), R
Yapham (E), DY 52
York (A), DC 47
  (Bedern,
  St. Andrew,
  St. John del Pike,
  St. John Hungate,
  St. John Ousebridge,
  St. Lawrence, (also SLH),
  St. Martin Coney Street,
  St. Mary Bishophill Junior,
  St. Mary Layerthorpe,
  St. Maurice,
  St. Michael le Belfry,
  St. Nicholas,
  St. Sampson,
  St. Wilfrid)
  also, SLH
  (All SS. North Street, and
  St. Giles Gillygate)

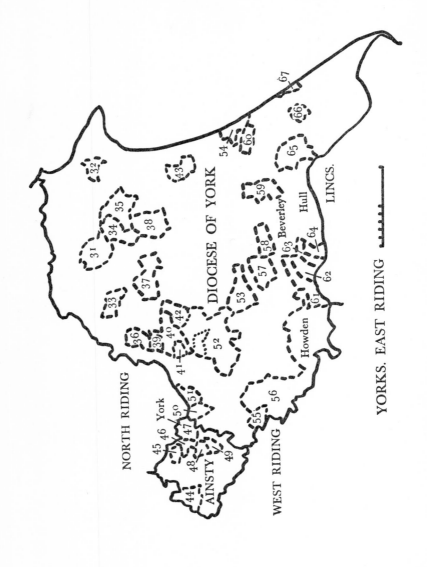

NORTH RIDING

DIOCESE OF YORK

31
32
33
34
35
36
37
38
39
40
41
42
43
44
45 46 York
47
48
49
50
51
52
53
54
59
60
Beverley
57
58
63
Hull
64
62
61
Howden
56
55
65
66
67

AINSTY

WEST RIDING

LINCS.

YORKS. EAST RIDING

THE EAST RIDING
AND THE CITY AND AINSTY OF YORK

The East Riding of Yorkshire and the City and Ainsty of York were wholly in the diocese of York and, apart from peculiars, in the jurisdiction of the exchequer court. The records of this and of nearly all the peculiars are now at the Borthwick Institute, York, and for those still in the York Minster Library prior application can be made at the Institute.

Prerogative Court of Canterbury and other courts having general jurisdiction – see page 1.

Prerogative Court of York and other courts having jurisdiction in the province – see page 150.

Exchequer and Chancery Courts of York – see page 155.

Court of the Dean and Chapter of York (DC) (Borthwick Institute, York, and York Minster Library)
> Jurisdiction included 14 parishes in York, 2 in the Ainsty, and 5 in the East Riding. A few records also survive from the time jurisdiction was exercised in Bubwith and Goodmanham.
> Indexes: wills, admons. and invs., 1438-1728, 1650-1857 (calendar; m/f at SG; new index in preparation).
> Printed indexes: wills and admons., 1524-1724, probate registers, 1321-1638, probate act books, 1559-1636 (Yorks. Arch. Soc. Record Series, vol. 38, pp. 73-96 – this is very incomplete, and the MS indexes above should also be consulted); wills in chapter act books, 1336-1429 (56) (Y.A.S.R.S., vol. 60, pp. 189-90).

Peculiar of the Dean of York (DY) (Borthwick Institute, York)
> Jurisdiction included 12 parishes in the East Riding. See also chancery court and court of the dean and chapter.
> Printed index: wills and admons. (act books), 1604-1722 (2,750) (Y.A.S.R.S., vol. 73, pp. 31-80).
> Other indexes: wills, 1531-1708, 1722-1857 (MS).

Peculiar of St. Leonard's Hospital, York (SLH) (York Minster Library)
> Jurisdiction included All SS. North Street, St. Giles Gillygate and St. Lawrence in the city of York; Rufforth in the Ainsty; and Carnaby, North and South Cave, Hotham, and Nunburnholme in the East Riding, pre-Reformation only, concurrent with exchequer and other courts.
> Printed index: wills, 1419-1523 (100) (Y.A.S.R.S., vol. 60, pp. 191-93).

Peculiar of Acomb (AC) (Borthwick Institute, York)
Wills, admons. and invs., 1456-1837 (calendar from 1709; m/f at SG).

Prebend of Ampleforth (AM) (Borthwick Institute, York)
See also chancery court and court of the dean and chapter.
Wills, admons. and invs., 1528-1827 (calendar from 1661; m/f at SG).

Manor of Askham Bryan (AS) (Borthwick Institute, York)
Index: wills, admons. and invs., 1715-1799 (calendar).

Prebend of Barnby (Barnby Moor) (BA) (Borthwick Institute, York)
See also chancery court and court of the dean and chapter; and after
1736, peculiar of the dean of York.
Wills, admons. and invs., 1610-1729 (calendar, 1670-1736).

Manor of Beeford (BF) (Borthwick Institute, York)
Printed index: wills, admons. and invs., 1561-1768 (150) (Y.A.S.R.S.,
vol. 68, pp. 213-16).

Peculiar of the Collegiate Church of St. John's Beverley (BG) (Borthwick
Institute, York)
A concurrent jurisdiction, ceasing by 1552, over a number of places
in the East Riding; at all times these places were also subject to the
exchequer or other peculiar courts.
Printed index: 1539-1552 (100) (Y.A.S.R.S., vol. 60, pp. 182-84).

Prebend of Bilton (BI) (Borthwick Institute, York)
See also chancery court and court of the dean and chapter.
Wills, admons. and invs., 1591-1849.

Peculiar of Bishop Wilton (BS) (Borthwick Institute, York)
Wills, admons. and invs., 1531-1824 (calendar, 1616-1857; m/f at SG).

Prebend of Bugthorpe (BU) (Borthwick Institute, York)
See also chancery court and court of the dean and chapter.
Wills, admons. and invs., 1544-1831 (calendar from 1669; m/f at SG).

Peculiar of South Cave (CA) (Borthwick Institute, York)
Wills, admons. and invs., 1558-1843 (calendar from 1579; m/f at SG).

Prebend of Driffield (annexed to the Court of the Precentor of York) (DR)
(Borthwick Institute, York)
See also chancery court and court of the dean and chapter.
Wills, admons. and invs., 1557-1852.

Prebend of Dunnington (DU) (Borthwick Institute, York)
See also chancery court and court of the dean and chapter; and
exchequer court after 1729.
Wills, admons. and invs., 1549-1729.

Prebend of Fridaythorpe (FR) (Borthwick Institute, York)
See also chancery court and court of the dean and chapter; and prebend of Wetwang after 1730.
Wills, admons. and invs., 1593-1730.

Prebend of Givendale (GI) (Borthwick Institute, York)
See also chancery court and courts of the dean and chapter and of the dean.
Wills, admons. and invs., 1661-1669.

Prebend of Grindal (GR) (Borthwick Institute, York)
See also chancery court and court of the dean and chapter; and exchequer court after 1628.
Wills, admons. and invs., 1623-1628.

Prebend of Holme Archiepiscopi (HA) (Borthwick Institute, York)
Jurisdiction in Withernwick only. See also chancery court and court of the dean and chapter.
Wills, admons. and invs., 1560-1836 (calendar 1663-1704 only).

Peculiar of (the dean and chapter, formerly prior and convent, of Durham in) Howden and Howdenshire (HO) (Borthwick Institute, York)
Wills, admons. and invs., 1521-1857 (calendar 1598-1622 only).

Prebend of Langtoft (LA) (Borthwick Institute, York)
See also chancery court and court of the dean and chapter.
Wills, admons. and invs., 1520-1845 (calendar 1647-1738 only).

Prebend of Laughton en le Morthen (annexed to the Court of the Chancellor of York) (LE) (Borthwick Institute, York)
Jurisdiction included Acklam near Malton and Wawne. See also chancery court and court of the dean and chapter.
Wills, admons. and invs., 1548-1857.

Peculiar of (the Archdeacon of the East Riding in) Mappleton (MA) (Borthwick Institute, York)
See also chancery court and court of the dean and chapter.
Index: wills, admons. and invs., 1571-1849 (calendar).

Prebend of North Newbald (NN) (Borthwick Institute, York)
See also chancery court and court of the dean and chapter.
Wills, admons. and invs., 1496-1851 (calendar 1633-1734 only).

Peculiar of (the Sub-Dean of York in) Preston in Holderness (PH) (Borthwick Institute, York)
See also chancery court and court of the dean and chapter.
Wills, admons. and invs., 1559-1837 (calendar 1676-1729 only).

Prebend of Riccall (RI) (Borthwick Institute, York, and York Minster Library)
   See also chancery court and court of the dean and chapter.
   Wills, admons. and invs., 1549-1833 (calendar from 1690 only; m/f at SG); wills, 1731, 1739 (2) (at York Minster).

Court of (the Succentor of York) in Tunstall (TU) (Borthwick Institute, York)
   See also chancery court and court of the dean and chapter.
   Wills, admons. and invs., 1557-1838.

Prebend of (Market) Weighton (WE) (Borthwick Institute, York)
   See also chancery court and court of the dean and chapter.
   Wills, admons. and invs., 1502-1857 (calendar from 1660 only; m/f at SG).

Prebend of Wetwang (WG) (Borthwick Institute, York)
   See also chancery court and court of the dean and chapter; and prebend of Fridaythorpe.
   Wills, admons. and invs., 1458-1850 (calendar 1659-1709 only).

Corporation of Kingston upon Hull (City Record Office, The Guildhall, Kingston upon Hull, HU1 2AA)
   Printed indexes: wills, 1329-1425 (36) (*Northern Genealogist*, vol. 2, pp. 181-83); wills, 1303-1791 (*Calendar of Ancient Deeds, etc., in the Archives of the Corporation,* ed. L. M. Stanewell, 1951).

Holderness
   Printed abstracts: wills, 1390-1446 (East Riding Antiq. Soc. Trans., vols. 10 (pp. 1-18) and 11 (pp. 1-18)).

York
   Printed abstracts: wills, 1385-1443 ('Some Early Civic Wills of York', Associated Architectural Socs. Reports, vols. 28 (pp. 827-71), 31 (pp. 319-39), 32 (pp. 293-317, 569-93), 33 (pp. 161-77, 473-92), 34 (pp. 201-17) and 35 (pp. 61-74).

THE NORTH RIDING

The North Riding of Yorkshire was split between the dioceses of York and (after 1541) Chester. The eastern part lay in the diocese of York, and was, apart from peculiars, in the jurisdiction of the exchequer court. The records of this, and of most of the peculiars, are now at the Borthwick Institute, York; for those still in York Minster Library prior application can be made at the Institute. The parish of Crayke was a peculiar of the bishop of Durham, and (until 1837) was administered by his consistory court, which also had jurisdiction over the North Riding chapelries of Over Dinsdale and Girsby in the parish of Sockburn (co. Durham). Records of this and of the peculiar of Allerton and Allertonshire (now North-allerton) are at the Department of Palaeography and Diplomatic in the University of Durham.

The western part of the North Riding was in the archdeaconry of Richmond, Eastern Deaneries, in the diocese of Chester, the records of which are now at the Leeds Archives Department. This also holds the records of the manor of Arkengarthdale and the peculiars of Masham and Middleham. The Department is situated above the Sheepscar Library, at the junction of Roundhay Road and Sheepscar Street North, to the north-east of the centre of Leeds. At present there is ample car-parking.

Prerogative Court of Canterbury and other courts having general juris-diction – see page 1.

Prerogative Court of York and other courts having jurisdiction in the province – see page 150.

Exchequer and Chancery Courts of York – see page 155.

Consistory Court of the Commissary of the Archdeaconry of Richmond, Eastern Deaneries (R) (Leeds Archives Department, Sheepscar Library, Leeds LS7 3AP. Tel. Leeds (0532) 628339)
> Jurisdiction: the deaneries of Richmond and Catterick, comprising the western half of the North Riding, except for peculiars; but including some jurisdiction over the peculiars of Arkengarthdale and Middle-ham.
> Indexes: wills, admons. and invs., c.1427-1857 (19th cent. calendar, including some wills no longer existing); wills, 1474-1490, 1503 (fragmentary), wills, admons. and invs., 1521-1610, 1711-1750 (card index, and in progress).

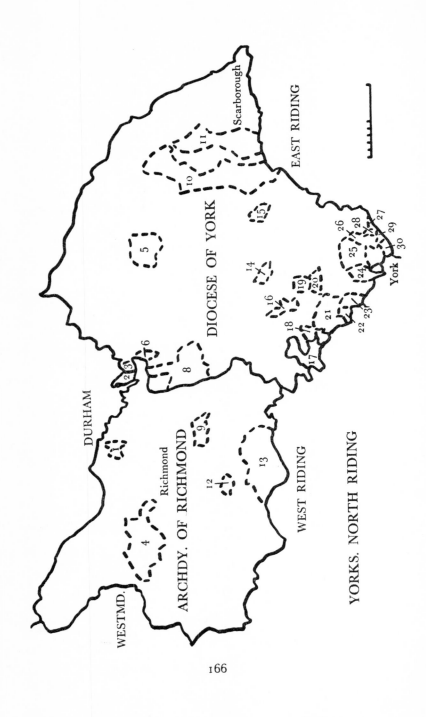

DURHAM

WESTMD.

Richmond

ARCHDY. OF RICHMOND

WEST RIDING

YORKS. NORTH RIDING

DIOCESE OF YORK

Scarborough

EAST RIDING

York

Archdeaconry of Richmond, Eastern Deaneries, contd.
Printed index: wills and admons., 1427-1616, A-G only (*Northern Genealogist,* vol. 2, supplement).
Printed abstracts: wills and invs., 1442-1579 (Surtees Soc., vol. 26); wills, 1438-1601 (*Northern Genealogist,* vols. 3-5).

Consistory Court of Durham with the Peculiar of Crayke (CD) (University of Durham, page 44)
Jurisdiction included Over Dinsdale and Girsby, chapelries in the parish of Sockburn (partly in Co. Durham); and, until 1837, the North Riding parish of Crayke.

Court of the Dean and Chapter of York (DC) (Borthwick Institute, York, and York Minster Library)
Jurisdiction included Helperby and Hornby in the North Riding; also prebend peculiars during inhibition. A few records also survive from the time jurisdiction was exercised in Dalton on Tees and Topcliffe.
Indexes: wills, admons. and invs., 1438-1728, 1650-1857 (calendar; m/f at SG; new index in preparation).
Printed indexes: wills and admons., 1524-1724, probate registers, 1321-1638, probate act books, 1559-1636 (Yorks. Arch. Soc. Record Series, vol. 38, pp. 73-96 – this is very incomplete, and the MS indexes above should also be consulted); wills in chapter act books, 1336-1429 (56) (Y.A.S.R.S., vol. 60, pp. 189-90).

Peculiar of the Dean of York (DY) (Borthwick Institute, York)
Jurisdiction included 7 parishes in the North Riding. See also chancery court and court of the dean and chapter.
Printed index: wills and admons. (act books), 1604-1722 (Y.A.S.R.S., vol. 73, pp. 31-80).
Other indexes: wills, 1531-1708, 1722-1857 (MS).

Peculiar of St. Leonard's Hospital, York (SLH) (York Minster Library)
Pre-Reformation jurisdiction included Burniston, Over Helmsley, Newton-on-Ouse, Pickhill and Topcliffe (most of the wills are for Newton), concurrent with exchequer and other courts.
Printed index: wills, 1419-1523 (100) (Y.A.S.R.S., vol. 60, pp. 191-93).

Peculiar of Aldbrough (in Stanwick St. John) (AD) (York Minster Library)
Printed index: wills, admons. and invs., 1610-1700 (32) (Y.A.S.R.S., vol. 60, pp. 181).

Peculiar of (the Bishop of Durham and of the Dean and Chapter in) Allerton and Allertonshire (AE) (University of Durham, page 44)
Index: wills and admons., 1666-1845.

Peculiar of Alne and Tollerton (AH) (Borthwick Institute and York Minster Library)
Printed index: wills, 1541-1553 (York Minster) (Y.A.S.R.S., vol. 38)
Wills, admons. and invs., 1458-1856 (calendar from 1601; m/f at SG).

Prebend of Ampleforth (AM) (Borthwick Institute, York)
See also chancery court and court of the dean and chapter.
Wills, admons. and invs., 1528-1827 (calender from 1661; m/f at SG).

Manor of Arkengarthdale (AR) (Leeds Archives Department)
See also consistory court of the archdeaconry of Richmond, Eastern Deaneries, above.
Index: wills and admons., 1698-1812 (modern MS); m/f of calendar, 1726-1808, at SG.
Printed abstracts: wills, 1698-1812, A-M only (*Northern Genealogist,* vol. 4, pp. 93-102. 116-131, vol. 5, pp. 24-29, and vol. 6, pp. 93-96).

Peculiar of the Collegiate Church of St. John's Beverley (BG) (Borthwick Institute, York)
A concurrent jurisdiction, ceasing by 1552, which included Gate Helmsley in the North Riding; see also prebend of Osbaldwick.
Printed index: 1539-1552 (100) (Y.A.S.R.S., vol. 60, pp. 182-84).

Prebend of Bugthorpe (BU) (Borthwick Institute, York)
Jurisdiction included Stockton on the Forest. See also chancery court and court of the dean and chapter.
Wills, admons. and invs., 1544-1831 (calendar from 1669; m/f at SG).

Peculiar of (the Dean and Chapter, formerly Prior and Convent, of Durham in) Howden and Howdenshire (HO) (Borthwick Institute, York)
Jurisdiction included Holtby in the North Riding.
Wills, admons. and invs., 1521-1857 (calendar 1598-1622 only).

Prebend of Husthwaite (HU) (Borthwick Institute, York)
See also chancery court and court of the dean and chapter.
Wills, admons. and invs., 1633-1842 (calendar from 1661; m/f at SG).

Manor of Linton on Ouse (LI) (Borthwick Institute, York)
Index: wills, admons. and invs., 1710-1735 (TS).

Peculiar of Masham (MF) (Leeds Archives Department)
A prebend of York until 1546 (so see also chancery court and court of the dean and chapter), then a lay fee belonging to Trinity College Cambridge.
Index: wills, admons. and invs., 1572-1857.

Deanery and Royal Peculiar of the Collegiate Church of Middleham (MI) (Leeds Archives Department)
See also consistory court of the archdeaconry of Richmond, Eastern Deaneries, above.
Wills and admons., 1722-1854 (28 only) (MS list).

Manor of Newton on Ouse with Beningbrough (NO) (Borthwick Institute, York)
See also peculiar of St. Leonard's Hospital, York, above, pre-1523.
Index: wills, admons. and invs., 1614-1812 (TS).

Prebend of Osbaldwick (O) (Borthwick Institute, York)
See also chancery court and court of the dean and chapter.
Wills, admons. and invs., 1549-1827 (calendar 1631-1739 only).

Peculiar of Salton (SA) (Borthwick Institute, York)
See also chancery court and court of the dean and chapter.
Wills, admons. and invs., 1531-1826.

Prebend of Stillington (SO) (Borthwick Institute, York)
See also chancery court and court of the dean and chapter.
Wills, admons. and invs., 1515-1843.

Prebend of Strensall (ST) (Borthwick Institute, York)
See also chancery court and court of the dean and chapter.
Wills, admons. and invs., 1528-1852 (calendar 1640-1739 only).

Prebend of Warthill (WD) (Borthwick Institute, York)
See also chancery court and court of the dean and chapter.
Wills, admons. and invs., 1548-1837 (calendar from 1681 only; m/f at SG).

Manor of Westerdale (WF) (location of records now unknown)
Printed abstracts: wills, 1550-1575 (23) (Y.A.S.R.S., vol. 74, pp. 49-64).
Printed index: miscellaneous wills and admons., 1669-1765 (31) (Y.A.S.R.S., vol. 74, pp. 65-66).

Abbotside
Printed abstracts: wills, 1552-1688 (Y.A.S.R.S., vol. 130).

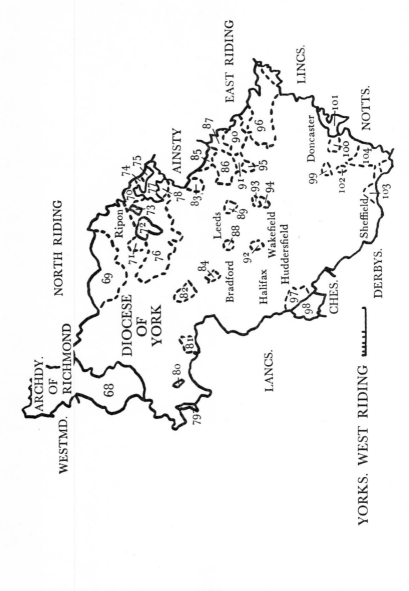

THE WEST RIDING

Nearly all the West Riding of Yorkshire lay in the diocese of York and, apart from peculiars, the jurisdiction of the exchequer court. The records of this and of most of the peculiars are now at the Borthwick Institute, York; for those still in York Minster Library prior application can be made at the Institute.

Four parishes in the extreme north-west were in the deanery of Lonsdale, one of the Western Deaneries of the archdeaconry of Richmond in the diocese of Chester. The records of these and of the consistory court of Chester, which had jurisdiction over some West Riding chapelries in the Lancashire parishes of Rochdale and Whalley, are now at the Lancashire Record Office at Preston.

The deanery of Boroughbridge, to the north-west of the city of York, was one of the Eastern Deaneries of the archdeaconry of Richmond, the records of which are now in the Leeds Archives Department. This also holds records of the peculiars of Altofts in Normanton, Hunsingore, Knaresborough, and Masham. The Department is situated above the Sheepscar Library, at the junction of Roundhay Road and Sheepscar Street North, to the north-east of the centre of Leeds. At present there is ample car-parking.

The West Riding parish of Rossington and chapelries in the Nottinghamshire parishes of Finningley and Blyth fell within the archdeaconry of Nottingham (diocese of York), most of whose records are now at the Nottinghamshire Record Office.

Prerogative Court of Canterbury and other courts having general juris-diction – see page 1.

Prerogative Court of York and other courts having jurisdiction in the province – see page 150.

Exchequer and Chancery Courts of York – see page 155.

Consistory Court of the Commissary of the Archdeaconry of Richmond, Eastern Deaneries (R) (Leeds Archives Department, Sheepscar Library, Leeds LS7 3AP. Tel. Leeds (0532) 628339)
  Jurisdiction: those parishes in the deanery of Boroughbridge not in peculiars.
  Index: wills, admons. and invs., c. 1427-1857 (19th cent. calendar, including some wills no longer existing); wills, 1474-1490, 1503 (fragmentary), wills, admons. and invs., 1521-1610, 1711-1750 (card index, and in progress).

Archdeaconry of Richmond, Eastern Deaneries, contd.
Printed index: wills and admons., 1427-1616, A-G only (*Northern Genealogist,* vol. 2, supplement).
Printed abstracts: wills and invs., 1442-1579 (Surtees Soc., vol. 26).

Consistory Court of the Commissary of the Archdeaconry of Richmond, Western Deaneries (RW) (Lancashire Record Office, Preston, page 74)
Jurisdiction: the deanery of Lonsdale.
Indexes: wills and admons., 1457-1720 (19th cent. calendar), 1720-1857 calendar. The indexes to the western deaneries printed by the Lancs. and Cheshire Record Soc. do not include non-Lancashire wills.
Printed abstracts: selected wills and invs., 1442-1579 (Surtees Soc., vol. 26).

Consistory Court of Chester in the Archdeaconry of Chester (CC) (Lancashire Record Office, Preston)
Jurisdiction: the West Riding chapelries of Whitewell (in Whalley) and Saddleworth (in Rochdale).
For records and indexes see pages 73-74.

Exchequer Court of York in the Archdeaconry of Nottingham (AN) (Nottinghamshire Record Office, page 101)
Jurisdiction included the West Riding parish of Rossington and parts of the Notts. parishes of Blyth and Finningley in the West Riding. Some records of the archdeaconry are at the Borthwick Institute, York, with other exchequer court records.

Court of the Dean and Chapter of York (DC) (Borthwick Institute, York, and York Minster Library)
Jurisdiction included 6 parishes in the West Riding; also prebend peculiars during inhibition.
Indexes: wills, admons. and invs., 1438-1728, 1650-1857 (calendar; m/f at SG; new index in preparation).
Printed indexes: wills and admons., 1524-1724, probate registers, 1321-1638, probate act books, 1559-1636 (Yorks. Arch. Soc. Record Series, vol. 38, pp. 73-96 – this is incomplete, and the MS indexes above should also be consulted); wills in chapter act books, 1336-1429 (56) (Y.A.S.R.S., vol. 60, pp. 189-90).

Peculiar of St. Leonard's Hospital, York (SLH) (York Minster Library)
Pre-Reformation jurisdiction included Gisburn and Saxton, concurrent with exchequer and other courts.
Printed index: wills, 1419-1523 (100) (Y.A.S.R.S., vol. 60, pp. 191-93).

Peculiar of Altofts in Normanton (AL) (Leeds Archives Department)
Printed index: wills, admons. and invs., 1622-1677 (25) (*Northern Genealogist,* vol. 1, p. 130).

Manor of Barnoldswick (BD) (Borthwick Institute, York)
Printed abstracts: will, 1678, admon., 1794, invs., 1660-1759 (47) (Y.A.S.R.S., vol. 118).
Printed list: the above, plus 20 other docs., 'not now forthcoming' (*Northern Genealogist*, vol. 1, pp. 113-114).

Manor of Batley (BE) (Bradford Central Library, Prince's Way, Bradford BD1 1NN)
Printed abstracts: wills, 1651-1694 (40) (Y.A.S.R.S., vol. 74, pp. 68-82); 1702-1753 (*Records of the Parish of Batley,* by M. Sheard, 1894).
Printed index: wills (in court rolls), 1615-1652, to the above, 1651-1753 (Y.A.S.R.S., vol. 74, pp. 81-85).

Manor of Crossley, Bingley, Cottingley and Pudsey (CR) (Borthwick Institute, York)
Printed abstracts: wills, 1600-1645 (Bradford Hist. and Ant. Soc. Local Records, vol. 1).
Printed index: wills, 1585-1676 (some) (*Northern Genealogist*, vol. 1, pp. 33-34).
Other index: wills and admons., 1585-1804 (calendar; m/f at SG).

Prebend of Driffield (*annexed to the Court of the Precentor of York*) (DR) (Borthwick Institute, York)
See also chancery court and court of the dean and chapter.
Wills, admons. and invs., 1557-1852.

Prebend of Fenton (FE) (Borthwick Institute, and York Minster Library)
See also chancery court and court of the dean and chapter.
Wills, admons. and invs., 1528-1854 (calendar, from 1617 only) (Borthwick Institute); m/f of calendar at SG.
Wills, 1731, 1738 (2), invs., 1757-1762 (4) (York Minster Library).

Manor of Hunsingore (HN) (Leeds Archives Department)
Index: wills, admons. and invs., 1607-1839 (19th cent. MS; m/f at SG).

Honour of Knaresborough (K) (Leeds Archives Department)
Printed index: wills and admons., 1640-1857 (Surtees Soc., vol. 110).
Printed abstracts: wills, admons. and invs., 1507-1668 (in manor court rolls in Public Record Office) (Surtees Soc., vols. 104 and 110).

Prebend of Knaresborough (K) (Borthwick Institute, York)
Wills and admons., 1546, 1560 (2 only) (TS).

Prebend of Laughton en le Morthen (*annexed to the Court of the Chancellor of York*) (LE) (Borthwick Institute, York)
See also chancery court and court of the dean and chapter.
Wills, admons. and invs., 1548-1857.

Manor of Marsden (MD) (Borthwick Institute, York)
  Printed index: wills and admons., 1664-1855 (*Northern Genealogist,* vol. 2, pp. 102-107, 168-71).
  Other index: wills and admons., 1655-1855 (calendar).

Peculiar of Masham (MF) (Leeds Archives Department)
  A prebend of York until 1546 (so see also chancery court and court of the dean and chapter), then a lay fee belonging to Trinity College Cambridge.
  Index: wills, admons. and invs., 1572-1857.

Peculiar of (the Archdeacon of York or of the West Riding in) Mexborough and Ravenfield (ME) (Borthwick Institute, York)
  See also chancery court and court of the dean and chapter.
  Index: wills, 1662-1740, 1760-1839 (calendar).

Peculiar of Selby (SE) (Borthwick Institute, York)
  Wills, admons. and invs., 1555-1857 (calendar from 1681).
  Printed abstracts: wills, admons. and invs., 1634-1710 (Y.A.S.R.S., vol. 47).
  See also British Museum Add. MS. 36,582.

Manor of Silsden (SI) (Borthwick Institute, York)
  Printed index: wills, admons. and invs., 1588-1737 (*Northern Genealogist,* vol. 1, pp. 37-38, 110-12).
  Other index: wills, admons. and invs., 1737-1809 (calendar; m/f at SG).

Peculiar of Snaith (SN) (Borthwick Institute, York)
  Index: wills, admons. and invs., 1568-1857 (calendar; m/f at SG).

Manor of Temple Newsam (TN) (Borthwick Institute, York)
  Printed abstracts: wills, admons. and invs., 1612-1701 (Thoresby Soc., vol. 33, pp. 241-82).
  Printed index: as above, 1612-1701 (*Northern Genealogist,* vol. 1, pp. 34-37).

Prebend of Ulleskelf (U) (Borthwick Institute, York)
  See also chancery court and court of the dean and chapter; and prebend of Wetwang below.
  Wills, admons. and invs., 1612-1751.

Peculiar of Wadworth (WA) (Borthwick Institute, York)
  See also chancery court and court of the dean and chapter; also prebend of South Cave (East Riding).
  Wills, admons. and invs., 1639-1819 (calendar 1708-1760 only).

Manor of Warmfield with Heath (WB)
  Printed index: wills, admons. and invs., 1642-1691 (*Northern Genealogist,* vol. 1, p. 129).
  Abstracts with Yorks. Arch. Soc.

Prebend of Wetwang (WG) (Borthwick Institute, York)
See also chancery court and court of the dean and chapter; and prebend of Ulleskelf.
Wills, admons. and invs., 1458-1850 (calendar 1659-1709 only).

Prebend of Wistow (WI) (Borthwick Institute, York)
Wills, admons. and invs., 1558-1842 (calendar 1617-1707 only).

Barwick in Elmet
Printed abstracts: wills, 1419-1748 (*Wills, Registers and Monumental Inscriptions of the Parish of Barwick-in-Elmet, Co. York,* by G. D. Lumb).

Bradford
Printed abstracts: wills, 1392-1496 (*The Bradford Antiquary,* vol. 1, p. 201 and vol. 2, pp. 19, 169, 218, and 247).

Halifax
Printed abstracts: wills, 1348-1559 (*Halifax Wills,* by J. W. Clay and E. W. Crossley, vols. 1 and 2).

Leeds, Pontefract, Wakefield, Otley and district
Printed abstracts: wills and admons., 1391-1561 (*Testamenta Leodensia,* Thoresby Soc., vols. 2, 4, 9, 11, 15, 19, 27); wills, pre-Reformation (arranged by places) (Thoresby Soc., vols. 22 (Leeds, and Aberford – Guiseley), 24 (Harewood – Otley), 26 (Pontefract) and 33 (Rothwell – Woodkirk)).

NORTH WALES

These six counties were in the province of Canterbury and mainly in the dioceses of Bangor and/or St. Asaph; but with a very few parishes also in the dioceses of Chester (before 1541 Lichfield), Hereford and St. David's.

Anglesey was wholly in Bangor.

Caernarvonshire was wholly in Bangor except for 3 parishes in St. Asaph.

Denbighshire was mainly in St. Asaph, with 17 central parishes in Bangor, and 1 parish in Chester.

Flintshire was mainly in St. Asaph; with the 6 parishes (or parts of parishes) in the southern detachment, and the peculiar of Hawarden, in Chester.

Merionethshire was in Bangor (22 western parishes) and St. Asaph (13 eastern parishes).

Montgomeryshire was mainly in St. Asaph, with 7 southern parishes in Bangor, 2 parishes in the consistory of the archdeaconry of Brecon (diocese of St. David's), and 9 parishes or parts of parishes in the episcopal consistory of Hereford.

The records of all these courts are at the National Library of Wales, except for any surviving pre-1541 records relating to Denbighshire and Flintshire parishes in the diocese of Lichfield. The National Library of Wales is a conspicuous building on the eastern outskirts of Aberystwyth, overlooking the town. There is ample car-parking. Prior application should be made for a reader's ticket.

Prerogative Court of Canterbury and other courts having general jurisdiction – see page 1.

Consistory Court of Bangor (National Library of Wales, Aberystwyth. Tel. Aberystwyth 3816)

    Jurisdiction: see introductory note. Anglesey; nearly all Caernarvonshire; 17 parishes in Denbighshire; the western part of Merionethshire; and 7 parishes in Montgomeryshire.

    Index: wills, admons. and invs., 1635-1680 (card index, and in progress), 1700-1857 (calendar).

    Chronological list: wills, admons. and invs., 1681-1699 (calendar).

Consistory Court of St. Asaph (National Library of Wales)
Jurisdiction: see introductory note. 3 parishes in Caernarvonshire; most of Denbighshire; 13 parishes in Merionethshire; and most of Montgomeryshire.
Indexes: wills, 1565-1623, wills, admons. and invs., 1625, 1637-1648 (MS, 19th cent., alphabetical by Christian name); admons. and invs., 1583, 1584, 1606, 1609, 1612, 1623, wills, admons. and invs., 1660-1729 (calendar, alphabetical by Christian name); 1729-1820 (card index, surnames); 1821-1857 (calendar, surnames); m/f of calendar, 1583-1857, at SG.
Unindexed: wills, admons. and invs., 1627, 1631, 1633, 1634, 1636; wills, 1557-1637 (30), 1611-1622 (80, cos. Montgomery and Merioneth).

Consistory Court of Chester (National Library of Wales)
Jurisdiction: from 1542, the parish of Holt in Denbighshire and the southern detachment of Flint. Records relating these Welsh parishes have been separated from those for the remaining, English, part of the diocese. See also prerogative court of York, page 150.
Index: wills, admons. and invs., 1546-1830 (TS, extracted from the printed indexes below).
Printed indexes: wills, admons. and invs., 1546-1830 (with the rest of the diocese – for details see page 23).
Unindexed: wills, admons. and invs., 1831-1857.

Episcopal Consistory Court of Hereford (National Library of Wales)
Jurisdiction: 9 parishes or parts of parishes in Montgomeryshire.
For records and indexes see page 59.

Consistory Court of the Archdeaconry of Brecon (diocese of St. David's) (National Library of Wales, page 182)
Jurisdiction: the southern Montgomeryshire parishes of Kerry and Mochdre.

Peculiar Court of Hawarden (National Library of Wales)
Jurisdiction: Hawarden in Flintshire, diocese of Chester. Never inhibited. See also prerogative court of York, page 150.
Printed index: wills, admons. and invs., 1554-1800 (Flintshire Hist. Soc., vol. 4).
Other indexes: wills, admons. and invs., 1801-1857.

Consistory Court of Lichfield (Lichfield Joint Record Office)
Jurisdiction: before 1542, those Denbighshire and Flintshire parishes subsequently in the diocese of Chester (see above). Also, throughout, Penley in Flintshire (a chapelry in the parish of Ellesmore, Salop.)
For records and indexes see page 119.

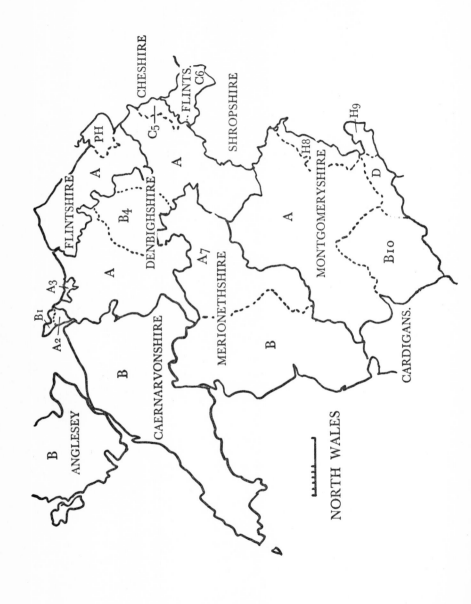

CHESHIRE

FLINTS.

C6

SHROPSHIRE

PH

C5

A

FLINTSHIRE

A

B4

DENBIGHSHIRE

H8

MONTGOMERYSHIRE

H9

A

D

B1

A3

B10

A2

A

A7

CAERNARVONSHIRE

MERIONETHSHIRE

CARDIGANS.

B

ANGLESEY

B

B

NORTH WALES

A=Diocese of St. Asaph; B=Diocese of Bangor; C=Diocese of Chester; D=Diocese of St. David's; H=Diocese of Hereford.

Caernarvonshire
Llandudno, B 1
Eglwys-Rhos, A 2
Llangystennin, A 2
Llysfaen, A 3

Denbighshire (B 4)
Clocaenog
Derwen
Efenechdyd
Gyffylliog
Llanbedr Dyffryn Clwyd
Llandyrnog
Llanelidan
Llanfair Dyffryn Clwyd
Llanfwrog
Llangwyfan
Llangynhafel
Llanhychan
Llanynys
Ruthin
Holt, C 5

Flintshire
Peculiar of Hawarden = PH
Southern Detachment, (C 5)
Bangor Iscoed
Hanmer
Overton
Threapwood
Worthenbury

Merionethshire (A 7)
Bettwys Gwerful Goch
Corwen
Gwyddelwern
Llandderfel
Llandrillo
Llanfawr
Llanger
Llangywer
Llanmawddwy
Llansanffraid-Glyndyfrdwy
Llanuwchllyn
Llanycil
Mallwyd

Montgomeryshire
Alderbury (partly Salop), H 8
Buttington, H 8
Carno, B 10
Churchstoke, H 9
Forden, H 8
Hyssington, H 9
Kerry (Ceri), D
Llandinam, B 10
Llangurig, B 10
Llanidloes, B 10
Llanwnnog, B 10
Mainstone (partly Salop), H 9
Mochdre, D
Montgomery, H 8
Penstrowed, B 10
Snead, H 9
Trefeglwys, B 10
Worthen (partly Salop), H 8

B=Archdeaconry of Brecon (Diocese of St. David's); D=Diocese of St. David's; H=Diocese of Hereford; L=Diocese of Llandaff.

Glamorgan (D 5)
Bishopton
Cheriton
Ilston
Knelston
Llanddewi
Llandeilo Tal-y-Bont
Llangenydd
Llangiwg
Llangyfelach
Llanmadog
Llanrhidian
Llansamlet
Loughor
Nicholaston
Oxwich
Oystermouth
Pennaen
Pennard
Penrice
Port Eynon
Reynoldston
Rhossili
Swansea

Radnor
Discoed, H 1
Knighton, H 1
Michaelchurch-on-Arrow, H 2
Norton, H 1
Presteigne, H 1
Old and New Radnor, H 1

Monmouth
Cwmyoy, B 3
Dixton Newton, H 4
Llanthony, B 3
Monmouth, H 4
Oldcastle, B 3

SOUTH WALES
AND MONMOUTHSHIRE

BRECKNOCK, CARDIGAN, CARMARTHEN, GLAMORGAN, MONMOUTH, PEMBROKE, RADNOR

These seven counties were in the province of Canterbury and almost entirely in the dioceses of St. David's and Llandaff, with eight parishes in the diocese of Hereford. Within the diocese of St. David's the archdeaconry of Brecon had its own independent consistory court.

Carmarthen, Cardigan and *Pembroke* (archdeaconry of St. David's) were wholly in the diocese of St. David's and the jurisdiction of its consistory court.

Brecknock was wholly and *Radnor* mainly in the archdeaconry of Brecon and the jurisdiction of its consistory court; 6 Radnorshire parishes were in the diocese of Hereford and the jurisdiction of the episcopal consistory of Hereford.

Glamorgan was mainly and *Monmouth* almost entirely in the diocese of Llandaff; but 23 parishes in the Gower peninsula in Glamorgan were in the diocese and consistory of St. David's (archdeaconry of Carmarthen), in Monmouth 3 parishes were in the archdeaconry of Brecon and 2 in the diocese and consistory of Hereford.

The records of all these courts are at the National Library of Wales. This is a conspicuous building on the eastern outskirts of Aberystwyth, overlooking the town. There is ample car-parking. Prior application should be made for a reader's ticket.

Prerogative Court of Canterbury and other courts having general jurisdiction – see page 1.

Episcopal Consistory Court of St. David's (National Library of Wales, Aberystwyth. Tel. Aberystwyth 3816)
>   Jurisdiction. Carmarthen, Cardigan and Pembroke; and the Gower parishes in Glamorgan. Occasional Brecon archdeaconry wills are to be found in this court, but they are very rare.

>   *Archdeaconry of Cardigan*
>>   Chronological lists: wills, admons. and invs., 1594-1596, 1600-1747 (cals.).
>>   Indexes: admons. (only), 1700-1740; wills and admons., 1746-1857 (cals.).

Episcopal Consistory Court of St. David's, contd.
  Archdeaconry of Carmarthen
    Chronological lists: wills, admons. and invs., 1594-1596, 1600-1816
    (cals.).
    Indexes: admons. (only), 1700-1733 (cal.); wills, admons. and invs.,
    1780-1816 (card index, in progress), 1817-1836 (card index), 1837-
    1857 (calendar); m/f of cal., 1600-1857 at SG.

  Archdeaconry of St. David's
    Chronological lists: wills, admons. and invs., 1594-1596, 1600-1629,
    1649-1653, 1700-1747 (calendars), m/f of calendar, 1694-1836, at
    SG.
    Indexes: admons. (only), 1700-1740, wills, admons. and invs., 1746-
    1857 (cal.).
  Index: unproved wills (all 3 archdeaconries), 1600-1857.

Consistory Court of the Archdeaconry of Brecon (National Library of
Wales)
  Jurisdiction: Brecknock, most of Radnor, and 3 parishes in Monmouth.
  Indexes: wills, 1570-1578, 1583-1589, 1612, 1620, 1621, 1632-1633,
  1637 (N.L.W. MS. 2911D); wills, admons. and invs., 1660-1677, wills,
  1694-1703 (calendars); wills, admons. and invs., 1733-1782 (endorsed
  'not reliable'); 1783-1857 (calendar).
  Chronological lists: wills, admons. and invs., 1678-1785 (calendars).
  Unindexed: wills, admons. and invs., 1603, 1609-1615, 1617-1618,
  1620-1658 (very few wills before 1620, or 1653-1658).

Consistory Court of Llandaff (National Library of Wales)
  Jurisdiction: most of Glamorgan and almost all of Monmouth.
  Index: wills, admons. and invs., 1575-1857 (calendar; m/f at SG).

Episcopal Consistory Court of Hereford (National Library of Wales)
  Jurisdiction: 2 parishes in Monmouth and 6 in Radnor.
  For records and indexes see page 59.

ISLE OF MAN

The Isle of Man was in the province of York and the diocese of Sodor and Man.

Until the end of 1884 it remained in the jurisdiction of the ecclesiastical courts, which alternated for parts of each year between those of the vicar general of the bishop and the official of the archdeacon.

The records of the two courts are kept together but are indexed separately. These continued without interruption at the time of the Commonwealth, although the see was vacant from 1644 to 1661 and the ecclesiastical officials were replaced by law 'judices' and a registrar. After the abolition of the archdeacon's court in 1874 the consistory court had sole jurisdiction, and from 1885 testamentary business has been in the High Court of Justice. Pre-1847 records are all now at the Manx Museum Library in Douglas, and later records are in the Deeds and Probate Registry.

Prerogative Court of Canterbury and other courts having general jurisdiction – see page 1.

Prerogative Court of York and other courts having jurisdiction in the province – see page 150.

Consistory Court of Sodor and Man (Manx Museum Library, Douglas)
  Indexes: wills, admons. and invs., 1659-1884 (after 1846 records are in the Deeds and Probate Registry).
  Unindexed: wills, admons. and invs., 1600-1659.

Archdeaconry Court of the Isle of Man (Manx Museum Library)
  Indexes: wills, admons. and invs., 1631-1884 (after 1846 records are in the Deeds and Probate Registry).

When the deceased lived or had property outside the island, his will might appear in a variety of other courts (in addition to the prerogative courts of Canterbury and York and their associated courts, mentioned above) – these include the Commissariot of Edinburgh (page 200), the prerogative court of Armagh (page 187) and the Irish Principal Registry (page 196), and the English consistory courts of Carlisle (page 27), Chester and Richmond (Western Deaneries) (pages 73-76); and, from 1858, the former Principal Probate Registry (page 6).

THE CHANNEL ISLANDS

The Channel Islands were in the province of Canterbury and diocese of Winchester, but have always been administered separately from that diocese.

Probate matters in Jersey were subject to the ecclesiastical court of the dean of Jersey as recently as 1949, and the records, which date from 1660, are now at The Greffe, Royal Court, in Jersey.

In Guernsey wills relating to personal estate only, and intestacies, are in the court of the commissary of the bishop of Winchester in the Bailiwick of Guernsey; the Bailiwick also include the islands of Alderney, Sark, Jethou and Herm. In this unique case the ecclesiastical court still retains jurisdiction in probate matters. Records date from 1660. Wills devising real estate, in Guernsey only, are to be found in the Royal Court of Guernsey, but records date from 1841 only. There can be no devise of real estate in Herm and Jethou, as these formerly belonged to the Crown and now to the States of Guernsey. In Sark all estates and any form of landed property whatsoever must descend intact to the heir until the fifth degree of kinship. Failing any such relatives the property reverts to the Seigneur absolutely. The widow has a right to dower on one third of real estate. There was a fixed rule of descent also for Alderney, so wills of realty were rare there, and in any case were all destroyed in the 1939-45 war.

Prerogative Court of Canterbury and other courts having general jurisdiction (in cases before 1858 when the deceased had property in England or Wales) – see page 1.

Ecclesiastical Court of the Dean of Jersey and (since 1949) *The Royal Court* (Judicial Greffe, Royal Court, Jersey. Tel. Jersey Central (0534) 33201, ext. 213)
  Indexes: wills of personalty, 1660-1964, admons., 1848-1964 (calendars, by volume); wills of personalty and admons., 1965-present day (card index since 1967). Wills of realty, 1851-present day (indexed with deeds of sale and hypothecation of real estate).

Court of the Commissary of the Bishop of Winchester in the Bailiwick of Guernsey (The Ecclesiastical Court of the Dean of Guernsey, 12 New Street, St. Peter Port, Guernsey. Tel. Guernsey (0481) 21732)
  Index: wills and admons., 1660 to the present day.

Royal Court of Guernsey (The Greffe, Royal Court, Guernsey)
  Index: wills, 1841 to the present day.

IRELAND

Before 1858 Ireland was subject to the over-riding jurisdiction of the archbishop of Armagh, and within his province there were some 28 dioceses with the normal consistory courts and at least two peculiars. There were no archdeaconry courts. Virtually all the records of these courts, and many of the records of their successors the Principal and District Probate Registries up to 1903 (for which see page 195), were destroyed by the explosion and fire which wrecked the Four Courts in Dublin in June 1922.

Indexes or calendars to most of these records survive in some form or other. There were already printed indexes to the prerogative court of Armagh to 1810 (for which MS abstracts of nearly all wills to 1800 survive); to the important diocese of Dublin (to 1857); and to eleven other southern and three northern consistory courts. Many of the calendars survived the explosion, and there are 19th century copies of others. In addition to most surviving material (some is at the Northern Ireland P.R.O.) the Irish Public Record Office in Dublin has consolidated indexes of wills and admons. from all Irish courts from October 1829 to 1879, and abstracts to 1839, originating in the Inland Revenue Office.

There are printed abstracts of surviving wills registered in respect of land at the Registry of Deeds, 1708-1785; printed indexes to will abstracts in the Genealogical Office at Dublin Castle; to miscellaneous will abstracts (mainly at the Society of Genealogists, before 1930), and printed abstracts of Quaker wills. The Public Record Offices in Dublin and in Belfast have printed lists of surviving and acquired wills, admons. and abstracts in various Reports, and both maintain card indexes and have sizeable collections of testamentary material.

Many testators also had property in England and Wales, and therefore also appear in the prerogative courts of Canterbury or York. Estate Duty Office will abstracts (mainly from P.C.C.) from 1821 to 1857 (and indexes from 1812) are at the Northern Ireland Public Record Office.

A Simple Guide to Irish Genealogy, by the Rev. Wallace Clare, 1937, 3rd edition revised by Rosemary ffolliott, 1966 (Irish Genealogical Research Society), and *In Search of Ancestry*, by Gerald Hamilton-Edwards (2nd edn., Phillimore, 1969), 'Irish Records', pp. 140-47, give valuable help with the special problems of Irish genealogy and records.

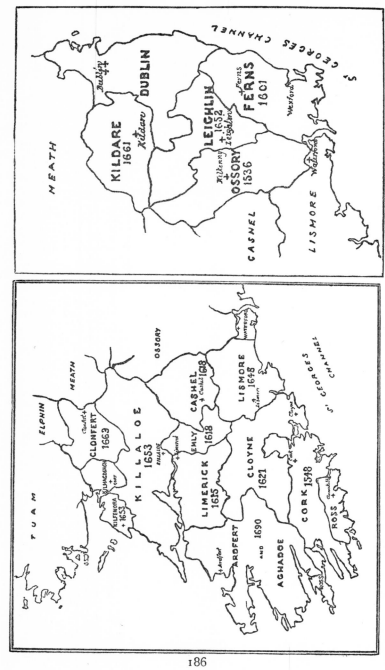

Dioceses in south-west and south-east Ireland, reproduced by kind permission, from Phillimore's *Irish Wills*, vols. 2 and 1.

Prerogative Court of the Archbishop of Armagh (Public Record Office, Dublin)

Virtually all the original records of this court were destroyed in 1922.

Jurisdiction: over-riding throughout Ireland.

Printed indexes: (destroyed) wills, 1536-1810 (42,000) (by Sir Arthur Vicars, 1897).

Surviving (copy) wills (not always complete), 1664-1684, 1706-1708, 1726-1729, 1777 (A-L), 1813 (K-Z), 1834 (A-E) (56th Report of the Deputy Keeper of Public Records in Ireland, pp. 79-197; also 14 orig. wills, in 55th Report, p. 30; these are all also included in *A Guide to Copies and Abstracts of Irish Wills*, by Rev. Clare Wallace, 1930, reptd. 1972).

Surviving (grant books of) admons., 1748-1751, 1839 (57th Report, pp. 62-324).

Other indexes to destroyed records: wills, 1811-1857, unproved wills, 1689-1857, invs., 1668-1857 (PRO Dublin).
'Additions to and corrections in Vicars' Index (TS, British Museum).
Wills (Northern Ireland testators), 1810-1857 (PRO Belfast).
Admons. (to which abstracts survive), 1595-1802 (5,000) (Irish Genealogical Research Soc., London).

Abstracts: (all) wills, 1536-1800 (37,000) (MS, by Sir William Betham, at PRO Dublin; annotated will pedigrees based on these abstracts, at the Genealogical Office, Dublin Castle, with another copy (unannotated) at PRO Belfast); wills in Greene MSS. (5 vols.) (at PRO Dublin, from Nat. Lib. of Ireland). Many other collections of abstracts are at the PRO Dublin and the PRO Belfast.
M/f of Betham's abstracts, from Phillipps' MS, partially indexed, at SG.

Consistory Courts

Virtually all the records of these courts were destroyed in 1922. Any surviving records are in PRO Dublin unless otherwise indicated.

ANTRIM. Mainly in diocese of Connor.

Printed index to surviving records: will and grant books, 1818-1820, 1853-1857 (56th Report, pp. 79-197); copies of wills, 1818-1820, also at PRO Belfast.

Other indexes (to destroyed records): wills 1661-1857, admons., 1636, 1661-1857 (copies also at PRO Belfast).

Printed indexes to abstracts: selected wills and admons., Crosslé colln. (in PRO Belfast, Reports of Deputy Keeper, 1925 Appx. F, 1933 Appx. B, 1938-45 p. 15), Swanzy colln. (at Genealogical Office, Dublin Castle, *Analecta Hibernica*, no. 17).

Small parts of the county were in the dioceses of Down and of Dromore (parish of Aghalee only) (see co. Down), and the parish of Ballyscullion only was in the diocese of Derry (see co. Londonderry).

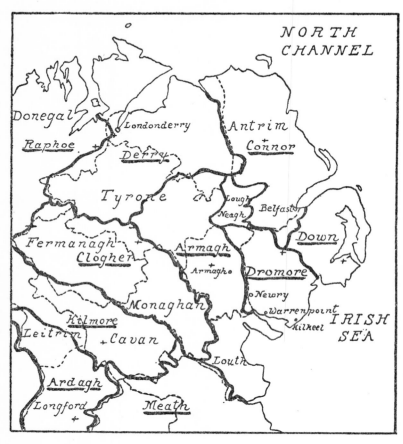

Dioceses and counties in north-eastern Ireland, reproduced, by kind permission, from Phillimore's *Irish Wills*, vols. 4 and 5. Names of dioceses are underlined, and their boundaries indicated by heavy lines; county boundaries by broken lines.

ARMAGH. Mainly in the diocese of Armagh.
   Indexes: wills, 1677-1857 (M-Y); 1687-1838 (19th cent. copy, at PRO
   Belfast, with photocopy at PRO Dublin); admons., 1600-1857 (PRO
   Belfast).
   Printed index to abstracts: selected wills and admons., Crosslé colln.
   (in PRO Belfast, Reports of Deputy Keeper, 1925 Appx. F, 1933
   Appx. B, 1938-45 p. 15).
   A small part of the county was in the diocese of Dromore (see Co.
   Down).

CARLOW. Entirely in the diocese of Leighlin.
   Printed indexes: wills, 1652-1800 (1,000) (Phillimore's Irish Wills, vol.
   1, pp. 36-61); admons., 1694-1845 (*The Irish Ancestor,* supp., 1972).
   Other indexes: wills (fragments), 1801-1857.

CAVAN. Mainly in the diocese of Kilmore.
   Indexes: wills, 1701-1857 (badly damaged); 1701-1838 (19th cent. copy,
   with photocopy also at PRO Belfast); admons., 1728-1857.
   Abstracts: selected wills and admons., 1694-1770 (Swanzy colln., at
   PRO Dublin, copies at PRO Belfast).
   Small parts of the county were in the dioceses of Ardagh (see co.
   Longford) and Meath (see co. Meath).

CLARE. Mainly in the diocese of Killaloe and Kilfenora.
   Printed index: wills, 1653-1800 (900) (Irish Wills, vol. 3, pp. 85-108);
   to surviving admons., 1845, and caveats, 1710-1714, 1722-1723 (57th
   Report, pp. 63-324).
   Other indexes: wills, 1801-1857 (fragments only), admons., 1704-1857.
   A small part of the county was in the diocese of Limerick (see co.
   Limerick).

CORK. Mainly in the dioceses of Cloyne, and of Cork and Ross.
   Printed indexes: wills, Cork and Ross, 1548-1800 (4,750); Cloyne, 1621-
   1800 (1,400) (Irish Wills, vol. 2).
   Other indexes: Cork and Ross, wills, 1801-1857, admons., 1612-1857;
   Cloyne, wills, 1801-1857 (damaged), 1808-1838 (19th cent. copy),
   admons., 1630-1857.
   A small part of the county was in the diocese of Ardfert (see co. Kerry).

DONEGAL. Mainly in the diocese of Raphoe.
   Printed index: wills, 1684-1857 (1,800) (Irish Wills, vol. 5, pp. 155-200).
   Other index: admons., 1684-1857.
   Surviving records: admon. grant book (with Derry), 1812-1857 (very
   badly damaged).
   Small parts of the county were in the dioceses of Derry (see co. London-
   derry) and Clogher (see co. Fermanagh).

Down. Mainly in the dioceses of Down and of Dromore, and the peculiar of Newry and Mourne.
Printed indexes: wills, Dromore, 1678-1857 (6,400), Newry and Mourne, 1727-1857 (600) (Irish Wills, vol. 4); to surviving wills, Down, 1850-1857 (56th Report, pp. 79-197); selected wills and admons., Down and Dromore, Crosslé colln. (in PRO Belfast, Reports of Deputy Keeper, 1925 Appx. F, 1933 Appx. B, 1938-45 p. 15), Swanzy colln. (863) (in Genealogical Office, Dublin Castle, *Analecta Hibernica,* no. 17).
Other indexes: Down, wills, 1681-1856, admons., 1684-1857 (also copies at PRO Belfast); Dromore, wills, 1801-1857 (damaged), admons., 1749-1857 (also copies at PRO Belfast), Newry and Mourne, admons., 1811-1845 (also copy at PRO Belfast), surviving will, 1826 (1).
Abstracts: Crosslé colln. (PRO Belfast), Swanzy colln. (Genealogical Office, Dublin Castle), as above.
A small part of the county was in the diocese of Connor (see co. Antrim).

Dublin. Entirely in the diocese of Dublin.
Printed indexes: wills and admons., 1638-1857 (30,000) (2 vols., appxs. to 26th Report (1895) and 30th Report (1899) of the Deputy Keeper of Public Records in Ireland); wills and invs., 1457-1483 (register at Trinity Coll., Dublin, Royal Soc. of Antiq. of Ireland, 1898).
Other index: admons., 1697-1845.

Fermanagh. Mainly in the diocese of Clogher.
Indexes: wills, 1661-1857 (also copy at PRO Belfast), 1658-1849 (19th cent. copy), admons., 1660-1857.
Printed index: selected wills and admons., Crosslé colln. (in PRO Belfast, Reports of Deputy Keeper, 1925 Appx. F, 1933 Appx. B, 1938-45 p. 15).
Abstracts: Crosslé colln., above; selected wills and admons., 1712-1750 (Swanzy colln., at PRO Dublin, copies at PRO Belfast).
A small part of the county was in the diocese of Kilmore (see co. Cavan).

Galway. Mainly in the dioceses of Clonfert and Kilmacduagh, and of Tuam.
Printed index: Clonfert and Kilmacduagh, wills, 1665-1857 (1,000), admons., c. 1778-1857 (500) (*The Irish Ancestor,* supp., 1970).
Other indexes: Tuam, wills, 1648-1857 (very badly damaged), admons., 1692-1857.
Small parts of the county were in the dioceses of Elphin (see co. Roscommon), and Killaloe and Kilfenora (see co. Clare).

Kerry. Entirely in the diocese of Ardfert and Aghadoe.
Printed index: wills, 1690-1800 (720) (Irish Wills, vol. 3, pp. 136-153).
Other indexes: wills, 1801-1857, admons., 1738-1837.

KILDARE. Partly in the diocese of Dublin (for which see co. Dublin) and partly in the diocese of Kildare.
Printed indexes: wills, 1661-1800 (500) (Irish Wills, vol. 1, pp. 128-142; and in *Journal of co. Kildare Arch. Soc.*, vol. 4, no. 6, 1905); admons., 1770-1848 (*Journ. co. Kildare Arch. Soc.*, vol. 5, no. 3, 1907).
Other index: wills, 1801-1857 (fragments).
Abstracts: wills, 1661-1826 (2 vols.).

KILKENNY. Mainly in the diocese of Ossory.
Printed indexes: wills, 1536-1800 (1,350) (Irish Wills, vol. 1, pp. 1-35); to surviving admons., 1845-1857 (57th Report, pp. 62-324).
Other indexes: wills, 1801-1857 (very badly damaged), admons., 1660-1857.
Abstracts: admons., 1738-1804 (in T.U. Sadleir collection, copied at PRO Dublin).
A small part of the county was in the diocese of Leighlin (see co. Carlow).

KING'S COUNTY (OFFALY). Mainly in the dioceses of Kildare (for which see co. Kildare), and Killaloe and Kilfenora (for which see co. Tipperary). Small parts of the county were in the dioceses of Clonfert (see co. Galway), Meath (see co. Westmeath) and Ossory (see co. Kilkenny).

LEITRIM. Mainly in the diocese of Kilmore (for which see co. Cavan) but partly in the diocese of Ardagh (see co. Longford).

LIMERICK. Mainly in the dioceses of Limerick, and (Cashel and) Emly.
Printed indexes: wills, Limerick, 1615-1800 (1,050) (Irish Wills, vol. 3, pp. 109-35), Cashel and Emly, 1618-1800 (vol. 3, pp. 1-36).
Other indexes: Limerick, wills, 1801-1857, admons., 1738-1837; Cashel and Emly, wills, 1801-1857, admons., 1644-1857, unproved wills, 1638-1856.
Surviving records: Cashel and Emly, probate and admon. grant books, 1840-1845.
A small part of the county was in the diocese of Killaloe (see co. Clare).

LONDONDERRY. The county was mainly in the diocese of Derry.
Printed index: wills, 1612-1857 ((6,150) (Irish wills, vol. 5, pp. 1-154).
Other indexes: admons., 1698-1857 (also copy at PRO Belfast).
Surviving records: admon. grant book, 1812-1851 (badly damaged).
Printed index to abstracts: selected wills and admons., Crosslé colln. (in PRO Belfast, Reports of Deputy Keeper, 1925 Appx. F, 1933 Appx. B, 1938-45 p. 15).
Small parts of the county were in the dioceses of Armagh (see co. Armagh) and Connor (see co. Antrim).

LONGFORD. Mainly in the diocese of Ardagh.
Printed index: wills, 1695-1857 (*The Irish Ancestor*, supp., 1971).
Other index: admons., 1697-1850.
A small part of the county was in the diocese of Meath (see co. Westmeath).

LOUTH. Mainly in the diocese of Armagh.
Indexes: wills, 1677-1857 (M-Y) (also copy from 1635 at PRO Belfast); 1666-1838 (A-L) (19th cent. copy at PRO Belfast, with photocopy at PRO Dublin); wills, Drogheda district, 1691-1846 (A-Y). Admons., 1600-1857 (at PRO Belfast).
Printed index to abstracts: selected wills and admons., Crosslé colln. (in PRO Belfast, Reports of Deputy Keeper, 1925 Appx. F, 1933 Appx. B, 1938-45 p. 15).
A small part of the county was in the diocese of Clogher (see co. Monaghan).

MAYO. In the dioceses of Killala and Achonry, and of Tuam.
Printed index: Killala and Achonry, wills, 1698-1838 (from 19th cent. copy), 1839-1857 (fragments only, from damaged calendar) (*The Irish Genealogist*, vol. 3, no. 12, pp. 506-19).
Other indexes: Killala and Achonry, admons., 1738-1837; Tuam, wills, 1648-1857 (very badly damaged), admons., 1692-1857.

MEATH. Mainly in the diocese of Meath.
Indexes: wills, 1572-1857 (fragments), 1635-1838 (19th cent. copy); admons., 1663-1857.
Small parts of the county were in the dioceses of Armagh (see co. Louth), Kildare (see co. Kildare) and Kilmore (see co. Cavan).

MONAGHAN. Entirely in the diocese of Clogher.
Indexes: wills, 1661-1857 (also copy at PRO Belfast), 1658-1849 (19th cent. copy), admons., 1660-1857.
Printed index: selected wills and admons., Crosslé colln. (in PRO Belfast, Reports of Deputy Keeper, 1925 Appx. F, 1933 Appx. B, 1938-45 p. 15).
Abstracts: Crosslé colln., above; selected wills and admons., 1712-1750 (Swanzy colln., at PRO Dublin, copies at PRO Belfast).

QUEEN'S COUNTY (LEIX). Mainly in the dioceses of Leighlin (for which see co. Carlow) and Ossory (for which see co. Kilkenny). Small parts of the county were in the dioceses of Kildare (see co. Kildare) and Dublin (see co. Dublin).

ROSCOMMON. Mainly in the diocese of Elphin.
Indexes: wills, 1650-1857 (fragments); 1669-1838 (19th cent. copy); admons., 1726-1857.
Small parts of the county were in the dioceses of Tuam and of Clonfert (see co. Galway), and of Ardagh (see co. Longford).

SLIGO. Mainly in the dioceses of Killala and Achonry (for which see co. Mayo) and of Elphin (for which see co. Roscommon). A small part of the county was in the diocese of Ardagh (see co. Longford).

TIPPERARY. Mainly in the dioceses of Cashel (and Emly), and of Killaloe (and Kilfenora).
Printed indexes: Cashel, wills, 1618-1800 (1,400) (Irish Wills, vol. 3, pp. 1-36); Killaloe, wills, 1653-1800 (vol. 3, pp. 85-108); to surviving admons., 1845, and caveats, 1710-1714, 1722-1723 (57th Report, pp. 63-324).
Other indexes: Cashel, wills, 1801-1857, admons. 1644-1857, unproved wills, 1638-1856; Killaloe, wills, 1801-1857 (fragments), admons., 1704-1857.
Surviving records: Cashel, probate and admon. grant books, 1840-1845; Killaloe, see printed indexes above.
A small part of the county was in the diocese of Waterford and Lismore (see co. Waterford).

TYRONE. Mainly in the dioceses of Derry (for which see co. Londonderry) and of Armagh (for which see co. Armagh). A small part of the county was in the diocese of Clogher (see co. Fermanagh).

WATERFORD. Entirely in the diocese of Waterford and Lismore, with the peculiar of the dean of Lismore.
Printed index: wills, 1645-1800 (1,900) (Irish Wills, vol. 3, pp. 37-84). Other indexes: wills, 1801-1857 (badly damaged), 1801-1838 (19th cent. copy); admons., 1661-1857 (peculiar of Lismore, 1766-1846 only); grants of probate and admon., 1650-1788, 1847-1857.

WESTMEATH. Mainly in the diocese of Meath.
Indexes: wills, 1572-1857 (fragments), 1635-1838 (19th cent. copy), admons., 1663-1857.
A small part of the county was in the diocese of Ardagh (see co. Longford).

WEXFORD. Mainly in the diocese of Ferns.
Printed index: wills, 1601-1800 (2,600) (Irish Wills, vol. 1, pp. 62-127). Other indexes: wills, 1801-1857 (fragments), admons., 1765-1833, grants of probate and admon., 1847-1857.
A small part of the county was in the diocese of Dublin (see co. Dublin).

WICKLOW. Mainly in the diocese of Dublin (for which see co. Dublin). Small parts of the county were in the dioceses of Ferns (see co. Wexford) and Leighlin (see co. Carlow).

193

Prerogative Court of Canterbury and other English ecclesiastical courts. Wills of many Irish dying or having possessions also in England or Wales are to be found, chiefly in P.C.C., but also in P.C.Y. and other courts.

Printed index: (P.C.C.) wills, 1634-1652 (*Journ. of Royal Soc. of Antiqs. of Ireland,* vol. 78, pt. 2, pp. 24-37).

Abstracts: (P.C.C.) wills, pre-1660, admons., 1559-1661 (by R. E. F. Garrett, at SG).

Other lists and indexes: (P.C.C.) wills, 1661-1700 (by R. E. F. Garrett, at SG); (P.C.C.) wills and admons., 1751-1775 (by R. M. Glencross, at Irish Genealogical Research Soc., London, and at Phillimore & Co. Ltd., Shopwyke Hall, Chichester).

Note. The printed index to wills in the Prerogative Court of Armagh (see above) includes some 1,500 'copy wills', where grants of double probate are recorded. These are most likely to be found duplicated in P.C.C., but will not necessarily appear in the index by R. E. F. Garrett.

Estate Duty Office (Public Record Office of Northern Ireland, 66 Balmoral Avenue, Belfast BT9 6NY. Tel. Belfast (0232) 661621)

The records of this office are described on page 4. Indexes and abstracts relating to Ireland were recently transferred to Belfast.

Indexes: (all English prerogative and consistory courts) wills, 1812-1857.

Abstracts: wills, 1821 (letter K on)-1857 (over 2,000) (the first 545 wills, 1812-1821, were destroyed).

Inland Revenue Office (Public Record Office, Dublin)

Indexes: (all prerogative and consistory) wills, 1828-1879 (26 vols.), admons., 1828-1879 (16 vols.).

Abstracts of the above: wills and admons., 1 Oct. 1828-31 Dec. 1839 (28 vols.). The abstracts 1840-1879 are missing.

Office of Charitable Donations and Bequests, Dublin

Abstracts (of all wills leaving a bequest of charitable nature): wills, from 1800 to date. Details published from about 1825 in the *Dublin Gazette.*

Indexes: 1800-1828, 1840-1857 (at PRO, Dublin – for 1828-1839 see Inland Revenue Wills, above).

Copy abstracts: 1805, 1814 (by T. U. Sadleir, at the Genealogical Office, Dublin Castle, and indexed in *Analecta Hibernica,* no. 17).

Registry of Deeds (Henrietta Street, Dublin)

This registry was established in 1708, and many will abstracts are included in its now gigantic collection.

Printed abstracts: wills, 1708-1785 (1,464) (Irish MSS. Commission, 2 vols.; 1786-1827, in preparation).

Index: grantors of wills, 1708-1800 (2,000) (MS, copies at PRO, Dublin, PRO, Belfast, and Genealogical Office, Dublin Castle).

Society of Friends (Friends' Meeting House, 6 Eustace Street, Dublin)
Printed abstracts: Monthly Meeting, Carlow, wills and invs., 1675-1740;
Edenderry, wills, 1628-1763; Mountmellick, wills, 1755-1795; co.
Wexford, wills, 1680-1760; Dublin, wills, 1683-1772 (224 in all)
(*Quaker Records, Dublin,* Irish MSS. Comm., 1957); wills, 1654-1860
(50) (*Guide to Irish Quaker Records,* Dublin, Irish MSS. Comm.,
1967).

Society of Friends (Friends' Meeting House, Railway Street, Lisburn)
Printed abstracts: Ballyhagan Meeting Book, wills, 1685-1740 (28)
(*The Irish Genealogist,* vol. 2, no. 8, Oct. 1950).

Public Record Office, Dublin
Printed indexes: miscellaneous wills received between 1922 and 1930
(2,960) (Appendixes to 55th, 56th and 57th Reports of the Deputy
Keeper).
Other index: wills (and other probate records) which survived the 1922
fire or have been acquired since (including the above) (around 20,000)
(card index).

Public Record Office, Belfast
Printed indexes: wills, etc., are indexed in the Reports of the Deputy
Keeper of the Public Records in Northern Ireland following their
receipt.
Other index: copy wills, etc., acquired since 1922 (card index).

The Genealogical Office, Dublin Castle
Printed index: wills in various MS collections (excluding the Betham
will pedigrees), some 7,500 in all (compiled by Miss P. B. Eustace,
Analecta Hibernica, no. 17, pp. 147-348, Irish MSS. Comm., 1949).

Representative Body of the Church of Ireland Library (Church of Ireland
House, Church Avenue, Rathmines, Dublin 6)
Abstracts (1,500) made by W. H. Welpley (57pp TS index) (copies of
many of these are at SG; many are at PRO Belfast, and others at
the Genealogical Office, Dublin Castle, and have appeared in the
printed indexes to these collections).

Wills and Admons. from 1858

As in England and Wales, from 1858 probate matters were transferred from ecclesiastical to civil jurisdiction. The Principal Registry
at Dublin also acted as a district registry for the Dublin area, and
there were in addition 11 separate district registries. In the 1922
explosion it was generally speaking the Principal Registry records
to 1903 that were lost, and the original wills from the district
registries. Fortunately the will books had remained in the district

registries, though these do not contain copies of all wills proved. There are also still surviving consolidated indexes of wills and admons. for both principal and district registries from 1858, and for district registry unproved wills. The most serious loss is for the jurisdiction of the Principal Registry, the counties of Dublin, Kildare, Wicklow, Meath and part of King's County or Offaly.

The surviving records are now divided between the Irish Public Record Office in Dublin and the Northern Ireland Public Record Office in Belfast. The latter hold the records of the district registries of Armagh, Belfast and Londonderry, and these include 19th century records of cos. Louth, Monaghan and Donegal, all now in Eire. Grant books of probate for these three district registries and some other records remain at the P.R.O., Dublin. Records of the remaining district registries are all now at the P.R.O., Dublin, including will books from 1858 (those for the Ballina district, most of cos. Mayo, Sligo and Leitrim, survive from 1865 only), some grant books of probate, and other testamentary material.

The consolidated printed indexes of the Principal and District Probate Registries for England and Wales, in London, also include many hundreds of Irish wills and admons. resealed in London. For the period 1858-1876 they are in a separate section following the letter 'Z', and thereafter in the main index. The same is the case in the Scottish commissary court of Edinburgh (see pages 197-200).

Principal Registry, Dublin (Public Record Office, Dublin)
   Jurisdiction: cos. Dublin, Kildare, Wicklow, Meath and part of King's County or Offaly.
   Indexes (to destroyed records): wills and admons. (principal and district registries consolidated), 1858-1906; unproved wills, 1858-1905.
   Surviving records: (copy) wills, 1874 (G-M), 1878, 1891 (G-M), 1896 (A-F); and from 1904 on. (Copy) (district) wills, 1869 (G-M), 1891 (M-P), 1901 (A-F). (Original) wills, etc., some for 1859, 1866, 1869, 1872-1873, 1875, 1878, 1881-1884, 1886-1887, 1891-1897, 1899, 1900 (all years very badly damaged); and from 1904 on. Admons., some for 1867, 1869, 1878, 1881-1882, 1888-1892, 1894, 1898-1900, 1903 (all years very badly damaged); and from 1904 on.
   Records of the district registries, including will books, called in after 1922, are also at PRO Dublin (or, for most of Northern Ireland, at PRO Belfast), as are surviving records from the Four Courts.

SCOTLAND

In Scotland, as in the rest of the British Isles, testaments were originally subject to ecclesiastical jurisdiction. The area in which each court functioned, named after the actual official commissary, was known as a 'commissariot', and although the bishops' authority was abolished in 1560, until 1823 these districts remained based on the old dioceses, which often did not coincide with county boundaries, and in some cases were intermingled.

The principal commissary court was that of Edinburgh, which had over-riding jurisdiction over the inferior courts, and over all persons without fixed domicile, or dying domiciled abroad ('furth' of Scotland) but with possessions in Scotland, in addition to a purely local jurisdiction. Indexes to this court, whose records commence as early as 1514, should always be consulted as well as those of local courts. The commissariot districts continued with some augmentation until 1823, and the Scottish Record Society has published indexes to 1800 of all surviving testaments in these courts. For the period 1801-1823 there are separate TS indexes at the Scottish Record Office (where all the pre-1823 records are) for the commissariots of Edinburgh (to 1829), Glasgow, Peebles (to 1827) and St. Andrews, and a consolidated TS index to the remaining commissariots throughout Scotland. After Edinburgh itself, the most important courts were Glasgow and St. Andrews, with considerable and early records; conversely, pre-1800 testaments for Ross are entirely wanting, survive for only a few years for Peebles, for Caithness, and for Orkney and Shetland, and are very few in number for Wigtown and for the Isles.

In 1823 the old commissariot jurisdictions were abolished, and replaced by commissary courts based on the sheriffdoms, at that time generally the same as the counties. From the start Perthshire and Argyll were each split into two sheriff court districts, and so was Angus from 1832.

The commissariot of Edinburgh was at first exempted from this reorganisation, and until 1830 continued its local jurisdiction over all the Lothians, when separate courts for Haddington and Linlithgow were established. The dual role of the court for the county or sheriffdom of Edinburgh, and over persons dying 'furth' of Scotland continued. From 1858 there is a separate class of 'probates resealed' for the wills of testators already proved in London or Dublin, but

SCOTLAND

Key numbers will be found
against each county in the text.

ORKNEY
AND
SHETLAND

*Commissariot
of the Isles*

(all islands except
Orkney and
Shetland)
Arran (Butes.), 33
Bute, 27 Harris (Inv.), 4
Lewis (Ross), 3
Mull (Arg.), 15 Skye (Inv.), 6

ISLES

CAITHNESS

ROSS

ABERDEEN

MORAY

INVERNESS

ST.ANDREWS
AND
BRECHIN

DUNKELD

ARGYLL

DUNBLANE

STIRLING

ST.ANDREWS

EDINBURGH

LAUDER

GLASGOW

LANARK

PEEBLES

DUMFRIES

KIRKCUDBRIGHT

ENGLAND

WIGTOWN

with possessions in Scotland as well as England, Wales or Ireland, which continued until 1971, and these did not need confirmation in the commissary court. Similarly many Scottish wills and admons. resealed in London are included in the consolidated printed indexes of the Principal and District Probate Registries for England and Wales (page 6). For the period 1858-1876 they are in a separate section following the letter 'Z' and a similar section of Irish entries, and thereafter are in the main index. The commissary or sheriff court of Edinburgh continued to have jurisdiction over all persons without fixed domicile, and it is therefore advisable to continue to search this in addition to any local court.

There are consolidated printed indexes to *Personal Estates of Defuncts* arranged in three groups : the Lothians, 1827-1865; Argyll, Bute, Dunbarton, Lanark and Renfrew, 1846-1865; and the remainder of Scotland, 1846-1867. These only give date of death and year of recording, but are an indication of the existence (or otherwise) of a confirmation.

From 1876 an annual consolidated calendar of confirmations has been prepared, either printed or (latterly) on microfilm, which can be examined in the Legal Search Room at the Register House in Edinburgh. The testamentary records themselves are still retained by the relevant sheriff clerk except where shown as having been deposited at the S.R.O. In the years since 1876 the sheriffdoms have been merged into much larger groupings, so that each now includes several counties which themselves form one or more sheriff court districts dealing in testamentary business and holding records. The *Scottish Law Directory* lists these and the parishes in each particular sheriff court district.

Under Scottish law before 1868 only personal (moveable) property could be bequeathed. Confirmation of a 'testament testamentar' was the equivalent of probate of an English will, and, in cases of intestacy, the appointment of an executor by the court (generally a near relative) was called a 'testament dative' (though this is likely to contain more information than English letters of admon.). The considerable records arising out of the Scottish laws of inheritance of real estate are outside the scope of this guide. They provide much information for the genealogist, and are fully described by Gerald Hamilton-Edwards, *In Search of Scottish Ancestry* (Phillimore, 1972), chapters 6-9, and by D. J. Steel, *Sources for Scottish Genealogy and Family History* (National Index of Parish Registers, vol. 12) (Phillimore, for the Society of Genealogists, 1970), pages 152-165. The former also gives a useful list of all pre-1855 parishes showing county and commissariot (Appx. D, pp. 201-12).

Commissariots and Sheriff Courts (Scottish Record Office, PO Box 36, HM General Register House, Edinburgh EH1 3YY. Tel. Edinburgh (031) 556 6585)
Records of the commissariots before 1823 are all in the S.R.O. Records of the commissary and sheriff courts after that date remain with sheriff clerks unless deposited at the S.R.O.

Commissariot of Edinburgh
Jurisdiction: see introductory note. Over persons without fixed domicile or dying 'furth of Scotland'; locally in the Lothians until 1830; originally also in Peebles and part of Stirlingshire. Pre-20th century records are now at the S.R.O.
Printed indexes: testaments, 1514-1600 (15,500) (Scottish Record Soc., vol. 1, and Index Lib., vol. 16), 1601-1700 (22,500) (S.R.S., vol. 2), 1701-1800 (14,800) (S.R.S., vol. 3). Miscellaneous executry papers preserved in HM Register House (not technically part of the commissariot records), 1481-1740 (170) (S.R.S., 1904).
Other indexes: testaments, 1801-1829 (TS; also MS, 1801-1830, at SG).
The parishes of Abercorn (Linlithgow) and Aberlady (Haddington) were in the commissariot of Dunkeld (see Perthshire).
From 1830 there were three courts, for the sheriffdom and county of Edinburgh (Midlothian) together with those dying 'furth' of Scotland, for Haddington (East Lothian) and for Linlithgow (West Lothian).
Printed indexes: to personal estates of defuncts (for all these courts, consolidated), 1827-1865.
Other indexes: Edinburgh, 1808-1901 (MS), probates resealed (see introductory note), 1858-1900 (TS); Haddington, 1830-1898 (TS); Linlithgow, 1831-1897 (TS).

ABERDEEN (10) AND BANFF (9). Until 1823 mainly in the commissariot of Aberdeen.
Printed index: testaments, 1715-1800 (3,450) (S.R.S., vol. 6).
Other indexes: testaments and invs., 1657-1747 (with gaps) (TS), 1801-1823 (TS).
The central Banff parishes of Aberlour, Botriphnie, Grange, Inveravon, Inverkeithny, Keith, Kirkmichael, Marnoch and Rothiemay, and the north-western Aberdeen parishes of Gartly, Glass and Rhynie were in the commissariot of Moray (see Moray and Nairn).
The post-1823 records of the former sheriffdoms of Aberdeen and Banff remain respectively at the sheriff courts of Aberdeen and Banff.
Printed index: personal estates of defuncts, 1846-1867.

ANGUS (OR FORFARSHIRE) (14) AND KINCARDINESHIRE. Until 1823 the commissariots of St. Andrews and Brechin had intermingled jurisdiction in most of Angus (see key to parishes). Kincardine was in the commissariot of St. Andrews (13) except for the parishes of Glenbervie and Strachan in the commissariot of Brechin (12).

ANGUS AND KINCARDINESHIRE contd.

Printed indexes: testaments, St. Andrews, 1549-1551, 1583-1676 (with gaps), 1681-1800 (S.R.S., vol. 8), Brechin, 1576-1800 (S.R.S., vol. 13).

Other indexes: testaments, St. Andrews, 1801-1823 (TS), Brechin, 1801-1823 (TS).

The Angus parishes of Auchterhouse, Fearn, Ruthven and Tealing were in the commissariot of Dunkeld (see Perthshire).

The records of the former sheriffdom of Angus or Forfar (from 1832 split into the sheriff court districts of Dundee and Forfar) are now at the S.R.O.

Indexes: Forfar, 1824-1958 (MS), Dundee, 1832-1958 (MS).

The post-1823 records of the former sheriffdom of Kincardine remain at the sheriff court of Stonehaven.

Printed index: personal estates of defuncts (both counties), 1846-1867.

The pre-1823 commissariot jurisdictions of parishes in Angus.
B=Brechin; K=Dunkeld; A=St. Andrews.

Aberlemno, A	Fearn, K	Lundie, A
Airlie, A	Forfar, A	Mains, A
Alyth, K	Glamis, A	Maryton, B
Arbirlot, A	Glenisla, B or A	Menmuir, K
Arbroath, A	Guthrie, B	Monifieth, A
Auchterhouse, K	Inverarity, A	Monikie, B
Barry, A	Inverkeillour, A	Montrose, B
Benvie, A	Kettins, A	Murroes, A
Brechin, B	Kingoldrum, A & B	Newtyle, A
Careston, B	Kinnaird, B	Novar, B
Carmyllie, B	Kinnell, A	Oathlaw, B
Clova, B	Kinnettles, A	Panbryde, B
Cortachy, B	Kirkden, A	Rescobie, A
Craig, A	Kirriemuir, A	Ruthven, K
Dun, A	Lethnot, B	St. Vigeans, A
Dundee, B or A	Liff, A	Stracathro, B
Dunnichen, B	Lintrathen, A	Strathmartin, A
Eassie, A	Lochlee, B	Tannadice, A
Edzell, A	Logie-Pert, A	Tealing, K
Farnell, B	Lunan, A	

ARGYLL. Until 1823 the mainland was in the commissariot of Argyll (16) and the islands were in the commissariot of the Isles (15).

Printed indexes: testaments, Argyll, 1674-1800 (2,350) (S.R.S., vol. 9), The Isles, 1661-1675, 1709-1800 (S.R.S., vol. 11); invs., Argyll, 1693-1702 (S.R.S., 1909).

Other index: testaments, 1801-1819 (TS).

Records of the former sheriffdom of Argyll (sheriff courts of Inveraray and Dunoon) are now at the S.R.O.

Index: Inveraray, 1815-1900 (TS).

Other records: Dunoon, from 1815.

Printed index: personal estates of defuncts, 1846-1865.

AYR (34), DUNBARTON (23) AND RENFREW (28). Until 1823 almost entirely in the commissariot of Glasgow.

Printed index: testaments, 1547-1555, 1563-1565, 1602-1692 1694-1701, 1706-1708, 1717-1800 (S.R.S., vol. 7).

Other index: testaments, 1801-1823 (TS).

The parish of Renfrew, part of Cathcart (Renfrews.), and part of Card-ross (Dunbarton), were in the commissariot of Hamilton and Campsie (see Lanarkshire); during the Commonwealth, testaments of the parish of New Kilpatrick (Dunbarton) are found in the commissariot of Stirling (see Stirlingshire).

Records of the sheriffdoms of Ayr (sheriff courts of Ayr and, since 1903, of Kilmarnock), Dunbarton (sheriff court of Dumbarton) and Renfrew (sheriff court of Paisley), are now at the S.R.O.

Indexes: Ayr, 1824-1938 (TS), Kilmarnock, 1903-1935; Dumbarton, from 1824 (indexes to individual vols. only); Paisley, 1824-1899 (TS).

Printed index: personal estates of defuncts, Ayr, 1846-1867, Dunbarton and Renfrew, 1846-1865.

BANFF (9). See with Aberdeen.

BERWICK (32). Until 1823 wholly in the commissariot of Lauder.

Printed index: testaments, 1561-1566, 1627-1634 (fragments); 1634-1800 (S.R.S., vol. 18).

Other index: testaments, 1801-1823 (TS).

The post-1823 records of the former sheriffdom of Berwick remain at the sheriff court of Duns.

Printed index: personal estates of defuncts, 1846-1867.

BUTE (27). Until 1823 wholly in the commissariot of the Isles.

Printed index: testaments, 1661-1675, 1709-1800 (500) (S.R.S., vol. 11).

Other index: testaments, 1801-1823 (TS).

The post-1823 records of the former sheriffdom of Bute remain at the sheriff court of Rothesay.

Printed index: personal estates of defuncts, 1846-1865.

CAITHNESS (1) AND SUTHERLAND (2). Until 1823 wholly in the commissariot of Caithness.

Printed index: testaments, 1622-1623 (3), 1661-1664 (300) (S.R.S., vol. 10).

Other index: testaments, 1803-1827 (TS).

The post-1823 records of the former sheriffdoms of Caithness and Sutherland remain at the sheriff courts of Wick and Dornoch respectively.

CLACKMANNAN (22). See with Stirling.

CROMARTY. See ROSS.

DUMFRIES (39). Until 1823 wholly in the commissariot of Dumfries.
Printed index: testaments, 1624-1800 (with gaps) (4,300) (S.R.S., vol. 14 – for 1693-1716 (250) see pp. 88-92).
Other index: testaments, 1801-1829 (TS).
The post-1823 records of the former sheriffdom of Dumfries remain at the sheriff court of Dumfries.
Printed index: personal estates of defuncts, 1846-1867.

DUNBARTON (23). See with Ayr.
EAST LOTHIAN (HADDINGTON) (31). See with Edinburgh, page 200.
EDINBURGH (MIDLOTHIAN) (30) See page 200.
ELGIN (8). See Moray.

FIFE (21) AND KINROSS (20). Until 1823 mainly in the commissariot of St. Andrews.
Printed index: testaments, 1549-1551, 1583-1676 (with gaps), 1681-1800 (21,000) (S.R.S., vol. 8).
Other index: testaments, 1801-1823 (TS).
For Aberdour, Leslie and Strathmiglo, in Fife, see also the commissariot of Dunkeld, and for Fossaway, in Kinross, see also the commissariot of Dunblane (both under Perthshire); for Muckhart, in Kinross, and Carnock, Saline and Torryburn, in Fife, see the commissariot of Stirling (under Stirlingshire).
Records of the former sheriffdom of Fife (sheriff court of Cupar) are now at the S.R.O. The county is now divided into the sheriff court districts of Cupar, Dunfermline and Kirkcaldy. Records of the former sheriffdom of Kinross are now at the S.R.O.
Indexes: Cupar, 1823-1892 (TS); Kinross, from 1847 (indexes to individual vols. only).
Other records: Kirkcaldy, post-1960 only.
Printed index: personal estates of defuncts (both counties), 1846-1867.

FORFAR (14). See Angus.
HADDINGTON (EAST LOTHIAN) (31). See with Edinburgh, page 200.

INVERNESS (11). Until 1823 mainland parishes were mainly in the commissariot of Inverness.
Printed index: testaments, 1630-1634, 1666-1670, 1676-1681, 1713-1800 (S.R.S., vol. 4, and Index Lib., vol. 20).
Other index: testaments, 1801-1824 (TS).
The isles (6) lay in the commissariot of the Isles (see Argyllshire). The mainland parishes of Glenelg, Kilmallie and Kilmonivaig were in the commissariot of Argyll (see Argyllshire), and the parish of Petty was in the commissariot of Moray (see Moray and Nairn).
The post-1824 records of the former sheriffdom of Inverness remain at the sheriff court of Inverness.
Printed index: personal estates of defuncts, 1846-1867.

KINCARDINE (12 and 13). See with Angus.
KINROSS (20). See with Fife.

KIRKCUDBRIGHT (40). Until 1823 mainly in the commissariot of Kirkcudbright.
Printed index: executry papers, 1663-1800 (1,400) (S.R.S., vol. 17).
Other index: 1800-1824 (TS).
The south-eastern parishes of Colvend, Kirkbean, Kirkpatrick-Durham, Kirkpatrick-Irongray, Lochrutton, New Abbey, Terregles and Troqueer were in the commissariot of Dumfries (see Dumfriesshire), and the extreme western parish of Minnigaff was in the commissariot of Wigtown (see Wigtownshire).
The post-1824 records of the former sheriffdom of Kirkcudbright remain at the sheriff court of Kirkcudbright.
Printed index: personal estates of defuncts, 1846-1867.

LANARK. Until 1823 the commissariots of Glasgow and of Hamilton and Campsie had intermingled jurisdiction in the north-western half of the county (29), and the south-eastern part was in the commissariot of Lanark (35) (see key to parishes).
Printed indexes: testaments, Glasgow, 1547-1555, 1563-1565, 1602-1692, 1694-1701, 1717-1800 (27,500) (S.R.S., vol. 7); Hamilton and Campsie, 1564-1576, 1591-1642, 1651-1800 (S.R.S., vol. 5, and Index Lib., vol. 20); Lanark, 1595-1602, 1620-1658 (with gaps), 1661-1800 (6,000) (S.R.S., vol. 18).
Other indexes: testaments, Glasgow, 1801-1823 (TS); Hamilton and Campsie, and Lanark, 1801-1823 (TS).
The records of the former sheriffdom of Lanark (sheriff court of Glasgow) are now at the S.R.O., as well as those of the sheriff courts of Lanark, Airdrie, and Hamilton, which were not established until 1888.
Printed indexes: Glasgow, personal estates of defuncts, 1846-1865.
Other indexes: Glasgow, from 1817 (indexes to individual vols. only); Hamilton, 1888-1899 (TS).
Other records: Lanark and Airdrie, post-1888.

The pre-1823 commissariot jurisdictions of parishes in Lanarkshire.
G=Glasgow; H=Hamilton and Campsie; L=Lanark.

Avondale, G	Covington, L	Lanark, L
Barony, G	Crawford, L	Lesmahagow, L
Biggar, L	Crawfordjohn, L	Libberton, L
Blantyre, G	Culter, L	New Monkland, H
Bothwell, G	Dalserf, H	Old Monkland, H
Cadder, G & H	Dalziel, G	Pettinam, L
Cambuslang, G	Dolphinton, L	Roberton, L
Cambusnethan, G	Douglas, L	Rutherglen, G
Carluke, L	Dunsyre, L	Shotts, H
Carmichael, L	Glasgow city, G	Stonehouse, G
Carmunnock, G	Glassford, G	Symington, L
Carnwath, L	Gorbals, H	Walston, L
Carstairs, L	Govan, H	Wandell, L
Cathcart (pt.), H & G	Hamilton, H or L	Wiston, L
	East Kilbride, H	

LINLITHGOW (WEST LOTHIAN) (26). See with Edinburgh, page 200.
MIDLOTHIAN (EDINBURGH) (30). See page 200.

MORAY (ELGIN) (8) AND NAIRN (7). Until 1823 wholly in the commissariot of Moray.
Printed index: testaments, 1684-1800 (1,400) (S.R.S., vol. 20).
Other index: testaments, 1801-1827 (TS).
The post-1827 records of the former sheriffdoms of Moray (sheriff court of Elgin) and Nairn remain respectively at the sheriff courts of Elgin and Nairn.
Printed index: personal estates of defuncts, 1846-1867.

ORKNEY AND SHETLAND. Until 1823 wholly in the commissariot of Orkney and Shetland.
Printed index: testaments and invs., Orkney, 1611-1684 (2,750), Shetland, 1611-1649 (1,000) (S.R.S., vol. 21).
Other indexes: testaments and invs., 1685-1689 (TS); confirmations, 1806-1823, invs., 1809-1831 (TS).
Records of the former sheriffdoms of Orkney (sheriff court of Kirkwall) and Shetland (sheriff court of Lerwick) remain at the sheriff courts.
Printed index: personal estates of defuncts, 1846-1867.

PEEBLES (36), ROXBURGH (38), AND SELKIRK (37). Until 1823 wholly in the commissariot of Peebles.
Printed index: testaments, 1681-1699 (600) (S.R.S., vol. 12).
Other index: testaments and invs., 1801-1827 (TS).
A few pre-Reformation testaments for these counties may be found in the commissariot of Glasgow (see Lanarkshire). Peebles-shire was originally in the commissariot of Edinburgh, page 200, but later was removed.
Records of the former sheriffdom of Peebles are now at the S.R.O.
Indexes: from 1814 (indexed by individual vol. only).
The post-1823 records of the former sheriffdoms of Roxburgh and Selkirk remain respectively at Jedburgh and Selkirk.
Printed index: personal estates of defuncts (all counties), 1846-1867.

PERTH. Until 1823 mainly in the commissariots of Dunkeld (the northern part) (17) and Dunblane (the southern part) (18), and with a number of parishes in the populous south-west in the commissariot of St. Andrews (19) (see key to parishes).
Printed indexes: testaments, Dunblane, 1539-1547, 1553-1558, 1598-1637, 1652-1800 (9,000) (S.R.S., vol. 15); Dunkeld, 1682-1800 (2,650) (S.R.S., vol. 16); St. Andrews, 1549-1551, 1583-1676 (with gaps), 1681-1800 (S.R.S., vol. 8).
Other indexes: testaments, Dunblane, 1655-1659 (TS), Dunkeld, 1663; Dunblane, 1801-1825, and Dunkeld, 1801-1823 (TS), St. Andrews, 1801-1823 (TS).

PERTH contd.

During the Commonwealth (1652-1659) a separate register was kept for the whole county, and this is included in the printed index of the testaments for the commissariot of Dunblane.

From 1824 the former sheriffdom of Perth was split into the sheriff court districts of Dunblane and Perth, records of which are now at the S.R.O.

Indexes: Dunblane, 1824-1900 (TS), Perth, 1824-1900 (TS).

Printed index: personal estates of defuncts, 1846-1867.

The pre-1823 commissariot jurisdictions of parishes in Perthshire.
A=St. Andrews; D=Dunblane; K=Dunkeld.

Aberdalgie, K	Dunblane, D	Lecropt (pt.), D
Aberfoyle, D	Dunkeld, K	Lethendy, K
Abernethy, D	Dunning, D	Logie, D
Abernytie, K	Errol, A	Logierait, K
Alyth, K	Findo-Gask, D	Longforgan, A
Arngask (pt.), K	Forgandenny, K	Madderty, K
Auchterarder, D	Forteviot, A	Meigle, K
Auchtergaven, K	Fortingall, K	Methven, A
Balquhidder, D	Foss, K	Moneydie, K
Bendochy, A	Fowlis-Easter, A	Monzie, D
Blackford, D	Fowlis-Wester, D	Monzievaird, D
Blair-Atholl, K	Glendevon, D	Moulin, K
Blairgowrie, A	Inchture, A	Muckhart, A
Callander, D	Kenmore, K	Muthill, D
Caputh, K	Killin, K	Perth, A
Cargill, K	Kilmadock, D	Port of Menteith, D
Cluny, K	Kilspindie, A	Rattray, K
Collace, A	Kincardine, D	Redgorton, K
Comrie, D	Kinclaven, K	Rhynd, A
Coupar-Angus, K	Kinfauns, A	St. Madoes, D
Crieff, K	Kinloch, K	St. Martins, K
Culross, D	Kinloch-Rannoch, K	Scone, A
Dowally, K	Kinnaird, A	Tibbermore, K
Dron, D	Kinnoul, A	Trinity-Gask, D
Dull, K	Kippen (pt.), D	Tulliallan, D & A
Dunbarnie, A	Kirkmichael, K	Weem, K

RENFREW (28). See with Ayr.

ROSS AND CROMARTY (5). Until 1823 mainland parishes were wholly in the commissariot of Ross.

Index: testaments, 1802-1824 (TS).

Other records: warrants of invs., 1682-1685, 1715-1770 (with gaps), 1784-1823.

Lewis and other islands were in the commissariot of the Isles (see Argyllshire).

Records of the former sheriffdom of Ross and Cromarty (sheriff courts of Dingwall and Stornoway) are now at the S.R.O.

Indexes: Dingwall, 1824-1900, Stornoway, 1827-1840 (TS).

Printed index: personal estates of defuncts, 1846-1867.

SCOTLAND

Roxburgh (38) and Selkirk (37). See with Peebles.

Shetland. See with Orkney.

Stirling and Clackmannan. Until 1823 the greater (eastern) part of Stirlingshire and nearly all Clackmannan were in the commissariot of Stirling (25) (see key to parishes).
Printed index: testaments, 1607-1800 (8,800) (S.R.S., vol. 22).
Other indexes: testaments, 1712 (TS supplement), 1801-1823 (TS).
The parishes of Balfron, Baldernock, Campsie, Drymen, Fintry, Killearn, Kilsyth and Strathblane, all in western Stirlingshire, were in the commissariot of Glasgow (24) (for which see Lanarkshire), though the commissariot of Hamilton and Campsie also had some jurisdiction over Campsie and Baldernock; and the Clackmannanshire parish of Tillicoultry was in the commissariot of Dunblane (see Perthshire). During the Commonwealth (1652-1659) testaments of the parishes of Baldernock, Buchanan, Killearn, and Campsie, are also to be found in the commissariot of Stirling. Part of Stirlingshire was originally in the commissariot of Edinburgh, page 200, but later was removed.
Records of the former sheriffdom of Stirling are now at the S.R.O.
Index: 1809-1900 (ST).
Post-1823 records of the former sheriffdom of Clackmannan remain with the sheriff court of Alloa.
Printed index: personal estates of defuncts (both counties), 1846-1867.

The pre-1823 commissariot jurisdictions of parishes in Stirlingshire.
G=Glasgow; H=Hamilton and Campsie; S=Stirling.

Airth, S	Drymen, G	Lecropt (pt.), S
Alva, S	Dunipace, S	Logie (pt.), S
Baldernock, G & H	Falkirk, S	Muiravonside, S
Balfron, G	Fintry, G	Polmont, S
Bothkennar, S	Gargunnock, S	St. Ninians, S
Buchanan, S	Killearn, G	Slamannan, S
Campsie, G & H	Kilsyth, G & S	Stirling, S
Denny, S	Larbert, S	Strathblane, G

Sutherland (2). See with Caithness.

West Lothian (Linlithgow) (26). See with Edinburgh, page 200.

Wigtown (41). Until 1823 wholly in the commissariot of Wigtown.
Printed index: warrants of testaments, 1700-1800 (800) (S.R.S., vol. 23).
Other indexes: warrants, invs. and settlements, 1801-1826 (TS).
Post-1826 records of the former sheriffdom of Wigtown remain with the sheriff court of Wigtown.
Printed index: personal estates of defuncts, 1846-1867.

INDEX TO COURTS

This index includes all major courts, but peculiars are excluded unless they had jurisdiction in more than one county or riding.

Abbreviations: archdy. = archdeaconry; bp. = bishop; commy. = commissary; comt. = commissariot; csty. = consistory; ct. = court; div. = division; ep. = episcopal; pec. = peculiar; prerog. = prerogative; regs. = registers.

Dumfries, comt., 203-4
Dunblane, comt., 203, 205-7
Dunkeld, comt., 200-1, 203, 205
Durham, csty., 30, 44, 150-4,
    156-9, 165-7

Edinburgh, comt., xiv, 183, 197,
    199, 200, 205, 207
Elphin, csty., 190, 192-3
Ely, archdy., 18-21; csty., 8,
    18-21, 65-6, 92-4
Emly, csty., see Cashel
Essex, archdy., 46-9
Estate Duty Office, vii, 4-5, 25-6,
    31-2, 112-3, 185, 194
Exeter, archdy., 31, 34-7; ep.
    csty., 25-6, 31-3, 35-7; ep.
    principal registry, 25-6, 31, 33;
    pecs. of dean and chapter, 25-6,
    31, 34, 37

Ferns, csty., 193
Freckenham, Isleham and, pec.,
    20-1, 65, 125-7

Glasgow, comt., 197, 202, 204-5,
    207
Gloucester, csty., 50-3, 135,
    138-40, 143-6
Guernsey, commy. of bp. of
    Winchester in Bailiwick, 184

Hamilton and Campsie, comt.,
    202, 204, 207
Hereford, csty. of dean, 58-9; ep.
    csty., 50, 53, 58-9, 108-9, 111,
    146-9, 176-83
Hereford, Little, and Ashford
    Carbonell, pec., 58-9, 109
Hexhamshire, pec., 44-5, 151
Hitchin div. of archdy. of
    Huntingdon, 60-3
Howden and Howdenshire, pec.,
    163, 168
Huntingdon, archdy., 8, 20, 61,
    65, 67, 97-8; see also Hitchin
Hurstbourne and Burbage, pec.,
    55, 142, 144-5
Husting, ct. of, 85-6

Inverness, comt., 203
Ireland, principal registry, 183,
    185, 195-6
Isleham and Freckenham, pec.,
    20-1, 65, 125

Isles, comt., 197, 201-3, 206

Jersey, ct. of dean, royal ct., 184

Kildare, csty., 191-2
Kilfenora, csty., see Killaloe
Killala and Achonry, csty., 192-3
Killaloe and Kilfenora, csty.,
    189-93
Kilmacduagh, csty., see Clonfert
Kilmore, csty., 189-92
Kirkcudbright, comt., 204

Lambeth Palace Library, 3-4, 8
Lanark, comt., 204
Langford, pec., 10-3, 105
Lauder, comt., 202
Laughton-en-le-Morthen, pec.,
    163, 173
Legacy Duty Office, see Estate
    Duty
Leicester, archdy., 77-8
Leighlin, csty., 189, 191-3
Lewes, archdy., 130-2
Lichfield, csty., 23, 73, 108,
    118-22, 134-6, 138, 150, 176-7;
    dean and chapter, 118-22, 135,
    138-9; pec. of dean, 118-22
Limerick, csty., 189, 191
Lincoln, csty., 7-8, 14-5, 60, 64-6,
    77, 79-80, 82-3, 96, 100, 104;
    dean and chapter, 7-8, 11, 15,
    66, 79, 81, 83, 97-8, 106; ep.
    regs., 8, 15, 64, 66, 79, 81, 98,
    106
Lismore, csty., see Waterford
Llandaff., csty., 180-3
London, archdy., 85-6, 88-91;
    commy. (Essex and Herts.),
    46-9, 60-4; commy. (London),
    46-9, 85-6, 88-91; csty., 14, 47,
    60, 64, 72, 85-6; ep. regs., 49,
    87; Husting, ct. of, 85-6;
    P.R.O., 1-5, 25-6, 31-2; pec. of
    dean and chapter of St. Paul's,
    46-9, 60-4, 85, 87-91

Maidstone, archdy., 68
Man, Isle of, archdy., 183
Masham, pec., 168, 174
Meath, csty., 189, 191-3
Middlesex, archdy. (Essex and
    Herts.), 46-9, 60-4; (Middx.),
    85-6, 88-91
Monks Risborough, pec., 15-7, 105

Moray, comt., 200, 203, 205

Newry and Mourne, pec., 190
Norfolk, archdy., 20-1, 92, 94-5,
125-7
Northampton, archdy., 96-7, 99
Norwich, archdy., 92-5, 125-7;
csty., 18-21, 92, 124-5
Nottinghamshire, archdy., 100-3,
154-9, 171-2

Orkney and Shetland, comt., 197,
205
Ossory, csty., 191-2
Oxford, archdy., 16, 104, 107;
csty., 10-1, 16, 104, 107;
Chancellor of the University, 4,
105; New College, 46-7

Peebles, comt., 197, 205
Peterborough, csty., 66, 96-7, 99
Principal (Probate) Registry, vii,
ix, 6, 183, 196, 199
Public Record Office, 1-5, 25-6,
31-2

Raphoe, csty., 189
Richmond, archd. (eastern deans.),
153-4, 156-9, 165-7, 171-2;
(western deans.), 27-30, 73-5,
153-4, 156-9, 171-2, 183
Rochester, archdy. and csty., 20,
68, 70-2, 130, 132-3
Ross (Ireland), csty., see Cork
Ross (Scotland), comt., 197, 206

St. Albans, archdy., 14, 60-4
St. Andrews, comt., 197, 200-1,
203
St. Asaph, csty., 108, 176-9
St. David's, csty., 58-9, 176-9,
180-3
St. Edmund's Abbey, ct. of the
sacrist, 125
St. Paul's, see London
Salisbury (Sarum), archdy., 140,
144; archdy. of sub-dean, 140-1,
143-5; csty., 10-1, 50, 104,
140-1, 144-5; pec. of dean,
10-3, 31, 35, 38-43, 141-5; pec.
of dean and chapter, 38-9, 42-3,
55, 141, 144-5

Shetland, comt., see Orkney
Shoreham, pec. deanery, 68, 70-2
Sodor and Man, csty., 150-3, 183
Stamp Duty Office, see Estate
Duty
Stirling, comt., 202-3, 207
Stow, archdy., 79-83, 97-8
Sudbury, archdy., 19, 124-7
Suffolk, archdy., 124-7
Surrey, archdy. and commy., 55,
89, 128-9

Taunton, archdy., 112, 114, 116
Thame, pec., 15-7, 105
Thorney, pec., 20, 65
Totnes, archdy., 31, 34, 36-7
Tuam, csty., 190, 192

Wantage, pec. of dean and canons
of Windsor, 10-3, 141, 144-5
Waterford and Lismore, csty., 193
Wells, archdy., 112, 114, 116;
csty. of dean, 112, 114, 116-7;
dean and chapter, 112, 115-7;
ep. csty. of Bath and Wells, 50,
53, 112-4, 116-7
Westminster, royal pec. of dean
and chapter, 49, 85, 87-91
Wetwang, pec., 164, 174
Wigtown, comt., 197, 204, 207
Wiltshire, archdy., 140-2, 144
Winchester, archdy. and csty.,
54-7, 129, 140, 143-5; see also
Guernsey, Jersey, and Surrey
Windsor, ct. of dean, 13; pec. of
dean and canons (in Wantage),
10-3, 141, 144-5
Worcester, csty., 50, 53, 108-11,
121-3, 134-5, 137-9, 146-9

York, Borthwick Institute, 44-5,
100-1, 150-75; dean and
chapter, 75-6, 100, 150-1, 154,
156-9, 161, 167, 172; chancery,
100-1, 150-1, 154-5; exchequer,
75-6, 100-3, 150-3, 154-6, 161,
165, 171; pec. of dean, 156-9,
161, 167; pec. of St. Leonard's
Hospital, 161, 167, 172; pec. of
precentor, 162, 173; prerog.,
vii, xiv, 3, 150-3; see also
archdy. of Richmond